Flowering and foliage
varieties for the home

INDOOR
PLANTS

Flowering and foliage varieties for the home

INDOOR
PLANTS

Halina Heitz

Consulting Editor: Dennis W. Stevenson, PhD
Director, Harding Laboratory
The New York Botanical Garden

Portraits and instructions for
care of the most popular
green and flowering plants
as well as novelties and rarities.
With glossary

350 Color Photographs
140 Drawings in color by Ushie Dorner

BARRON'S

CONTENTS

The bellflower (*Campanula isophylla*) is one of the few houseplants that can tolerate alkaline water.

6

The plants on pages 4–5 from left to right:

Mediterranean Window with Sun-loving Houseplants
back row: Calamondin orange (*x Citrofortunella mitis 'Varieta'*), bougainvillea (*Bougainvillea*), Rosette succulent (*Aeonium arboraum 'Atropurpureum'*), kangaroo thorn (*Acacia armata*), bougainvillea hybrid, passionflower (*Passiflora caerulea*).
front row: china rose (*Rosa chinensis*), desert rose (*Adenium obesum*), china rose (*Rosa chinensis*), lavender (*Lavandula angustifolia*), crimson bottlebrush (*Callistemon citrinus*), wax-flower (*Chamelaucium*), oleander (*Nerium oleander*), Livingston daisy (*Dorotheanthus bellidiformis*), echeveria (*Echeveria*), stonecrop (*Sedum species*).

Lycase skinneri, an epiphytic mountain orchid from Central America.

The graphic leaf of a fan palm (here: *Washingtonia*).

The fruit of the kumquat (*Fortunella margarita*) is edible. New plants can be grown from their seeds.

How can you have better success with indoor plants? In this guide the author and the editors have reduced the complex answer to this question to one common denominator: appropriate culture. This means nothing more than learning the natural living conditions of the particular tropical or subtropical plant and then imitating them. For instance, did you know that some plants have a rest period, whereas others do not? That a plant's

Appropriate Culture

Houseplants were as costly and rare as gold when they were first brought from distant lands and taken indoors. We still prize them highly today, for they beautify our homes. But many plant lovers have forgotten that our indoor plants are almost exclusively from tropical or subtropical regions and therefore have special living requirements. Anyone who knows this possesses the key to success as an indoor plant gardener.

growth pattern and leaves indicate its light or water requirements? By learning the origins and life requirements of your plants you will understand what's best for them and will avoid basic mistakes. The essential part of this book is the plant culture section. More than 300 houseplants for home, office, and conservatory—popular, well-known ones, as well as interesting novelties and enchanting rarities—are shown and described in brilliant color photographs and precise instructions that guarantee success even to the novice indoor gardener. But this isn't all: The Glossary provides the plant lover with easy-to-understand, concise, useful information. The How To pages use informative step-by-step drawings to show transplanting, watering, and propagating procedures. Pests and diseases can be quickly managed with the help of pictures of symptoms and precise instructions for treatment. The superb color photographs—taken exclusively for this book—show how splendid houseplants can look with proper care. At the same time, they offer a wealth of ideas and decorative possibilities—from hanging plants and combinations of plants in containers to dreamy groupings in windows. The author and the editors wish you much pleasure and success with houseplants.

About the Author

Halina Heitz, the author and an indoor plant expert, was for 15 years the editor of the houseplant department of the leading German garden magazine *Mein schoner Garten*. Through her collaboration with gardeners and botanists, as well as hundreds of thousands of contacts with readers, she is familiar with all questions about the care of ornamental plants. Author and publisher are grateful to the photographer Friedrich Strauss for the numerous handsome photographs, which he took especially for this book, and to Ushie Dorner for the informative drawings. Special thanks go to all our advisors:

Dr. Susanne Amberger-Ochsenbauer, Agricultural Engineer in the area of horticulture, specializing in ornamental plants; formerly scientific fellow in ornamental plant horticulture at the Technical University of Munich.

Franz Becherer, cactus specialist.

Emil Luckel, President of the German Orchid Society.

Prof. Werner Rauh, former Director of the Institute of Systematic Botany and Plant Geography of Ruprecht-Karl University, Heidelberg.

Important: To keep your pleasure in your hobby unclouded, please read the Important Note on page 240.

White Hydrangea
Its enchanting flower umbels consist of sterile single flowers. Hydrangeas like slightly acid soil and must be watered thoroughly.

Making its way from
its natural habitat in
South America to us,
the amaryllis has had
to adapt to fat and
lean times.

ALL ABOUT INDOOR PLANTS

Magnificent flowers do not happen by themselves. Some knowledge is needed to crown the love of plants with success at cultivating them. An understanding of native conditions is one of the great secrets of plant culture. On the following pages you will learn everything worth knowing about growing houseplants.

11

Venerable rubber trees with aerial roots reaching to the ground (see photograph, page 141); man-high hedges of flaming red poinsettias (see photograph, page 89); coconut palms on sandy golden shores (see photograph, page 205); green swamps full of umbrella sedge; gigantic tropical forests thick with magnificently colored orchids and bromeliads (see photographs, pages 13 and 213); woods of eucalyptus, Norfolk Island pines, and bamboo;

Learn to Know Your Plants

Botany and plant history are more exciting and instructive than many believe. Anyone who knows where a plant comes from, how it lives, what its structure is, and why it looks one way and not another, can better understand its needs.

cactus monuments in sparkling desert light (photograph, page 223)— these are the native habitats of our houseplants.
So foreign visitors that are supposed to feel at home indoors in pots must get used to poor winter light and air dried by our heating systems. Therefore, never be angry with your houseplants when occasionally they let their leaves hang limp. Try to make them feel at home and gain insight into their needs. This is very easily done if you know more about your exotic foreigner and observe it carefully.

Habitats and Climate Zones
Indoor plants are not winter hardy and so must be protected all year long from low temperatures. They originate in tropical and subtropical regions and are imprinted by their habitats. An overview of the most important climate zones follows, but don't forget that these zones can frequently overlap or that islands of different types of climate can occur within others because of geographical oddities.

Tropical Habitats
The zones on both sides of the equator are designated tropical. The borders are the Tropics of Cancer and of Capricorn at latitudes of $23\frac{1}{2}°$ north and south, respectively. The tropics circle the "belly of the earth" like a wide belt and make up

about 40 percent of the earth's surface. The climatic conditions of this zone are quite various and range from the sultry, humid climate around the equator, to the climate of the savannahs and grasslands—which are characterized by rainy and dry spells—to the hot, dry, high-lying prairies and cool, damp mountain forests within these regions. So the tropical plants can occur in very different native conditions, as far as rain, temperature, and humidity are concerned. However, two life requirements are the same for all of them:
• Tropical plants do not undergo any seasonal change of temperature and light.
• Tropical plants receive a uniform daylight all year long, for in the tropics the length of the day and night is always the same.
Plants from the tropical rain forest live in a natural greenhouse. The rain forest extends on both sides of the equator and is delineated by steamy, leaden heat with marked nightly cooling, humidity between 90 and 99 percent, and copious rainfall without any real dry season. The luxuriant flora consists of evergreen trees, lianas, epiphytes, and on the ground gigantic shrubs and plants, often large-leaved forms, which live above one another in three stories, or layers. Rain forest plants kept indoors tolerate sun and the dryness of house heating very poorly. They do not require a resting period but are bound, compelled by our darker seasons, to check their growth in fall and winter.
Plants from tropical regions with rainy and dry spells. Plants from savannahs and steppes belong to this group, but so do those from areas that can be influenced by winds like the monsoon and the trade winds. These plants are accustomed to considerable alternation of humidity and dryness.
Plants from the tropical mountain forests have still other requirements. Their natural habitat is distinguished by rainfall, mists, strong sunlight, and coolness, which can even extend to frost in the higher altitudes. Therefore tropical mountain plants in the house also need much light and high humidity, along with coolness.
Plants from desert regions are of necessity experts at survival.

Epiphytes like the staghorn fern, *Dendrobium*, and *Tillandsia* establish themselves in the forks of tropical trees.

Deserts offer broiling heat in the daytime, with temperatures up to 120° F (50° C) in the shade, a mercilessly glaring sun, often a stiff breeze, and a water evaporation rate that is far greater than the yearly rainfall. These, as well as night temperatures that go almost to the freezing point, are indeed inhospitable conditions for plant life. Often there is no rainfall for months at a time, in fact even for years, and when there is, it comes in such cloudbursts that the ground cannot take up the water.

Desert plants have therefore learned to manage with condensed water, fog, or dew. Thus, anyone who grows them should not overwater them in summer and must keep them almost dry in winter. That they need full sun is obvious.

Subtropical Habitats

This refers to the region lying between the tropics and the temperate zone, in which we live. The average temperature in the coldest months ranges from 50° to 64° F (10° to 18° C), with rainfall and hours of daylight varying according to season. There are areas with warm summers and mild winters as well as others with rainy winters and summers. The rainy-winter regions lie in the Mediterranean area, South Africa, and California; the rainy-summer regions in the southern United States, New Zealand, and in parts of China.

Subtropical plants are frequently equipped with water reservoirs and protection against evaporation. They love cooler temperatures at night and they go through a rest period. Plants of the rainy-summer regions need warmth and water in summer and in winter must be kept cool and relatively dry; those from rainy-winter areas need water in winter too—as well as sufficient light and warmth.

My Tip: To anyone who would like to learn more about the various climate zones with their characteristic flora, I recommend a visit to the nearest large botanical garden. There you will find splendidly represented not only the principal zones but the intermediate and special zones as well.

HOW TO

Botany from root to flower

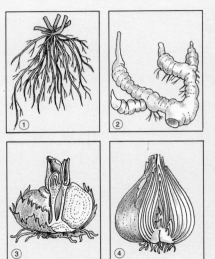

Below-Ground Plant Parts
1 Roots, consisting of main and side roots.
2 Rhizome with roots.
3 Tuber with roots.
4 Bulb with roots.

The Above-Ground Parts of a Plant
main stem, side stems (branches), leaves, flowers, and fruits.

The Life Goal of Plants
The purpose of a plant's life is growing, blooming, and producing fruit—that is to reproduce and continue the species. This is the single task toward which every cell and every organ in the organism is directed. In nature, above- and below-ground plant parts have worked harmoniously together toward this goal for millions of years. If this cooperation is disrupted, the organism attempts to reach its life goal through constant regeneration. Many blooming plants thus allow themselves to be outwitted. Cutting their flowers induces them to produce more flowers. The flower—often the goal of all our culture—is only a necessary transition stage for the plant. It is the beginning of its sexual maturity, whose purpose is reproduction.

Life Underground
The below-ground parts of the plant— roots, bulbs, tubers, or rhizomes (see drawings, Below-Ground Plant Parts)—have no contact with light and are mostly brown or white. How they are shaped and whether they root near the surface or deeply, strongly or weakly, is a result of species and its location.
The roots provide for anchoring in the ground and for the intake of water and nutrients.

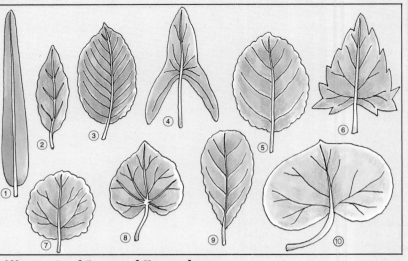

Different Leaf Forms of Houseplants
1 linear (*Chlorophytum*), 2 long (*Brunfelsia*), 3 ovate (*Beloperone*),
4 arrow-shaped (*Caladium*), 5 roundish (*Saintpaulia*), 6 triangular (*Ficus deltoidea*), 7 shield-shaped (*Jatropha*), 8 heart-shaped (*Sparmannia*),
9 wedge-shaped (*Euphorbia milii*), 10 kidney-shaped (*Ceropegia woodii*).

Other below-ground plant parts. Some plants have root tubers, metamorphosed stems (rhizomes or stem bulbs/tubers) or bulbs, which serve as underground storage places for water and nutrients for the plant.

Important: If a part of the root is damaged, for example by overwatering or injury during transplanting, the above-ground plant parts will suffer injury as well and may even die.

Life Above Ground

All the above-ground plant parts like stems, leaves, flowers, and fruit are light oriented. Those with deposits of the plant pigment chlorophyll are green and can transform carbon dioxide and water into sugar in the presence of light.

Stems (also called sprouts or shoots), like all other plant parts, display a wealth of variety in natural forms. They can be branching or unbranching, thin as a thread or thick as a bottle, herbaceous and juicy or woody and hard; they can creep, climb, or twine. Their function is to bear the leaves and flowers, to provide them with nutrients, and to position the leaves for the best possible access to light.

Leaves vary widely in size, shape, and color (see drawing, Leaf Forms) and are often very attractive. Whether they are small and needle-fine (see *Asparagus,* page 146), large and flat (see *Alocasia,* page 143), parchment-thin (see Maidenhair Fern, page 196) or thick as your arm (*Agave*), they are always the central nervous system and the green lungs of the plant. For it is mainly here that photosynthesis (see Glossary) and respiration (see Glossary) take place.

Flowers frequently reflect nature's almost incredible refinement. They are structured exclusively to fertilize and be fertilized. To this end they are provided with male pollen grains and female egg cells (see drawing, Structure of a Flower). Color, shape (see drawing, Different Flower Forms), and scent have proved lively seduction ploys. They attract animals, which then pollinate the flowers. When it flowers, the plant becomes sexually mature and internally prepares for fertilization. All energies are directed toward later fruiting and seeding, which is why a blooming shoot will often reduce its growth.

Fruit and seeds are the result of successful fertilization. The often colorful fruits serve as an attraction for the animals that will distribute the seeds. Development of fruits and seeds costs the plant a great deal of strength. Therefore, if you don't plan to propagate your houseplants, you should remove the flowers when they have finished blooming.

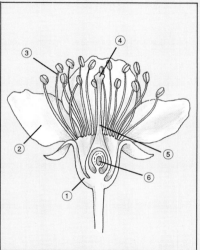

Structure of a Flower

1 Calyx with sepals.
2 Corolla with petals.
3 Male stamens with anthers and filaments.
4 Stigma.
5 Pistil.
6 Ovary with ovule. Stigma, pistil, and ovary are the female parts of a flower and all together are called the pistil.

Different Flower Forms

1 Bell-shaped (*campanulate*) flower, for example flowering maple (*Abutilon*).
2 Funnelform flower, for example cape primrose (*Streptocarpus*).
3 Butterfly-form (*papilionaceous*) flower, for example broom (*Cytisus*).
4 Tubular flower, for example basket plant (*Aeschynanthus*).

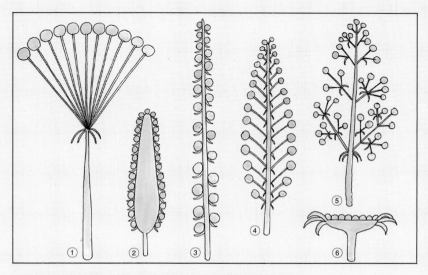

Schematic Drawing of the Important Inflorescences

1 Umbel (*Pentas, Clivia, Ixora, Pelargonium grandiflorum*). 2 Spadix (*Anthurium, Spathypyllum*). 3 Spike (*Acalypha, Crossandra, Pachystachys, Vriesea*). 4 Raceme (*Cymbidium, Smithiantha*). 5 Panicle (*Phalaenopsis, Medinilla*). 6 Composite (*Chrysanthemum, Gynura, Senecio*).

What the Appearance Tells You

Variety in plants is a result of the diverse habitats to which plants have had to adapt, each according to its species. As organisms bound to one spot plants were compelled over millions of years to perfect their rhythms, length of life, growth form, and appearance until the survival of their species was ensured.

For their innumerable problems they invented amazing solutions, which offer us important hints for their care (see box below).

Growth Form and Life Expectancy

Every plant, depending on its species, has its own genetic program that determines how old and how large it will become and what shape it will take. For instance, trees and shrubs that grow to the heavens in their own habitat will generally attain only a fraction of their potential size in the confined area of a pot. In appearance, they will remain more or less juvenile plants and will rarely bear fruit.

The important growth forms:
• upright, for example ti plant (*Cordyline*),
• climbing or twining, for instance grape ivy (*Cissus*),
• creeping or ground-covering, for example baby's tears (*Soleirolia*),
• trailing, such as basket plant (*Aeschynanthus*) or columnea (*Columnea*).

Furthermore, plants can live to various specific ages. They grow as annuals, biennials, or perennials, remain herbaceous or become woody like subshrubs, shrubs, or trees.

Annual plants such as *Browallia grandiflora* or biennials such as German violets go through a complete cycle of sprouting, growth, blooming, formation of fruits, and ripening of seeds in one or two years, respectively. After that they have fulfilled nature's reproduction requirement and they die. Naturally annual or biennial plants do not live longer as houseplants either, so the plant lover must replace or propagate them after one or two years.

Perennial plants like shrubs (for example, *Anthurium scherzeranum* hybrids, *Campanula*, *Chrysanthemum* hybrids, *Cyperus*) or bulbs (for example, *Hippeastrum*) form surviving roots, tubers, or bulbs that bring forth new growth during every growing season. With optimum care these plants can last for years, even as indoor plants.

Subshrubs (for example *Asparagus setaceus*, *Beloperone*) possess herbaceous parts that die back and woody parts that can put out new growth every year. These are also relatively long lived in pot culture.

Shrubs and trees (for example, *Araucaria*, *Ardisia*, *Cupressus*, *Gardenia*, *Grevillea*, *Ficus*, *Medinilla*, *Sparmannia*) are particularly long-lived evergreen or deciduous woody plants that can, with good culture, achieve a quite remarkable age, even in exile.

Plant Survival Strategies

Protection from Light. To this end plants provide themselves with hairy growth, frosting, fuzzy coats, or a silvery to blue-greenish waxy coating (for example, *Echeveria, Agave, Crassula*).
This tells us: Plants that look like this tolerate full light.

Protection from Water Evaporation. To diminish the loss of humidity, plants develop waxy coatings, many small or tough leaves reduced to thorns or needles, leathery leaves as well as thick hairy growth (for example, cactus and euphorbia, *Hoya, Ixora, Leptospermum, Myrtus*).
This tells us: These plants tolerate dry air.

Quest for Light. For this reason many rain forest plants leave the ground and locate in forks of trees. Still others provide themselves with gigantic leaves, which are regular light catchers, or they develop vines that enable them to travel up to the treetops.

This tells us: Tree dwellers (such as epiphytic orchids, bromeliads, and ferns) do not belong in soil; plants with huge leaves such as *Alocasia, Fatsia, Ficus lyrata, Ficus elastica* and vines like *Philodendron* and *Tetrastigma* need relatively little light.

Protection from Dry Periods. Some plants arm themselves with underground storage organs (*Achimenes, Cyclamen, Gloriosa, Sinningia, Zantedeschia*), succulent leaves (*Crassula, Hoya, Kalanchoe*) or stems (*Beaucarnea, Jatropha, Pachira*).
This tells us: Plants that store water must be watered sparingly.

To Take Up Atmospheric Humidity some plants developed absorption scales (for instance bromeliads), aerial roots (as in orchids), or hairs (as with African violets).
This tells us: These plants need damp air.

Enchanting Azaleas

Rhododendron Simsii hybrids are available in countless colors and forms.
  1 'Euratom',
  2 'Rosa Perle',
  3 'Rosalie',
  4 'Memoria Karl Glasen',
  5 'Schnee', 6 'Rex',
  7 'Flamenco',
  8 'De Waele's Favorite',
  9 'Stella Maus',
  10 'Leopold Astrid'.

Nomenclature—A Plant's Calling Card

Plants not only have one or several national or popular names in each country, but as proper citizens of the world they also possess a valid international passport: the botanical or scientific name, consisting of the capitalized genus name, which always appears first, and the lowercased species name, which always comes second. For example, *Clivia miniata* for clivia. Hybrid varieties also have a third name, the varietal or cultivar name, which carries single quotation marks, for example *Camellia japonica* 'Barbara Clark'. Additionally, an *x* mark usually precedes the name of a genus or species to indicate hybrids derived from two plants of a different genus or species, respectively.

Carl von Linnaeus, who is known as the Father of Botany, introduced this binomial (two-name) nomenclature in 1753 in his work *Species Plantarum*. Since that time no longer are there lengthy and wordy descriptions of plants, such as *Cyclamen orbiculato folio inferne purpurascente,* which translated means: sphere with circular leaves purple on the underside—a descriptive name for *Cyclamen purpurascens,* the wild alpine violet.

But the names, which contain Greek and Latin elements, have remained descriptive and colorful. They are derived from the names of the discoverer, patrons, or first describer; indicate the region of origin, characteristic qualities, or the appearance of the plant; or are Latinizations of the language of the native country. The species descriptions are particularly individual and informative.

Visitors from All Over the World

From South America come bush begonias and *Dieffenbachia*, from tropical Africa, *Dracaena* and umbrella sedge (in background from left to right). Baby's tears (front left) is native to the Mediterranean region, *Davallia* (front right) to China.

The History of Indoor Plants

It's hard to believe, but the indoor culture of plants began in Scandinavia, where for centuries people brought plants into the house when the desolation of the long winter began. Of course in the beginning they were certainly not exotic plants. These first reached Europe when the great ships roamed the seas and the continents were explored. In any event, the cactus story began with the discovery of America; presumably Christopher Columbus on his *Santa Maria* carried home a number of plant rarities from the new world.

• In 1570 an English apothecary offered as a botanical rarity a *Melocactus,* which probably came from the legacy of the *Santa Maria.*

• In 1620 the belladonna lily was introduced from the Cape Colony.

• In 1644 arum lilies were already growing in the Royal Garden in Paris.

• In 1690 the pineapple was already successfully bred in princely gardens and the sea grape (*Coccoloba*) was introduced in Europe.

• In 1698 *Aloe arborescens* was already growing in European greenhouses.

• In 1733 the first tropical orchid bloomed in Europe. It was *Bletia verrecunda* from the Bahamas.

• In 1770 the Swiss botanist Frederik Allamand collected seeds in South America and sent them to Linnaeus. These were later named *Allamanda* for him.

• In 1774 and afterward numbers of fragrant-leaved pelargoniums were introduced from the Cape Colony.

• In 1779 Captain Cook and Sir Joseph Banks took home the Norfolk Island pine from New Zealand.

• In 1819 an *Amaryllis* species was taken to Europe from Brazil.

Serious development of houseplants, or plants for indoor use, really began around the nineteenth century. The invention of heating and the greenhouse made it possible to keep exotic plant visitors without injury.

Certainly the tale of the ways plants first reached us reads like an adventure story. Gardeners, botanists, missionaries, and explorers risked their lives for them, but so did fortune-hunters and mercenaries utterly uninterested in plants. To acquire the highly prized rarities they had to cope with tropical illness, insects, poison snakes, predators, hostile natives, and the unpredictable climatic conditions. In addition there was ruthless competition, corruption, espionage, and possibly, because of the astronomical prices some plants commanded, even murder to be reckoned with.

And for the plants the long sea journey was equally terrible. They languished for months in unventilated wooden boxes, were eaten by vermin or insects, or they simply rotted. This changed when the English physician and naturalist Nathaniel Ward, through an accidental discovery, invented a closable glass container in which the soil retained constant dampness. The "Wardian case" entered into the history of botany and became the ideal means of transporting tropical plants that were found and was later the prototype of English ferneries as well as our modern window greenhouses, vitrines, and terrariums.

E xcept for the impulsive purchase of a beautiful plant for the sheer joy of it, several considerations should precede any plant purchase so that the right plant gets to the right spot and the future "cohabitation" will be a mutual pleasure for plant and human.

The first consideration must therefore always be: What conditions (light and temperature) do I have to offer my chosen plant and

this means 1860 footcandles (20,000 lux) and over.
• Bright = a place directly in a window with a short period of sun in the morning or in the evening, as is provided by an eastern or western location. Expressed as a light intensity of 930 to 1,860 footcandles (10,000–20,000 lux).
• Semishade = a place in a north window or in the vicinity of a window without direct sun. Light intensity ranges from 465 to 930 footcandles (5,000–10,000 lux).
• Shady = a place in a small north window or a location in a room with a light intensity of 230 to 465 footcandles (2,500–5,000 lux). On cloudy winter days the light intensity can be as little as 37 to 46 footcandles (400–500 lux); on the other hand, on sunny summer days it can be as high as 8,365 footcandles (90,000 lux). The minimum light that a plant needs for life ranges from 65 to 93 footcandles (700–1,000 lux), but many plants only begin to thrive at 930 footcandles (10,000 lux).

Tips for Planning, Buying, and Placement

Things you can do with houseplants: Bring a bit of nature from far-away places into your home; create colorful focal points and restful green areas; enrich your home with exotic fragrances; or merely call attention to the beauty of your own furniture. The most important prerequisite for success: the location must be right.

does it to some degree match the conditions and circumstances in its natural habitat?

The second consideration: What plants fit the size of my home and the style of my furnishings?

It Depends on the Light

Light is the plant's bread. In the natural environment it receives light from all sides, in the house often only from one. Let's not forget either that many houseplants come from tropical regions that have days and nights of the same length so that our fall and winter seasons mean a noticeable light deficiency for them. Plants always thrive best when they receive the light they would normally enjoy in their native locations. They've adapted to these conditions over many thousands of years—their leaves, particularly, are structured for this purpose. The light requirements of many plants can be determined from the leaves (see pages 26–27). When you choose and buy a plant that you don't know, pay attention to its leaves to be safe; also find out about its light requirements. Frequently plants are sold with printed care instructions in which their light requirements are characterized as follows:
• Sunny = a place in a south window with maximum light intensity or a location in full sun out of doors. Expressed in numbers

What Determines the Amount of Light

The compass points toward which the windows or other light sources are oriented naturally determine the light supply and are, therefore, also the "classical" photometers. The light value of such sources must of course vary from living area to living area, for they only really prove consistent where light can enter freely and unhindered. So an unimpeded north window on the fourth floor of an apartment house will receive far more light than a south window on the ground floor with a balcony extending over it or a large chestnut tree in front of it.

If you don't want to put a plant directly in front of a window, you must bear in mind that not only closely woven draperies but even sheer curtains as well as jalousies filter out considerable light. Besides, the light intensity diminishes according to the distance from the source of light:
• at a distance of 39 in. (1 m) the plant receives 80 to 50 percent of the light
• at a distance of 59 in. (1.5 m) 50 to 25 percent
• at a distance of 79 in. (2 m) 25 to 10 percent

Long Stems with Yellow Candles of Flowers

Pachystachys lutea wants a very bright but never sunny location. What many people don't know: The real flowers are the little white points that peep out of the sun-yellow bracts.

My Tip: Before you decide to buy a large, expensive houseplant, check its future location with a lux-meter. This light measuring instrument, which is comparable to the light meter used in photography, is a one-time purchase that you can use for any future houseplants. You should get plants that need sunny or bright locations only if you can offer them a place in a window that faces south, east, or west—or if you have a plant light. If you want to place them in the dark for a short period, for instance as a table decoration, you need not supply additional light.

Room Temperature is Important

Also check the warmth of the location for your future houseplant. In summer, there should not be a window behind whose pane a heat pool quickly develops. In winter, there are more things to consider. Turning down the heat at night, as is done in most households, is not a problem. This often matches the conditions of the plant's natural habitat and is accepted by all. Heating units under the window or baseboard heating, especially, offer the rising warmth plants like, since it helps to warm their soil. What is bad, however, is the drying of the air and the soil that goes along with it. Many plants need increased humidity during this period (see page 43).

A number of plants like to be overwintered in a cool, bright situation. Before you buy such plants, consider whether you can set up the appropriate winter quarters for them.

Types of Locations

In every household and in every room, individual light and temperature conditions determine which plants will thrive there. Here are some common types of locations:

The warm all-year-round, sunny place offers mean daytime temperatures above 68° F (20° C) and night temperatures that do not fall under 59° F (15° C). As a rule these conditions are present in a window location in a constantly used living area and in the comfortably heated greenhouse. In a room, the plants are set out in the sun for several hours a day: in the south window at midday, in the east window in the morning, in the west window in the afternoon and evening; in the heated conservatory, nearly all day long. For the hot south window with its strong midday sun the only plants suitable are those that live in the hot sun in their native habitat, for example flame nettle (*Coleus*) or ponytail (*Beaucarnea*). East and west windows, on the other hand, are ideal locations for all light-loving plants that can't stand the full glare of the sun.

Cool, sunny to bright places—for example a window in a weakly heated bedroom, in a bathroom that is only warm periodically, in a hall-way, or the conservatory that is not part of the living area—offer several hours of much light, in summer warmer and in winter cooler temperatures between 50° to 59° F (10°–15° C). Plants of the subtropics flourish here, as do those of the Mediterranean region and of the tropical high mountain regions—plants such as flowering maple (*Abutilon*), Norfolk Island pine (*Araucaria*), orange trees (*Citrus*), Monterey cypress (*Cupressus*), sago palm (*Cycas*), dendrobium (*Dendrobium*), silky oak (*Grevillea*), myrtle (*Myrtus*), azaleas (*Rhododendron* hybrids).

A warm, shady place provides temperatures of 59° to 70° F (15°–21° C) and receives no sun, on the whole. It can be shaded, or in the middle of a very bright room. Forest dwellers thrive here, since they are used to filtered light; these include ferns, tropical palms, and members of the arum family.

A cool, shady place. This can be any area that is slightly heated in winter, shady in summer, or be a room or conservatory that faces north, east, or west. Plants that thrive in average temperatures of 50° to 59° F (10°–15° C) and in shade are those from tropical and subtropical mountain forests, such as barroom plant (*Aspidistra*), bird's-nest fern (*Asplenium*), ivy (*Hedera*), Cretan bracken (*Pteris cretica*), reed rhapis (*Rhapis*), and baby's tears (*Soleirolia*).

A humid, bright place offers much light without direct sun, humidity over 60 percent, and temperatures that never go below 64° F (18° C). This environment can be achieved in a climate-controlled plant window, vitrines, and greenhouse rooms. Tropical rain forest dwellers like marantas, ferns, many gesneriads, and members of the arum family as well as epiphytic orchids, bromeliads, and tillandsias flourish admirably here.

Planning and Decorating with Indoor Plants

When selecting and buying house-plants, you should also note if they possess decorative characteristics with which you can define or emphasize the atmosphere and furnishings of your home. If you analyze carefully, as an interior decorator or designer would do, you will find in every plant some essential feature, or characteristic form, or color that will harmonize particularly well with a certain lifestyle (see box, page 25).

Indoor Plants Need Space

No plant stays the size it was when you bought it. How large it will become depends on several factors: its genetic growth program and the container in which you cultivate the houseplant as well as on the care that you bestow on it (see Growth Factors, page 36). Species that in their native habitat grow into high trees or shrubs—like dagger plant (*Yucca*), *Ficus* species, African hemp (*Sparmannia africana*) or sentry palm (*Howea*)—can also, with good care, reach the ceiling indoors or grow very broad—like the screw pine (*Pandanus*). So when choosing and buying your future houseplant, keep two things in mind: space and style. Reserve a place for it where it can flourish undisturbed and where its own individual style of growth will be the most effective visually. The space requirement of a large solitary plant is comparable to that for a piece of furniture.

Unusual combination of leaf plants and container.

Charming arrangement of flowering bulbs.

More Decorating Tips
• Large plants work best as solitary or key plants. In small areas use one at the very most.
• Large-leaved plants mitigate busy wallpaper patterns and form a plain background for small-leaved ones.
• The graphic contours of palm fronds, ferns, or *Yucca* crowns are particularly well set off by backlighting.
• Smaller plants look nicer in groups. For example, a basket or dish with a dozen African violets (see photograph, page 128), spring primulas, mini cyclamen, or cape primrose hybrids in various violet and pink shades.
• Repeat the colors of curtains, wallpaper, sofa cushions, pictures in flower colors, or set up points of contrast, for instance red flamingo flowers (*Anthurium*) with black furniture.

• Make your entryway inviting with beautiful plants. Install plant lights, if you haven't enough light.
• Make your walls green with climbing plants, if they receive enough light. A classical espalier trellis to help plants climb is the prettiest. You can also anchor a trellis in a large box and use it as a room divider, covered with plants.
• Hang greenery under the eaves of old houses.

Furniture for Plants
When the garden grows out over the windowsill and the nicest places on chests of drawers or consoles are already occupied, you can still resort to "plant furniture." Today the market offers a variety of flower benches, side tables, planters, flower stands, or etagéres (see photograph, page 146). Plants on glass shelves that allow the light to shine through produce a very attractive effect. Columns of pottery or flower holders of wood are very good for single plants, especially for gracefully trailing ones such as spider plants (see photograph, page 151), sword fern (see photograph, page 200), or classic hanging plants.

Attractive Cachepots and Containers
Beautiful cachepots are decorative elements that set off houseplants to the best effect. They come in enchanting colors and wonderful forms and are available in a wide variety of materials, ranging from pottery, porcelain, wood, wicker, and rattan to plastic, metal, and glass.
Make sure when you choose cachepots that they are larger than, the plant pot (there should be a finger's thickness of free space between plant pot and cachepot) and that plant and container harmonize with each other in color and shape. Always good: white cachepots, terracotta pots, and naturally colored baskets. Here are a few tips for variation:
• For colored leaved plants such as croton (*Codiaeum*), flame nettle (*Coleus*), or rex begonia (*Begonia*) choose a monochrome pot in the dominant leaf color, for instance red or purple.
• Put very sturdy and Mediterranean-looking plants like silver jade plant (*Crassula*) or miniature orange (*Citrus*) in plain pots of clay, stoneware, or glazed pottery.
• Old-fashioned plants like alpine violet (*Cyclamen*), fragrant-leaved

Plants enliven the work area and can improve the climate of a room.

geranium (*Pelargonium*), miniature roses (*Rosa*), or African violets (*Saintpaulia*) look pretty in porcelain cachepots with flower patterns or lacquered baskets in the appropriate color.
• Olive or sea-green containers go well with green-white or green-silvery variegated plants like aglaonema (*Aglaonema*) or fittonia (*Fittonia*).
• Such decorating favorites as palms, dagger plant (*Yucca*), Ficus species, and African hemp (*Sparmannia*) might, in the right situation, also be planted in square or round metal drums.
• Cactus, as long as they are not blooming, look especially jolly in brilliantly colored small pots.

Tips on Buying
It doesn't matter where you buy your plants. Just observe how they are handled there.

• Don't buy any plant that is standing in a dark corner or a drafty passageway.
• Green plants should have tight growth, with several shoots and juicy, spotless leaves. Don't take plants with yellow-brown spots on the leaves or leggy shoots (long shoots with wide intervals between leaves).
• Blooming plants should have lots of buds that are just about to open. Don't choose one in full bloom or one with "left-behind" (dried-out looking) buds.
• Only take plants that are insect-free. Inspect ends of shoots carefully (aphids) and undersides of leaves (spider mites, scale). On the flowers, small elongated thrips are the easiest to recognize.
• Also avoid plants whose soil is completely dried out or is covered with moss. In both cases the roots can be damaged.
• Especially recommended: Plants labeled with name and care instructions.

Availability
While as a rule you can obtain foliage plants all year around, flowering plants are only available at their natural blooming time or when forced by florists. Some flowering plants like the African violets (*Saintpaulia*), winter-flowering begonias (*Begonia*), flamingo flowers (*Anthurium*), or Palm-Beach-bells (*Kalanchoe*) bloom for months at a time or are obtainable in bloom almost all year long.

From Mini to Maxi

Thanks to the pressure of fashions and trends, houseplants have become extremely varied. Breeders and growers no longer attempt merely to manipulate flowering seasons or to achieve new flower colors and forms or variegations of leaves through hybridization. They "invent" plants that do not exactly conform to species norm but are decorative or they keep them small, either by reduction of the pot size (for example by culture in almost thimble-sized pots), by treatment with inhibiting chemicals, or through breeding. Here are some examples of what is available:

Flowering plant minis of chrysanthemum, *Spathiphyllum* (see photograph, page 133), flamingo flower, *Kalanchoe* (see photograph, page 120), roses (see photograph, page 128), African violets (see photograph, page 128), and nonhardy azaleas.

Foliage plant minis of dracaena, ferns, croton, palms, and dwarf pepper.

Tree forms of chrysanthemum (see photograph, page 101), broom, *Pachystachys lutea* (photograph, page 21), hibiscus, poinsettia, and nonhardy azaleas.

Hanging baskets of plants that have a creeping, climbing, or trailing growth habit (see photographs, pages 30–31).

Bonsais of various *Ficus* species (photograph, page 48), bottle tree, myrtle, lady palm, nonhardy azaleas, and Norfolk Island pine.

Minsais of *Aeonium,* balsam apple, ponytail palm, rubber plant, Ixora, and croton. Here we are dealing with bonsai-like miniatures with a special irrigation system.

Plants trained on hoops, of bougainvillea, mandevilla (see photograph, page 106), jasmine (see photograph, page 119), climbing lily (see photograph, page 112), *Stephanotis* (see photograph, page 133), glory-bower, passionflower (see photograph, page 124), and *Hoya.*

Twisted or braided stems in *Ficus* species (see drawing, page 44).

Planted dishes or other arrangements (see photographs, pages 23 and 29), in which often more attention has been paid to the visual effect than to having the correct conditions for the particular plants.

Miniature greenhouses planted with mini plants (see photograph, page 39) that need high humidity.

Planted lava flows, which provide optimal dampness for the plants and also furnish them with a background. They are available in various sizes from the nursery supply houses.

My Tip: Very often tillandsias are sold fastened to stones. Aside from the fact that these are usually plants that have been plundered from their native habitats (endangered species), this is not the correct culture for these plants. A real tillandsia lover only buys plants that are domestically reproduced from seed or vegetative propagation and are bound to branches (see photograph, page 46). The American Bromeliad Society can give you information.

Positive Effects of Plants

Plants are not only wonderful decorative objects, they also contribute to our well-being. Their beauty is a spiritual pleasure, and taking care of them diverts one from stress and worry and offers a little contact with the soil and closeness to nature. A study involving plants in the workplace showed that houseplants had a noticeably positive effect on the health and mood of the test subjects. But plants can do still more:

They improve the air. They humidify dry centrally heated air and filter out dust, which settles on the leaves and can be sluiced off or wiped away. Besides, they produce oxygen all day long, even if in relatively small amounts.

They filter pollutants from the air. A study completed by NASA proved that the spider plant, philodendron, ivy, and mother-in-law's tongue could clearly lower the formaldehyde concentration in the air. Chrysanthemums and gerbera displayed the best effect against benzene and trichlorethylene.

Houseplants for Every Lifestyle

For "classical decor" with furniture in the English or French style, the following are especially good: cyclamens, azaleas, begonias, ivy, ferns, gloxinias, camellias, palms, and African violets.

With austere art deco and with art nouveau use plants whose contours are sharply outlined or that have an ornamental, elegant effect, for example *Alocasia, Amaryllis,* flamingo flower, *Spathiphyllum, Monstera,* gardenia, calla, *Stephanotis,* string-of-hearts, and passionflower.

Exotic furniture of rattan harmonizes well with all tropical and subtropical plants, but especially with members of the arum family, bromeliads, *Ficus* species, blooming gesneriads, marantas, medinillas, orchids, palms, and passionflowers.

Furniture with an Oriental look goes well with austerely formal or Oriental plants like azaleas, bamboos, calamus, lady palms, and bonsais.

Contemporary designer furniture of steel, glass, and marble needs plants with a graphic or sculptured effect, for instance *Asparagus,* dracaenas, euphorbias, ferns, monsteras, large *Ficus* species, cacti, palms, scheffleras, aspidistras, radermacheras, yuccas, indoor linden, Norfolk Island pine, and grape ivy.

Rustic furniture needs cheerful, colorful flowering plants like cyclamens, winter-flowering begonias, kalanchoes, impatience, campanulas, Easter and Christmas cacti, geraniums, primulas, winter-flowering begonias, poinsettias, billbergia, or sturdy green plants, such as staghorn fern, schefflera, and Japanese fatsia.

Mediterranean furniture of pine harmonizes particularly well with *Agave, Aloe, Bougainvillea,* baby's tears, echeverias, elephant's foot, euphorbias, sedums, jade plants, hibiscus, cacti, myrtle, button fern, *Yucca,* and with miniature orange and lemon trees as well.

The Leaves Reveal the Light Needs

Almost all leaves constitute the real charm of a plant. Often, to the knowledgeable observer, they also reveal the plant's light needs:

<u>Leaves that are fleshy or are reduced to thorns:</u> Full sun and light. Examples: *Echeveria, Sedum* (1), *Kalanchoe*, cacti, euphorbias, *Nematanthus, Sansevieria.*

<u>Leathery leaves:</u> Much light, but no sun. Examples: Rubber plant, *Ixora*, coffee tree, camellias, *Stephanotis, Hoya* (2).

<u>Small, often needle-fine leaves:</u> Full sun. Examples: *Asparagus*, crown-of-thorns, myrtle (3).

<u>Large, usually soft leaves:</u> No sun, bright to semishady. Examples: Windowleaf, flamingo flower, *Gloxinia, Philodendron, Aspidistra*, Japanese fatsia, indoor linden (4).

<u>White or yellow-green variegated leaves:</u> Never sunny but always brighter than the green-leaved varieties. Examples: Ivy (5), pothos, spider plant, piggyback plant, *Syngonium*, screw pine, spindle tree, *Tradescantia*. Exceptions: Dieffenbachia, *Aglaonema*, which do better in semishade.

<u>Colored leaves:</u> Bright to semi-shade but never sunny. Examples: Rex and other rhizomatous begonias, *Calathea, Ctenanthe*, dracaenas, *Hypoestes*, croton, marantas (6), neoregelias, nidulariums, pepper, *Stromanthe*, earth star. Exceptions: *Coleus* and bloodleaf, which like full sun.

<u>Pinnate leaves:</u> No sun, bright to semishady. Examples: Ferns (7), *Polysicas*, palms.

<u>Gray-green leaves:</u> Much light. Examples: Silky oak, rosary vine (8), gray tillandsias.

<u>Soft leaves arranged in a rosette:</u> Semishady. Examples: cape primrose, primulas, African violets (9).

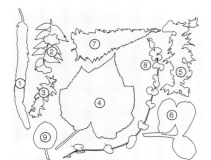

Houseplants for Hot and Sunny Locations

Desert rose, *Adenium* (see page 91)
Aeoniums, *Aeonium* (see page 142)
Aloes, *Aloe* (see page 144)
Ponytail palm, *Beaucarnea* (see page 147)
Bougainvillea, *Bougainvillea* (see page 139)
Bottle tree, *Brachychiton* (see page 149)
Crassulas, *Crassula* species (see page 155)
Echeverias, *Echeveria* species (see page 107)
Euphorbias, succulents *Euphorbia* species (see pages 108, 163)
Blood lily, *Haemanthus* (see page 113)
Star cactus, *Haworthia* (see page 168)
China rose, *Hibiscus* (see page 113)
Bottle plant, *Jatropha* (see page 119)
Palm-Beach bells, *Kalanchoe* (see page 174)
Shaving-brush tree, *Pachira* (see page 174)
Passionflower, *Passiflora* (see page 124)
Fragrant geraniums, *Pelargonium* (see page 176)
Canary Island date, *Phoenix canariensis* (see page 210)
Swedish ivy, *Plectranthus* (see page 180)
Groundsel, *Senecio* (see page 193)
Yuccas, *Yucca* (see page 190)

Fragrant Plants

Dwarf orange, *Citrus* (see page 102)
Alpine violet, *Cyclamen* (see page 105)
German violet, *Exacum* (see page 110)
Gardenia, *Gardenia* (see page 111)
Wax plant, *Hoya bella, Hoya carnosa* (see page 115)
Jasmine, *Jasminum* (see page 119)
Fragrant geraniums, *Pelargonium* (see page 176)
Madagascar jasmine, *Stephanotis* (see page 133)

Houseplants for Shady Locations

Maidenhair ferns, *Adiantum* species (see page 196)
Aspidistras, *Aspidistra* (see page 147)
Rhizomatous begonias, *Begonia* (see page 148)
Spider plant (green variety), *Chlorophytum* (see page 151)
Venezuela treebine, *Cissus rhombifolia* (see page 152)
Holly fern, *Cyrtomium* (see page 198)
Ball fern, *Davallia* (see page 198)
Dragon tree, *Dracaena marginata* (see pages 160, 161)
Aralia ivy, *x Fatshedera*
Japanese fatsia, *Fatsia* (see page 163)
Sentry palm, *Howea* (see page 209)
Microlepia, *Microlepia* (see page 199)
Radiator plant, *Peperomia* species (see page 177)
Heart-leaf, *Philodendron scandens* (see page 178)
Staghorn fern, *Platycerium* (see page 202)
Brake, *Pteris* (see page 203)
Piggyback plant, *Tolmiea* (see page 189)

Plants for Indoor Water Gardens

Water and Floating Plants
Water trumpets, *Cryptocoyrne wendtii, Cryptocoryne ponte-deriifolia*
Sword plants, *Echinodorus* hybrids
Water lily, *Nymphaea daubenyana*
Water lettuce, *Pistia stratiotes*
Swamp Plants
Papyrus and umbrella sedge, *Cyperus papyrus, Cyperus alternifolius, Cyperus haspan, Cyperus pumilus*
Anubias species
Bullrushes, *Scirpus* (see page 185)
Humidity-loving Houseplants
Grassy-leaved sweet flag, *Acorus gramineus* (see page 142)
Jaburan lily, *Ophiopogon jaburan* (see page 193)
Spathe flower, *Spathiphyllum* (see page 133)

My Tip: For small plants a dish 2 in. (6 cm) deep will be sufficient; larger ones need a deeper container. Important: The location must be very bright.

Plants for Children

The plants most exciting to children are the ones that do something.
The peanut (*Arachis hypogaea*) blooms for only a few hours and wilts after self-pollination. After that it lengthens its flower stalk, sinks it toward the ground, and burrows into the earth, where the ripening of the seed takes place (hence the name the Europeans use, "ground nut"). If you want to show your children this strange behavior, sow peanuts in February (unsalted ones, of course!). Remove the brown hull from the seed and put a group of three in a pot. Place the pot in a warm, light place and keep damp.

Cotton (*Gossypium herbaceum*), like the peanut, can be sown in the spring. It blooms about six months after sowing, with a mallowlike creamy yellow flower that is self-fertilizing. After nine weeks, a green capsule forms; later this bursts and white "cotton wads" are released.

Mimosa (*Mimosa pudica*) reacts if you touch it with a finger or shake the pot a little. It then quickly claps shut its feathery leaves; with stronger irritants it even drops the four lobed leaf, together with the stem.

Venus's fly-trap (*Dionaea muscipula*), when touched, snaps shut the lobes of its flower, which is furnished with sensitive hairs. In general it isn't very easy to main-tain as a houseplant (see page 192).

Decorative Idea— Plants in the Paludarium

A glass container filled with water-retaining clay gravel is ideal for bulrushes, sedges, and calla lily, which all love constant humidity. If you want the calla to bloom again, however, you must be sure to remove it from the paludarium at the end of May and keep it dry in another container for two months. Then you can repot it with the others again.

BASKETS

No more room on the windowsill? Hanging baskets are the best way to get plants up high.

The display of the Palm-Beach bells (*Kalanchoe manginii*) delights the eye from February to March.

Streptocarpus saxorum loves a sunny place and indicates by its fleshy little leaves that it requires very little water. Keep cool in winter!

Cascades of Flowers and Foliage

Hanging baskets offer trailing, climbing, and creeping plants the chance to develop on all sides. The leaves may then cascade like a waterfall, flowers foam over, and offspring or shoots dangle freely. Of course, hanging plants aren't exactly easy to take care of. How much to water becomes a question of instinct. Because the plants are often very leafy, they evaporate a lot of water; furthermore, they dry much faster in their lofty location than down below. Thus, when temperatures are warm, it is advisable to water them twice a week. For this purpose it's best to use a plastic English greenhouse watering can, which has a curving waterspout of about 23$\frac{1}{2}$ in. (60 cm) in length. Important: Only give as much water as the plants are able to use up—don't forget, most hanging pots have no drainage holes. So to avoid standing water, put a three-quarter inch (2 cm) layer of clay pot shards in a solid-bottomed ceramic pot before setting the flowerpot in it. For containers with a drainage hole, it's best to take them down once a week, put them in the bathtub, and spray them thoroughly with a gentle, lukewarm spray. To protect furniture and

The hallmarks of the strawberry begonia (*Saxifraga stolonipera*) are the threadlike runners.

floors, rehang the plants only when they've stopped dripping.

Recommended Plants to Hang

Especially robust plants are: *Asparagus, Billbergia, Ceropegia, Chlorophytum, Cissus, Hoya, Saxifraga stolonifera,* succulent *Senecio* species, *Setcreasea, Tradescantia, Zebrina.*

Hanging plants for areas that are only moderately warm: *Ampelopsis, Ficus pumila, Hedera, Jasminum, Pelargonium odoratissimum, Peperomia, Schlumbergera* hybrids, *Scirpus, Tolmiea.*

Hanging plants that need warmth and high humidity: *Aeschynanthus, Columnea, Hypocyrta, Dipladenia, Episcia, Epipremnum, Ficus sagittata, Monstera, Nepenthes, Philodendron, Syngonium,* as well as rhizomatous and winter-flowering begonias and, of course, many ferns.

Since it's difficult to mist the plants because of the furniture, the use of a humidifier is recommended.

My Tip: If you mount a plant spotlight on a side wall, it's even possible to have hanging plants in the middle of the room.

The root ball of parrot's beak (*Lotus berthelotii*) should never be allowed to dry out.

Pothos (*Epipremnum pinnatum*) can grow as long as 33 ft (10 m).

One of the popular names for *Sedum morganianum* is burro's tail.

31

Cultivating Houseplants Successfully

Proper watering, fertilizing, repotting, and pruning are important and must be learned. But cultivation also includes observation, instinct, and knowledge of what the individual plant needs.

An old nugget of farmers' wisdom says, "Your garden wants to see you every day." This applies to the plants in the house too. Like pets, plants need human care and suffer when they don't get it. But this doesn't consist only of watering and fertilizing. Rubber plants and cyclamens thrive demonstrably better in a relaxed, positive atmosphere. So be sympathetic toward them—or better, only deal with plants that you really like.

Cultivating a plant you are fond of is not work but a constant pleasure for which you will gladly sacrifice a little time.

First Care After Purchase

Let us imagine ourselves in the situation of a houseplant. How much stress it has already suffered before it comes under our protection! At first it was pampered in a horticultural factory with every possible refinement. Then it was snatched from this not native, to be sure, but nevertheless fostering, environment to be stacked in palettes in a truck and sent cross-country for hundreds of miles. Finally it stopped over—so to speak—at the garden center, was sold, transported again, and finally came to rest on our windowsill. Each time it has to get used to a new environment, that is, light, temperature, location, and water quality change.

Acclimate every newly acquired plant for several days in a "neutral" place. That is, one that is semi-shaded and where the temperature is around 64° F (18° C).

If it's wintertime, don't put the new plant in an artificially heated room, even if it likes warmth. In a florist shop plants are often kept at cooler temperatures than those prescribed. Great temperature changes are shocks to which many plants will react with flower, bud, or leaf drop.

Examine the pot ball. If it's dry, water once thoroughly and after half an hour pour away the water that has drained through. Orchids should only be misted at first.

Do not transplant, even if the plant is completely potbound and the pot seems to be too small. Wait about two weeks until the plant has gotten used to your living conditions. Do not repot plants bought in fall and winter until the end of February. The nutrients in the new soil are then available to the plant at the right time—the beginning of the growth period. When you're repotting, don't use too large a pot. Plants in pots that are too large usually—depending on the pot size—retain too much water.

Dish gardens usually contain various species and varieties, which often enough do not have the same care requirements. Place these gift arrangements in bright, warm (around 68° F [20° C]), but not sunny places. Separate the plants before their roots get intertwined and pot them singly or in roomier containers—best done in the spring.

What You Need for Care

- Handrake and trowel
- Watering can with long, thin spout
- Spray bottles for spraying water, insecticides, and foliar fertilizer
- Watering can with filter
- All-purpose household shears
- Garden shears
- Sharp knife
- Wood and bamboo stakes
- Florist's wire, twine, string
- Charcoal powder (for disinfecting cut ends)
- Fertilizer
- Water softeners
- Various soils, soil components, or additives
- Plant lights (for very dark locations)
- Vacation or delayed-action watering systems

These delightfully marked maranta plants will not tolerate dry heated air.

Get to Know the Plant

Plants are extraordinarily adaptable and don't suffer if you don't follow the care plan exactly every now and again. But naturally they thrive best when care is right. So you should learn the basics about every new plant arrival in your home.

• Read over the care directions in the particular plant portrait (see pages 84–299) carefully.

• Compare the statements with your conditions and care habits.

• Besides individual timetables for culture, take into consideration basics like growth factors (see page 36) and vegetative rhythms (see right).

• Try to improve less favorable locations by installing plant lights (see page 45), increasing the humidity (see page 43), shading, and insulating windowsills (see page 45).

Vegetative Rhythm and What It Means for Care

The Growing Season

For all plants the growing season depends on light. For our indoor plants it begins when the days grow longer.

Distinguishing signs: Fresh green new shoots, increasing growth.

Implications for care: Beginning in spring, slowly increase the amount of water and begin fertilizing.

The Resting Period

For many plants, for example those from tropical and subtropical latitudes with unfluctuating climate, there is no rest period. As house-plants in our latitude they are forced into a resting period, which is conditioned by the decreasing amount of sunshine and the shorter days in the fall and winter months. But a rest period can also be part of the genetic program of some species.

Beautifully Colorful—Green on Green

The plants on pages 34–35 from left to right:

Back row: *Calathea veitchiana*, sword fern (*Nephrolepsis exaltata*), stromanthe (*Stromanthe* 'Stripe Star'), rose geranium (*Pelargonium graveolens*).

Front row: Sword fern (*Nephrolepsis exaltata* 'Linda'), bulrush (*Scirpus cernuus*), inch plant (*Callisia repens*), guzmania (*Guzmania*), baby rubber plant (*Peperomia obtusifolia*), coral moss (*Nertera granadensis*), umbrella sedge (*Cyperus*), brittle maiden-hair fern (*Adiantum tenerum*), umbrella sedge (*Cyperus*).

This is true in the case of plants that die back and regenerate themselves from tubers and bulbs (like amaryllis, cyclamen, and many gesneriads) or of deciduous plants like *Bougainvillea glabra*. Also, plants that in their native habitat must survive periods of drought manage to live through these resting periods. Furthermore, these rest periods do not always occur in our fall and winter. In the case of the calla lily, for instance, the rest period doesn't begin until the end of May.

<u>Recognizable signs</u>: Growth decreases until it is at a standstill. Yellowing of leaves. Leaf drop.

<u>Implications for care</u>: Many houseplants require the maintenance of the resting period to be able to begin to grow again and to set flowers. This means that the houseplant gardener must provide a dry, cool period. Since the life process diminishes with the diminution of light, the other growth promoters such as water and warmth must be reduced at the same time or even taken away entirely. Moreover, fertilizing is stopped because a plant in resting condition or with light deficiency cannot deal with nutrients at all. For example, cacti that are compelled by warmth and nutrients to grow during the winter do not produce any very hardy tissue and do not bloom the following year.

My Tip: You can give plants from the tropical rain forest, which do not need a resting period, excellent, appropriate care under plant lights, which provide constant optimal light for growth. Of course constant warmth and a consistently high humidity are the important concomitant measures.

The Five Growth Factors

The growth factors of light, warmth, water, air, and nutrients are the engine that gets plant life started and keeps it going. They are mutually dependent on each other and mutually influence each other. Thus, they must be coordinated correctly for the species and for the time of the year. The growth factors are so important that the care plans in the plant portraits section (pages 84–229) are arranged according to them.

1. Light

By means of light, through photosynthesis, the plant manufactures the carbohydrates that it needs for growth. Light affects the direction of growth, influences the shape of the plant, leaf color, and flower development. Diminish the light intensity and the life processes are reduced to a pilot light. Light intensity is expressed in footcandles or lux and can be measured with a meter (see drawing, page 45). The minimum light needed by plants lies between 65 to 93 footcandles (700–1,000 lux). Below this, growth and flower development stagnates. Optimal growth becomes possible above 930 foot-candles (10,000 lux).

The duration of light a plant needs varies with the individual and depends on its natural habitat. On the average, a plant needs 12 to 16 hours of light daily.

Tips for care: The brighter a plant's location, the more vigorously it will grow, therefore the more warmth, water, and fertilizer it tolerates. In a darker position, the other growth factors should be diminished accordingly.

2. Warmth

Warmth promotes growth, nutrient uptake, and root vigor. Plants from the tropical rain forest need constant warmth; other tropical and subtropical plants like it if we turn down the heat a few degrees in winter; tropical mountain-dwellers and Mediterranean species must be cool when the dark season begins. Important for all is bottom warmth. The soil temperature should not fall below room temperature.

Tips for care: The warmer and brighter a plant's location, the more water it needs. Water less when it's cool. Coolness plus dampness is poison for houseplants.

3. Water

Water is a main constituent of the plant, serves as the transporter of nutrients (also of fertilizer), and maintains the pressure in the cells. If it's lacking, the plant wilts. If there's too much of it, the same symptom appears, for the water actually squeezes out the oxygen that the roots need for respiration. Water is constantly evaporated, more in sunny places, in high temperatures, and in dry air than in shady places with lower temperatures and humid air, and from large, soft, and thickly foliaged plants more than from small- and hard-leaved ones.

Tips for care: Water plants more during the growing season and water those in a bright location, in heat, and when the air is dry. Water them less during the rest period, and when they are in a shady spot, in cool areas, or where humidity is high.

Varieties of Camellia japonica

1 'Ima Kumagai'
2 'St. Ewe'
3 'Imbricata Rubra'
4 'Jury's Yellow'
5 'C. M. Wilson'
6 'Bob Hope'
7 'Fred Sander'
8 'Ezo Nishiki'
9 'Betty Sheffield Supreme'

4. Air and Humidity

Air and humidity are essential needs for plant life.

Air is needed by plants to breathe and to remain healthy. Stagnant air, on the other hand (as when the plants are crowded together), promotes pests. Drafts and air that is contaminated with exhaust or poisons (cigarette smoke) can produce leaf, flower, or bud drop.

Humidity is important for all houseplants that are not furnished with their own protection against evaporation (see page 16), or that can take up water from atmospheric moisture alone (epiphytes), or that come from the constantly moist rain forest and are not at all adapted to our dry heated air.

The humidity requirement of some tropical inhabitants lies between 60 and 80 percent. Most houseplants need between 50 and 80 percent humidity. A healthy house climate for people, animals, and plants should contain 50 to 60 percent humidity. In summer, in good weather the humidity ranges around 50 percent; on dark and stormy days, from 60 to 80 percent. In winter, the humidity in a centrally heated room is around 40 to 50 percent-problematic, dry air that most plants cannot tolerate. You can measure with a hygrometer whether there is enough moisture in your home. The apparatus can be found in a "weather station" with a thermometer and barometer or by itself (in a garden center that handles orchid equipment).

Tips for care: The higher the humidity is, the more warmth a plant can tolerate.

5. Potting Medium and Fertilizer

The plant obtains its nutrients from the potting medium. Furthermore, it serves to hold the roots and should be so constituted that the roots are always surrounded by slight dampness but air can also get to them. This means that a good potting medium should be able to retain moisture and be air permeable.

Potting medium can be produced by the gardener from various components or bought ready-mixed. In my experience, plants grow best in commercial potting soils and in the ready-made special mediums for particular plant groups (see page 40). Use only high-quality commercial potting soils for your houseplants. Inexpensive ones may not have satisfactory water retention capacity and porosity for air circulation, sufficient nutrient content, pH value, hygienic condition, or humus content.

Other plant materials or soil additives: Coarse peat, loam, bark humus, expanded clay bits and clay gravel, perlite, vermiculite, Styrofoam fragments, sphagnum moss, roots of the *Osmunda* fern as well as cork oak bark, and tree-fern boards for supporting epiphytes.

Environmental tip: Our peat regions are rapidly becoming depleted. Therefore substitute for peat-rich soil an alternative potting medium, for example chipped bark or clay gravel (see page 40). Sphagnum, *Osmunda*, and tree-fern are protected species and are only available from old stocks. Alternatives are aquarium filter fiber, Styrofoam fragments (unfortunately also not good for the environment), and bark.

Tips for care: Never allow mediums containing peat to dry out! Peat does of course have good water storing capacity, but once it is completely dry, it takes up water very poorly.

Fertilizer is necessary because the earth in a pot offers only limited nutrients, and plants, if they are to grow, need a fresh supply.

The principal nutrients are N (nitrogen), P (phosphorus), K (potassium), and Mg (magnesium).

Nitrogen makes the plants grow, provides for the growth of shoots and leaves and for the development of chlorophyll. But too much makes the tissue soft and subject to disease.

Phosphorus is necessary for the development of roots and buds as well as for the ripening of fruits and seeds. Flowering plants need more of it than do green plants.

Potassium makes the plant tissue strong and resistant to disease and insect pests and is important for photosynthesis.

Magnesium is a significant nutrient that the plant uses principally in the formation of chlorophyll.

Trace elements are those nutrients that the plant must have for life but nevertheless takes up only in "trace" amounts. For the smooth-running operation of the life processes the plant requires iron, copper, manganese, molybdenum, zinc, and boron.

A good complete fertilizer must contain the four chief nutrients and all the trace elements necessary for life. They can of course be supplied in various dosages. Growth-promoting fertilizers always contain more phosphorus and potassium than nitrogen. Fertilizers are available in various combinations and forms. Especially easy to use are liquid fertilizers, which can be watered in, or fertilizer sticks, which you simply poke into the soil.

The correct dosage depends on the plant roots' sensitivity to salts. For most plants .07 oz or $\frac{1}{2}$ teaspoon (2 gm or 2 ml) of fertilizer to 1 qt (1 l) of water is enough. Follow the manufacturer's instructions, use the measuring spoon provided, and make the solution too weak rather than too strong. You can work out the proportionate ounces (oz), quarts (qt), milliliters (ml), or gallons (gal). Salt-sensitive plants like orchids and ferns should receive very low dosages.

Small fern garden in an aquarium. A lava rock provides for humidity and good health.

Tips for care:
• The rule of thumb is: Feed houseplants every two weeks during the growing season. However, vigorously growing plants can even be fed weekly; slow-growing ones should only be fertilized every four weeks.
• Never fertilize a dry root ball or in full sun.
• It's better to feed often and at low concentrations than to do it seldom and in high dosages.
• Only feed when the plant is growing.
• Fertilize less when the plant is receiving less light than it needs for growth. When light is deficient the nutrients are not taken up and with inorganic fertilizers the soil can become oversalted.
• Plants without rest periods also need fertilizer once a month in winter.
• Important: Feeding does not take the place of repotting.

Should You Talk to Plants?
I know many plant lovers who attribute their success to the fact that they talk to their charges. Every so often even I "talk to myself" with plants in the garden or in the house. Trials with lie detectors have shown that plants react "anxiously" to attacks (fire, cutting implements). It still is not clear what kind of sensory apparatus plants possess. But little by little, new discoveries are being made. So far the following things are known: Ultrasound stimulates growth, an anesthetized tree survives transplanting better, and plants thrive better with chamber music than with hard rock. Why this is so is not clear. Yet, why could it not be that what today we cannot see, hear, or demonstrate by means of technology, tomorrow may prove to be the case? Even today it is possible to hear the

sound made by thirsty plants. In England a sensor was developed that picks up the alarm sound of plants that need water. The tone, which lies in the region of ultrasound at 1 MHz, arises from the stress on the fine water columns rising in the capillaries that provide for the whole plant. Human hubris is thus inappropriate because we know so pitifully little about all living things. Therefore, speak to your plants, and stroke their leaves gently. The evidence that it does them harm has not yet been produced.

HOW TO

Potting medium and techniques of repotting

Potting soil consisting mainly of peat, sand, and nutrients grows most plants well. You can tell this by the fact that the earth is quickly permeated by healthy roots and many new shoots develop.

Expanded clay induces many houseplants to thrive. The water-retentive clay bits (available in three sizes: balls, pellets, and granules) give the roots support. Their nutrients consist of water and the nutrient solution.

Epiphyte medium provides good rooting conditions for tree dwellers and air-rooted plants like ferns, bromeliads, or orchids. They are especially attractive if bound to an epiphtye support of gnarled wood or a piece of bark.

What You Should Know About Potting Mediums

The potting medium is both culture medium and foundation. A good potting medium should be well aerated, warm, and permeable to water. Also, it should be water retentive, rich in nutrients, and slightly acidic.

Potting mediums:
- All-purpose potting soil. A mixture blended to achieve a well-balanced soil that meets the need of the greatest variety of plants. Although commercial formulas do vary, such a mix basically consists of peat moss, humus, vermiculite, and sand. It may also include nutrients and other additives.
- Soilless potting mixes. This medium (sometimes called the Cornell mix) usually contains peat moss, vermiculite, and perlite to which fertilizer and trace elements are added. Soilless mixes are often used for propagating plants.
- African violet mix. A medium formulated for gesneriads, but other plants that prefer a slightly acidic medium do well in this. It is similar to all-purpose mix but more porous and acidic.
- Cactus soil mix. A sandy blend.
- Epiphyte planting materials. A blend of chopped sphagnum moss, Osmunda fern roots, and coarse shredded peat.
- Orchid soils. A mixture of shredded peat, bark, hardwood charcoal, Styrofoam flakes, and mineral materials like vermiculite, perlite, and, if available, even ground mussel shells or ground pumice.
- Expanded clay bits. Balls, pellets, or granules of clay that are water retentive, aerated, and stable in structure (proof against rotting).
- Clay pot shards for hydroculture.

As you gain experience, you should not be afraid to make simple variations to the standard all-purpose mixture for adapting it to specific plant preferences.

Root Ball in Clay Pellets
Ideal for all who usually water too much or too little. Spongelike, the pea-sized clay fragments suck up 130 percent of their own weight in water and release it to the roots as needed.

How to Transplant to Water

1 Thoroughly wash the dirt out of the root ball under running water.
2 Shorten roots that are too long, cut away rotten (brown) ones.
3 Set plant on washed expanded clay pellets and fill basket around it.
4 Place the basket pot in an outer pot and fill with lukewarm water.

How to Repot

It's time to repot when
- the earth is almost completely filled with roots,
- the soil smells moldy,
- the plant has root sickness,
- the plant bursts the pot or the roots are growing out of the drainage hole.

The ideal repotting time for most plants is spring. Otherwise it's fair to say: Always repot after blooming.

The new container should be about ³/₄ in. (2 cm) larger than the old one. Soak clay pots two hours before repotting.

This is how it's done: Water the plant several hours beforehand. Turn the pot over and rap it sharply or break it if necessary. Cut open a plastic pot. Crumble away the topmost layer of soil. Loosen a tight network of roots with a small, sharp instrument, such as a screwdriver.

Trimming the roots is necessary when the roots are brown-black and rotten or with very old plants that you don't want to keep putting into larger pots. Powder the cut end with charcoal. Finally cut back the branches as well, so that the balance will be maintained.

Cutting back is recommended for leafless plants (see page 44).

Important: Drainage. Lay a piece of broken flower pot over the drainage hole or cover it with a finger-thick layer of expanded clay bits (for large pots, 2 to 4 in. [5–10 cm]), pebbles, or cut-up Styrofoam for drainage. Pot the plant, water, keep in a bright place where the roots will be warm, but do not put it in a sunny spot. Ground warmth promotes the development of roots.

Further Care: Only water enough so that the earth doesn't dry out. As soon as new growth appears, begin care according to plant's requirements. Fertilize six to eight weeks after transplanting!

Replacing the top layer of earth is recommended for large plants that, for reasons of space, you don't want to keep on repotting in larger pots and for plants that should not be repotted (palms).

Converting to hydroculture demands careful washing of the root system (see drawings, How to Transplant to Water). Transplanting to clay pebbles (see drawing, Root Ball in Clay Pellets) offers no stress to the plant because the completely intact root ball is merely set into the new potting medium.

Epiphytes are potted in pots with holes or latticed baskets or bound on bark, tree-fern blocks, or moss boards.

Repotting Foliage and Flowering Plants

1 Hold your hand over the potting soil. Turn pot upside down. Carefully remove root ball. Untangle root network. Do not crumble away soil that is permeated with roots, trim away injured roots, shorten ones that are too long.
2 Provide drainage by covering the drainage hole with a curved piece of broken flower pot or a layer of expanded clay pellets.
3 Put in some soil. Place the plant in the middle of the pot and at about the same level it was at before. Fill up with soil and press firmly. Leave ¹/₂ in. (1 cm) of space to allow for watering.

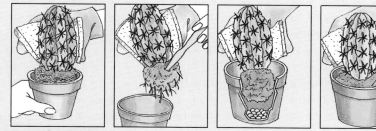

Repotting Cactus

1 Lift cactus out of pot with pieces of Styrofoam.
2 Make holes in the root ball and remove roots that are sick or dried out.
3 Arrange drainage on the bottom of the pot. Set cactus in the pot at the same height as before.
4 Fill in with potting medium and press firmly.

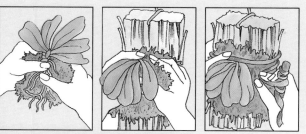

The Correct Way to Fasten Orchids

1 Wrap the air roots with plant material.
2 Fasten the plant to the piece of bark in such a way that no water can run into its center—danger of rot!
3 Bind it to the bark, not too firmly, with a strip of nylon stocking.

HOW TO

**Watering,
softening
water,
and providing
humidity**

Watering from the top is recommended for most houseplants. The potting medium will thus be dampened uniformly and the fertilizer in the water can be evenly distributed. Tip: A watering can with a long spout keeps the leaves from getting wet.

Watering from the bottom is good for plants with tubers, stems, or leaves that are particularly susceptible to dampness (for example, African violets). Disadvantage: The fertilizer salts will be pulled upwards and will crystallize on the surface of the soil as the water evaporates.

Soaking is the best way to provide thorough watering for epiphytes and orchids, which have a particularly porous potting medium. It is also an ideal method for hanging plants that are often in pots or baskets that do not have a sufficiently large saucer beneath them.

Ten Golden Rules of Watering

How much water a plant needs depends on its individual requirements, its vegetative rhythms, and the potting medium, as well as on light, temperature, and humidity.

1 It is high time to water when the earth looks light or has drawn away from the edge of the pot, if the pot is light, or if the plant wilts.

2 Water most plants from the top; in some exceptional instances, water from the bottom. It's best to soak dried-out plants, epiphytes, and hanging plants.

3 The ideal water is at room temperature and soft; you can find out about hardness from your local waterworks.

4 If water from your tap has more than 13 mg/L of dissolved salts, you should soften it.

5 In general tap water should be left to stand overnight so that the chlorine evaporates and the lime precipitates.

6 Plants in dry, warm air, in bright, sunny places, abundantly leaved and large-leaved plants, plants in clay pots, plants with high water requirements (usually planted in clay- or peat-rich soils) must be watered more often.

7 Plants in high-humidity, low-temperature, or light-poor locations as well as plants in plastic pots and plants with low water requirements, which are frequently planted in sandy soils, should be watered less often.

8 During the growth period, water plants thoroughly but not too often. Small quantities of water only dampen the surface and run out before the water reaches the fine roots in the interior.

9 As a rule the amount of water should be decreased in fall and winter.

10 Always remove the superfluous water in saucers and outer pots.

Water Bromeliads in the Cup

For any other plant, standing water of this sort would be lethal—not for bromeliads. From their water-proof cups—so-called cisterns—they supply themselves with water and nutrients.

Three Ways to Soften Water for Your Plants

1 With peat. Fill a garbage bag with 1 q (1 L) of dried peat and suspend it in 10 q (10 L) of water overnight.

2 With a filtered watering can, which contains an ion exchanger, so that limestone, chlorine, and other impurities are removed.

3 With the addition of a softening agent in liquid or solid form. Afterward, let the water stand for several hours.

How You Can Improve Humidity

A humidity of 60 to 70 percent is the ideal climate for most indoor plants. In summer, low humidity is less of a problem, but in winter in a warm room it can very quickly drop to under 40 percent—causing problems for plants.

Direct humidity can be provided by spraying (see drawing 4, Humidity). This way you imitate the falling of dew, which is indicated for tillandsias and other epiphytes, for example.

Important: Use soft water and a fine spray. Do not spray flowers or spray in sunlight.

Indirect humidity is appreciated by most houseplants. Besides the methods illustrated (see drawings 1–3, Humidity), there are still the following other possibilities:

• Installation of an electric humidifier, aquariums, room fountains, lava blocks.
• Large-leaved plant neighbors and swamp plants.
• Placing plants on saucers with peat, sand, or pebbles that are constantly damp.

My Tip: If you want to increase the humidity by spraying, you should not direct spray onto leaves that are particularly sensitive to water (for example, begonias, *Streptocarpus*, gloxinias, mimosas, *Miltonia*). Spray only in their vicinity (see drawing 3, Humidity). In this case it's even better to use some other method of indirect humidity.

Watering While You're on Vacation

If you're only going to be away from home for several days, water the plants thoroughly, give them a cooler place, or tuck the plant into clay granules, which can take up 130 percent of its own weight in water (see drawing, Root Ball in Clay Pellets, page 40).

For longer absences there are various "plant sitters," which all work on the principle of capillary action. When the potting medium is dry, the plant sucks water from a reservoir through an inserted clay cone (see drawing 3, Automatic Watering), a wick (see drawings 1 and 2, Automatic Watering), a woolen cord, a fleece strand, or porous wood. Underlaid pieces of felt can also be used in this way (see drawing, Watering During Vacation, page 43).

Important: Try it out ahead of time to see if it works and how long the water supply lasts.

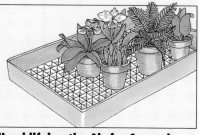

Humidifying the Air for Several Plants

Lay a rack in a tray and add water until it comes just to the bottom of the grating. The plants will have dry feet but be enveloped by evaporating water.

Humidity for Individual Plants

1 Embed pot in a larger pot containing expanded clay pellets, peat, or clay granules.
2 Put the plants on an overturned saucer in a larger, water-filled container.
3 Use indirect misting, that is, not on the plant itself but only in its environment.
4 Spraying the plant directly. Important for tillandsias and epiphytes.

Two Ideas for Automatic Watering

1 Introduce a Fiberglas wick through the drainage hole of the pot with a large needle.
2 Spread the wick along the surface of the soil and cover it with earth. Allow the bottom of the wick to hang down into the water container.
3 Plants will suck water from a dish through a clay cone when they are dry.

Watering During Vacation

Place a water absorptive mat on the kitchen counter so that the end hangs in the water-filled sink. The mat can take care of a whole row of plants. Important: The mat must not hang over the outside edge of the sink so that no water goes on the floor.

Cutting, training, and culture tricks

Cutting, Pinching Back, Trimming
1 The place to cut is just above a bud.
2 Pinching back: Nipping off the end of a shoot, especially in a young plant, so that it will branch.
3 Trimming: For rejuvenating, shaping, or making smaller, especially for older plants.

Training Plants on a Hoop
Suitable for: Twining and Climbing Plants
1 Form wire into a hoop and insert it deep into the pot.
2 Carefully wind shoots around hoop and tie them if necessary.

Establishing a Moss Stake
Suitable for: Air plants
1 Insert the moss stake (available from garden suppliers) in the pot and anchor it with soil.
2 Set the plant in next to it and fasten the shoots to it.

A Tree with Intertwined Trunks
The still-pliable trunks of the young weeping fig can be braided to make a charming standard.

Proper Cutting
Plants are cut back both to make them grow bushier and to keep them short.
The optimum time for pruning is spring, before the plant begins to put out new growth, or the time just after blooming (often the fall).
The correct cut is made with a clean, sharp knife diagonally and very close to the bud (see drawing 1, Cutting). Large cut areas are best disinfected with charcoal powder. With plants that "bleed" (*Ficus* species, euphorbias), spray the cut areas with water.
How much to take off? This depends on the kind of plant, its growth, and what you have in mind.
• In pinching back (see drawing 2, Pinching Back) the ends of the shoots are nipped back with the fingers.
• In pruning (see drawing 3, Trimming), if you want to shape the plant, cut only the tips; if you want to rejuvenate it, cut back as much as $^2/_3$ of the plant. The most drastic pruning is recommended when the plant grows very vigorously, is bare underneath, or has formed straggly shoots with large intervals between the leaves.
• In a bushy plant with two shoots very close together, one shoot should be removed entirely.

Training Plants Well
For binding on a frame (see drawings, Hoop) or espaliering, choose plants with long, soft shoots.
Moss stakes (see drawings, Moss Stake), which can be purchased, are ideal for *Philodendron* and *Monstera*.
Make your own standard (see drawings, Training a Standard). It often may take five years to achieve a finished standard. To allow for possible losses, it's a good idea to begin with several plants at the same time.

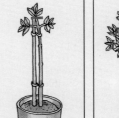

Training a Standard
1 Keep removing the side shoots of a sturdy young plant.
2 Introduce a support and secure it with string loops at intervals. When the desired height is reached, prune the top.
3 Keep pruning back the side shoots so that a thick crown will develop.

Ten Tricks for Successful Culture

Usually the expenditure of time doesn't seem at all large when it has to do with facilitating optimal growth of one's houseplants.

1 The trick with the apple (see drawing 1, Culture Tricks). Ripening apples and citrus fruits give off ethylene gas (see page 68), which is a plant hormone that bromeliads need to develop flowers. Shut your bromeliads in a transparent plastic bag with an apple for one to two weeks. Some four months later the flower development will occur.

2 Regularly remove old flower heads (see drawing 2, Culture Tricks). The development of the seed actually costs the plant a great deal of energy and impedes a possible second flowering.

3 Making a mark on the pot (see drawing 3, Culture Tricks) is a help in orienting the pot so that it is replaced facing the light the same way, after it has been moved for sluicing off, dusting, or window washing. Important for sensitive plants like Clivia, azalea, and gardenia, which otherwise react very easily with flower drop.

4 Styrofoam boards (see drawing 4, Culture Tricks), are the simplest way to protect from cold windowsills. Still better are electric warming pads, which are available in garden supply stores.

5 Dusting, washing, or a warm June rain (see drawing 1, Plant Cosmetics) allow the leaves to "breathe" again. The plants can assimilate better afterward.

6 Remove browned leaf tips (see drawing 2, Plant Cosmetics). Leave a small brown margin, since otherwise the freshly cut area will dry out again.

7 A thorough rinsing of the potting medium (see drawing 1, Rinsing and Soaking) under a slow stream of lukewarm water washes out the superfluous fertilizer salts. Helpful with plants that can't be repotted often such as palms or that you don't want to repot anymore because of their location.

8 A tub bath (see drawing 2, Rinsing and Soaking) is often the last resort for a limp plant with a completely dried-out root ball.

9 A plant light (see drawing 1, Measured Light) allows you to put both green and flowering plants even in dark corners.

10 The light meter (see drawing 2, Measured Light) is indispensible for measuring the supplementary light from plant lights as well as for determining the light values in dubious locations.

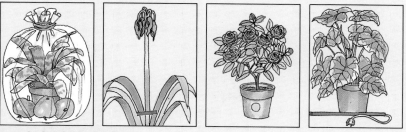

Practical Culture Tricks

1 The scent of apples induces bromeliads to flower. The plastic bag confines the aroma.
2 Remove spent flowers. The development of seeds costs the plant energy.
3 A mark (light mark) indicates the window side of the pot.
4 Styrofoam sheets or electric warming mats insulate against cold from below.

Plant Cosmetics

1 Wipe off smooth-surfaced leaves frequently with lukewarm water. Dust hairy leaves with a cosmetic brush.
2 When cutting off brown leaf tips, leave a margin.

Rinsing and Soaking

1 Remove superfluous fertilizer salts by allowing a great deal of water to run through the potting medium.
2 If the root ball has become dried out, sink the pot in a container of lukewarm water, deep enough so that water rises above the edge of the pot, and leave it until bubbles no longer rise to the surface.

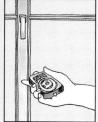

Measured Light

1 Plant lights distribute light that is necessary for growth and good health.
2 The brightness of a location can be measured precisely with a lightmeter (available from garden supply houses).

Something for the Enthusiast: The Tillandsia Tree

A bizarre, twisted branch that has been fixed in a sturdy pottery container with plaster or cement is a perfect place for gray tillandsias. They are best attached with fine cord made of cut-up nylon stockings. Since they take up water through the absorptive scales on their leaves, they should not be watered but misted all over with soft, room-temperature water.

Mistakes in Culture that Make Plants Sick

- Too little light in too warm a location
- Sun for shade-loving plants
- Shade for children of the sun
- Aggressive spring sun
- Fluctuating temperatures
- Heat pool at the windowpane
- Cold caged between window-pane and curtain
- Cold feet
- Cold, hard irrigation water
- Too much water in too cool a location
- Sogginess
- Oxygen-poor air in a poorly ventilated room
- Dry artificially heated air
- Poisoned air (gas from leaky gas lines or stoves, vapors from wood preservatives)
- Drafts or positions at drafty windows
- Too small or to large a container
- Musty, moldy, and clumped potting medium
- Not maintaining winter rest
- Open windows in May when aphids come out

Clay Pellets Instead of Soil

Clay pellets have long been used in hydroculture (expanded clay bits in various sizes) as well as for a combined soil-gravel culture. With the latter, the plant is simply transplanted from its soil-filled pot into the potting medium, which it soon fills happily with roots (see drawing, page 40).

Advantages of clay pellets:
- They have a plant-friendly pH value somewhere between 6.0 to 6.5.
- They do not rot or clump (and therefore are aerated and stable in structure).
- They provide for optimal supply of oxygen and water to the roots. Standing dampness is prevented by regular hand cultivation.
- A water gauge (for expanded clay bits) or a humidity gauge (for other plant pellets) indicates when the plants must be watered again.
- The water supply lasts for one to two weeks, as a rule, so that you can be away for short trips without worrying.
- Special long-acting nutrient solutions last four to six months with expanded clay bits and two months with other plant pellets.
- It isn't necessary to repot so often.

Switching from soil culture to hydroculture. This process is not without problems and works best when the plants are young, growing well, and healthy. Furthermore, all soil must be completely removed from the roots (see drawings, page 40), so they don't begin to rot. Use only special hydropots for repotting. Best time: March to September.

A number of green and flowering plants are suitable for this type of culture (see Plant Portraits, pages 84–229), with the symbol ⌗).

Switching from soil culture to clay pellets is much simpler, since the plant roots are not disturbed. You can also transplant older plants to this new potting medium.

Important: The new pot must be distinctly larger and without a drainage hole (see drawings, page 40). Ideal: $1/3$ earth ball, $2/3$ clay pellets. Best time for repotting: March to September. All houseplants that thrive in soil can also be cultivated this way. Clay fragments, expanded clay bits and other pellets of clay, hydroculture equipment, and chemicals necessary for this type of culture are obtainable in many garden supply outlets.

My Tip: Because the salt content of clay pellets varies widely, they must be rinsed thoroughly before being used.

Bonsai—A Very Large Small World

Translated, *bonsai* means a tree in a dish. It is not the "immature" juvenile form of a tree but a miniaturized tree with a very characteristic growth. A bonsai can be 5 years old and appear as if the storms of decades had passed over it. It looks curious when a bonsai blooms and fruits. While branches and leaves remain small, the flowers and fruits develop at their original size.

Every bonsai tells a story if you look more closely at it. The story can be called "The Whisper of the Leaves—The Quiet of the Forest," like the little sageretia forest on the next page. They can tell of a forested island on a high plateau of rock, of the trees' struggle for light, in which the outermost ones are victorious and bear abundantly leaved branches almost to the ground, while those inside are bare at the bottom. The shadow-loving moss remains unaffected by them and spreads a thick green carpet over the entire crown to the drip line, swallowing the whisper of the sageretia leaves—the stillness of the forest. The fact that this snippet of nature, made small as though by enchantment, brings the magical form of the tree closer to us and that one can do this oneself are perhaps the most fascinating aspects of the art of bonsai.

In the original country of bonsai, Japan, the minitree has been an object of meditation for almost 2,000 years. There they use outdoor plants exclusively, such as pine or maple, which remain outside year in and year out. When bonsai was transplanted to Europe, at first there was bitter disappointment when these outdoor plants were brought inside in order to admire their beauty. The plants perished. Thus bonsai gardeners came to the idea of creating a so-called indoor bonsai. What could be more appropriate than to choose tropical, subtropical, or Mediterranean trees or shrubs that had already demonstrated their usefulness as indoor plants? After years of experimental bonsai, experts discovered the best candidates.

Bonsai—Exotic Miniature Trees

What You Need to Know About Bonsai Culture

Basically, bonsai plants have the same requirements for light, water, temperature, and nutrients as do the normal pot plants of the same name (see Plant Portraits, pages 84–229). Very generally it holds true that:

Mediterranean shrubs are imprinted by their habitat in the Mediterranean, South Africa, Chile, and California. They love the freshness of summer outdoors but must be brought inside before first frost and wintered over in a bright, cool place (average about 50° F [10° C]).

Subtropical shrubs come from regions with hot, humid summers and mild, rainy winters. They also summer happily outdoors and should be moved indoors in September and wintered over in a place that is bright and somewhat warmer (around 59° F [15° C]).

Chinese elm with leaning trunk.

Tropical shrubs are used to warm, damp air the whole year around. Some can get along with astonishingly little light. Cultivate these in the house all year long, keeping them warm and in as much light as possible, but never in the sun. Provide humidity (see page 43).

Shrubs from the dry plains are used to dry periods and don't mind if you forget to water them once in a

Semicascade: Profusely blooming *Serissa foetida*.

while. They do best in a sunny place that is not too warm in winter.

Palms are really not suited for use as bonsais. Only the runner-producing lady palm (see Plant Portraits, page 210) permits development of a tiny forest form.

In the pomegranate (*Punica granatum*) the flowers appear on 1-year-old wood.

Plants Suitable for Bonsais

Mediterranean shrubs: Monterey cypress (*Cupressus macrocarpa*), myrtle (*Myrtus communis*)

Subtropical shrubs: Camellia (*Camellia japonica*), (*Carmona microphylla*), kangaroo vine (*Cissus antarctica*), tender azalea (*Rhododendron simsii* hybrids), Chinese elm (*Ulmus parvifolia*), sagretia (*Sageretia thea*), serissa (*Serissa foetida*)

Tropical shrubs: Weeping fig (*Ficus benjamina*), box-leafed fig (*Ficus buxifolia*), *Ficus neriifolia*, creeping fig (*Ficus pumila*), glossy-leaf fig and subspecies (*Ficus retusa*), schefflera (*Brassaia actinophylla*), ming arelia (*Polyscias fruticosa*)

Shrubs from the dry plains: Desert rose (*Adenium obesum*), silver jade plant (*Crassula arborescens*),

Gnarled 23½ in. (60 cm) high specimen of *Ficus retusa*.

spurge (*Euphorbia balsamifera*), narrow-leaved bottle tree (*Brachychiton rupestris*)

Palms: Lady palms (*Rhapis excelsa* and *Rhapis humilis*)

Extra Culture Tips for the Bonsai Gardener

In the cultivation of all bonsai, it is most important to be sure that they be set in very little soil in a very shallow dish. This means that the soil dries out faster than it would in a normal pot and nutrients will be used up faster. Therefore:

• Mist the soil well before watering. Otherwise the water can't penetrate and will run down the hill of earth unused and erode the piled up potting medium.

• Preferably you should fertilize very weakly and often, preferably

Sageretia in the form of a small forest, about 30 years old and 17¹/₂ in. (45 cm) high.

with a special bonsai fertilizer (available from specialty suppliers). This will avoid root-burning damage and salt deposits in the substrate.
• On principle, do not fertilize just shortly before and during blooming, after repotting, after root pruning, or if the bonsai look sick.

Bonsai Clubs Give Advice
If you have bought an indoor bonsai and would like to know more about these special houseplants, you had best turn for advice to a bonsai gardener in your area or a bonsai club.

Fruit-bearing brush cherry (*Syzygium paniculatum*).

49

The main reasons for disease and parasites in plants—as I know from the countless letters from readers that I have answered in the course of 15 years—are mistakes in culture and poor plant locations (see box, page 47). These weaken the plant and make it vulnerable. Therefore pay close attention to the culture instructions in the plant portraits (pages 84–229) and choose the best possible location.

which makes controlling them considerably easier. If you are at all in doubt, use a magnifying glass.
Breathing space. Avoid putting plants too close together. Air must be able to circulate between them.
Isolate if necessary. Sick plants must be separated from the healthy ones so that they cannot infect them or transfer parasites.

Control Procedures

Don't always reach for the poison. In many instances you can get the same results with "harmless" methods.
Mechanical controls should always be the first step. These include:
• Removing the infested or ailing parts of the plant.
• Collecting or wiping off insect pests. Also rinsing in the shower.
• Submerging the above-ground plant parts in lukewarm water with a shot of dishwashing detergent added. First put the pot in a plastic bag and fasten it to keep the pot and soil from getting wet.
Alternative control methods involve use of standard household materials, but they don't always prove successful.
• You can spray plant lice with an extract of stinging nettles (see box, page 52).
• Horsetail broth (see box, page 52) combats mildew. Use it once a week.
• Garlic is a powerful fungicide. Press a peeled clove into the soil.
Biological controls consist of using benign insects. Some examples follow:
• Ichneumon flies against whitefly
• Predatory mites against spider mites and thrips
• Predatory gallflies, gauze flies, or ichneumon flies against plant lice
• Specific nematodes (eelworms, threadworms) against snout weevils and fungus gnats.
Agents containing pyrethrum, which is derived from a chrysanthemum of that name, work against all chewing and sucking insects, especially against plant lice and white-flies. But such agents must not come into contact with open wounds or diseased skin. If they get into the bloodstream they are highly poisonous.
Biotechnical controls make use of the natural reactions of the parasites to physical or chemical stimuli.
• Yellow boards or yellow stickers

First Aid for Your Plants

All plants are susceptible to ailments and parasites. But you can act to protect against them: Avoid mistakes in culture, nourish the plants, if something goes wrong, find out the reason, remove and combat the villain zealously. The spider mite can be exterminated in the saunalike air of a closed plastic bag.

Preventive Measures

The best prevention is to give the plant the care it requires. Besides this there are several other measures to prevent disease or to help you recognize it early.
Hygiene. Regularly remove leaves or flowers that have dried out, rotted, or look sick, to avoid sources of blight. Cut stems off cleanly at the base. Always disinfect the cut places with charcoal. Keep pots and soil clean. Loosen the surface of the soil with a fork now and again so that algae or moss can't take hold. Regularly wash lime and salt deposits off the outsides of clay pots.
Strengthening the tissue. Water your plants with a brew made from horsetails, which contains silica crystals and strengthens tissue. Or spray your plants with a perfume atomizer containing aromatic vegetable oils. These have been demonstrated to work outstandingly well against bacteria and fungi, and their hormones activate vegetable growth. There are also specially formulated strengthening mixtures that contain valuable minerals, silica crystals, and rare trace elements such as molybdenum or selenium.
Regular check-up. Take time for your plants and observe any changes. Shoot tips and buds are easily attacked by aphids. Be sure to turn all leaves over. This way you will often detect insects and disease in the beginning stages,

Ferns—an ideal trimming for a warm, humid but unquestionably bright bathroom.

are insect traps that are smeared with glue, which attract whiteflies, miners, fungus gnats, and other flying pests with their yellow color.

• In the "plant sauna" (see drawing, page 50) you can destroy spider mites through extremely high humidity. To use this method, water the plant well, enclose it in a transparent plastic bag (for large plants use a dry cleaner's bag), tie it, and leave the plant there for several days. Important: Not all plants will tolerate this procedure. Watch out for mold!

Chemical means are used only when other measures have not worked.

• Insecticides kill insects and can be sprayed, watered in, scattered over the potting medium, or stuck into the ground as a stake.

• Acaricides kill mites.

• Fungicides are agents that destroy fungi.

• Bactericides are for bacterial diseases. There are no agents to treat viral illnesses.

• Substances containing oil, for example white oil or soap solutions (see box for recipe, page 52) clog the insects' breathing organs or destroy their protective waxy covering. Oily sprays for making leaves shine also work similarly to oil sprays, and these can now be found without aerosols or with propane/butane as the propellant.

My Tip: Usually the indoor plant gardener doesn't need more than $^1/_2$ qt ($^1/_2$ L) of a plant spray. The ordinary dilution is 0.1 percent. Get yourself a dropper and put four drops of undiluted preparation into $^1/_2$ qt ($^1/_2$ L) of water. It is the right dosage.

Precautions to Observe

• Do not use any highly poisonous agents.

• Follow the instructions for use and the dosage requirements exactly. Observe the recommended treatment intervals so as to destroy the second generation of pests.

• Do not use aerosol sprays, to protect the environment.

• Only spray out of doors.

• Wear gloves and do not inhale the insecticide fumes.

• Keep the insecticides in their original packages, out of the reach of children and animals, and under lock and key.

• Do not keep the unused portion of the spray (the effectiveness of the preparation diminishes very quickly), but do not throw it in the household trash. Take it to a toxic waste collection facility.

Alternative Home-made Sprays

Extract of Stinging Nettles for Plant Lice (Aphids)

Let 17 1/2 oz (500 g) fresh stinging nettles (before blooming) soak in 5 qt (5 L) of water for 12 to 14 hours. Spray fresh and undiluted to combat plant lice. (Also available from specialty stores as herbal extract.)

Horsetail Broth for Mildew

Soften 17 1/2 oz (500 g) fresh or 5 1/4 oz (150 g) dried field horsetails (scouring rush) in 5 qt (5 L) of water for about 24 hours, then boil for one-half hour. Allow to cool, strain, and thin 1:5 for spraying. (Also available from specialty stores as herbal extract.)

Spirits-Soap Solution for Scale and Mealybugs

Dissolve 1 tablespoon of soft soap or a strong squirt of dish-washing detergent in some warm water. Add 1 qt (1 L) of water and 1 tablespoon of rubbing alcohol. Dip a brush in the solution and dab the scale or woolly webs with it. Or spray the whole plant with it, not forgetting the undersides of the leaves. Rinse tender-leaved plants after 15 minutes with clear, lukewarm water to diminish injury from burning.

Caution: Do not smoke while handling. Spirits are combustible, even when diluted.

Treatment for Physiological Injury

Failure to grow: Eliminate errors in location or culture as well as root injury resulting from same (see below) or control root lice with insecticide.

Sunburn: Remove spotted leaves. Place plant in a bright but not sunny location. Don't water leaves of plants that are in the sun—burning-glass effect.

Iron deficiency (chlorosis): Dissolve chelated iron (from the garden center) in water according to directions, spray over leaves or water the plant with it. Soften the irrigation water (see page 42). Repot plants in spring.

Corky growths/tumors: Remove affected leaves. Keep plants in a brighter location and keep uniformly damp.

Root injury: Unpot the plant, remove ailing roots with a clean, sharp knife, dust with charcoal, and repot in fresh soil.

Accordion growth (in orchids): Cut off injured roots, dust with charcoal, and resettle in new potting medium.

Blossom rot: Eliminate culture errors such as wrong location, fertilizer too rich in nitrogen, disregarding rest period, wrong overwintering.

Treatment for Insects

Scale, mealybugs, and soft scale: Keep plants cooler and brighter. Scratch off scale or paint with spirits-soap solution (above box). Use pyrethrum spray or insecticide; for hard-leaved plants use white oil or leaf-polishing spray.

Plant lice: Use stinging nettle extract (see above box) for gauze flies, predatory gall flies, ichneumon flies. Use also a soap solution, pyrethrum spray, or other insecticide.

Root lice: Remove potting medium and clean roots. Repot, after about two weeks, irrigate with insecticide, repeat several times.

Thrips: Rinse off with lukewarm water. Use yellow sticky bars, predatory mites, or insecticide.

Spider mites (for instance, red spider): Increase humidity (see page 43), use plant sauna (see page 51), perform multiple rinsings with lukewarm water. Use mite predators or spider mite sprays, changing sprays if necessary, because mites quickly develop resistance.

Whiteflies: Lower the temperature, use yellow sticky boards, ichneumon flies, or insecticide.

Soft-skinned mite: Lower temperature and humidity. Remove and destroy infected plant parts.

Root mites: Dip infested roots, bulbs, or rhizomes in the appropriate acaricide, then pot plant in new medium.

Leaf eelworms (nematodes): Remove injured leaves and destroy them. Don't get water on the leaves.

Root eelworms (nematodes): Destroy the plant.

Fungus gnats: Use yellow sticky boards.

Springtails (Collembola): Decrease water in winter. Sluice through the potting medium (see page 45).

Snout weevils: Search out larvae and beetles at night with a flashlight. Introduce beneficial nematodes.

Slugs: Collect them in the evening. In greenhouses set out beer traps.

Treatment for Fungus Infections

Powdery and downy mildew: Remove afflicted leaves and destroy them. Use horsetail broth (see recipe in box above), or specific fungicide.

Gray mold (Botrytis): Remove infected plant parts. Place in airier, brighter location and lower humidity.

Leaf spot fungus: Remove infected plant parts. Use specific fungicide.

Rust fungus: Remove fallen leaves. Use specific fungicide.

Sooty mildew: Remove completely blackened leaves, wash the less blackened ones with warm water. Get rid of causal agent (aphids, scale, soft scale, or whitefly).

Rot in roots, tubers, stalk, or stem base. There is no cure.

Mold: Scratch off the superficial milky white layer on the surface of the potting medium. Raise the temperature, water well, but allow to dry out slightly between waterings. Repot in the spring.

Yellow mushroom: Remove the mushrooms. Raise the temperature, water less, and only from underneath. Change the soil in the spring.

Orchids—Always a Dream

Beauties that also thrive on a windowsill. Here among the green of the ferns grow hybrids of *Dendrobium nobile* and *Phalaenopsis*, the multigeneric hybrid *Vuylstekeara cambria* 'Plush' as well as *Odontoglossum* hybrids.

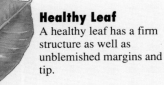

Healthy Leaf
A healthy leaf has a firm structure as well as unblemished margins and tip.

IMPROPER CULTURE: Brown Leaf Margins
Causes: Too little water or too much, overfertilization, exhausted soil, dry air. Remedy: Correct culture.

Brown Leaf Tips
Causes: Air too dry, root ball too dry. Remedy: Provide higher humidity (see page 43) and water.

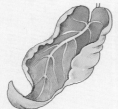

Yellow Leaves
Causes: Overwatering, too little nitrogen, too dark, too warm, or too cool a location. Remedy: Water less, fertilize, improve location.

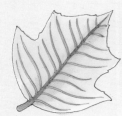

Curled Leaves
Causes: Air too dry, root ball too dry, root injury. Remedy: Correct mistakes in culture, repot as needed.

Pale Leaves (Chlorosis)
The leaf veins are still green. Causes: Water too hard, iron deficiency. Remedy: Use chelated iron in irrigation water.

Light Spots on Leaves
Causes: Temperature shocks, water too cold or too warm, spraying in sunlight. Remedy: Improve location, correct culture mistakes.

Silvery Spots
In some plants also may be red or brown spots. Causes: Sunburn, thrips. Remedy: Improve location, shade, do not water in sunlight.

Corky Growths
Causes: Flagrant temperature changes, too much water in too little light, too wide a fluctuation of dampness in potting medium. Remedy: Correct mistakes in culture.

PESTS: Spider Mites
Symptoms: Webs on backs and between the leaves. Cause: Air too warm and dry. Remedy: See page 52.

Scale
Symptoms: Brown scale, which covers the insect, leaf drop. Cause: Air too dry. Remedy: See page 52.

Aphids (Plant Lice)
Symptoms: Sticky leaves, deformed leaves. Causes: Draft, open windows in spring, air too dry. Remedy: See page 52.

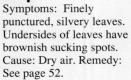

Thrips
Symptoms: Finely punctured, silvery leaves. Undersides of leaves have brownish sucking spots. Cause: Dry air. Remedy: See page 52.

Mealybug Aphids and Soft Scale
Symptoms: Cottony formations, stunted growth. Cause: Air too dry. Remedy: See page 52.

Whitefly
Symptoms: On undersides of leaves small white flies with wings overlapping like roof tiles. Cause: Spread from contaminated plants. Remedy: See page 52.

Soft-skinned Mite
Symptoms: Rolled, crumpled leaves, cessation of growth. Causes: Contagion, promoted by warmth above 73° F (23° C) and humidity over 85 percent. Remedy: See page 52.

Leaf Eelworms
(Nematodes)
Symptoms: Glassy spots, later becoming brown, bordered by the leaf veins, leaf drop. Cause: Contagion, promoted by damp leaves. Remedy: Keep leaves dry.

Slugs
Symptoms: Eaten leaves, slimy trails. Cause: Brought in from outside. Remedy: Look for the slugs in the evening.

FUNGUS DISEASES: Powdery Mildew
Symptoms: White to dirty-brown powdery deposits on tops and undersides of leaves. Cause: Airborne fungus spores. Remedy: See page 52.

Downy Mildew
Symptoms: White to dirty-brown powdery deposits on undersides of leaves. Cause: Airborne fungus spores. Remedy: See page 52.

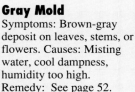

Gray Mold
Symptoms: Brown-gray deposit on leaves, stems, or flowers. Causes: Misting water, cool dampness, humidity too high. Remedy: See page 52.

Leaf Spot Fungus
Symptoms: Scattered yellow to brown leaf spots, partly with encircled spore deposits. Cause: Infection. Remedy: See page 52.

Rust Fungus
Symptoms: Rust colored little heaps of powder on undersides of leaves, light spots on tops of leaves. Cause: Brought in from outside. Remedy: See page 52.

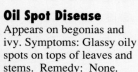

Sooty Mildew
Symptoms: Blackish, dirty deposit on the leaves. Causes: Aphids, scale, and whitefly. Remedy: See page 52.

BACTERIA AND VIRUSES: Bacterial Damp Rot
Appears on cyclamen, dieffenbachia, and calla. Symptoms: Rot at base of stem and later all over. Remedy: None.

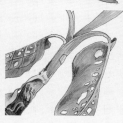

Oil Spot Disease
Appears on begonias and ivy. Symptoms: Glassy oily spots on tops of leaves and stems. Remedy: None.

Mosaic Virus
Especially afflicts flamingo flowers, orchids, hydrangeas, gloxinias, amaryllis. Symptoms: Light- and dark-green spots. Remedy: None.

Leaf Curl Disease
Afflicts fuchsias and geraniums particularly. Symptoms: Stunted, unnaturally curled leaves. Remedy: None.

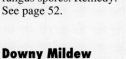

A nyone who does his or her own propagating is continually astonished at how eager plants are to reproduce. They propagate themselves in two ways: Vegetatively or asexually from plant parts, from which develop young plants that are copies of the mother plant down to a hair. Generatively or sexually from seeds, in which a completely new individual plant is produced, with

Propagation Made Easy

Propagation is not only fun, it also helps you to duplicate your favorite plants or to provide many a green memento. Especially interesting is planting the seeds of exotic fruits.

the young plants inheriting the characteristics of the father and mother plant.

Vegetative Propagation
With many plant species, this is the best way to get plants that are ready to bloom in a relatively short time. Propagation is done by division of the plant or by rooting a cutting in water or soil (see page 59).
The most difficult form of vegetative propagation is meristem culture, in which an entirely new plant is produced from a microscopically small unit of cells. Since laboratory equipment is necessary for this, it remains the province of the experts.
Rooting works this way: Almost all plants can develop roots from the cambium, the growth tissue under the outer skin. The process is induced by a wound, a cut, or a tear. This stimulates the wound-healing development of callus, which is a prerequisite for root development. Some plants like African violets, begonias, cape primroses, or sansevierias even regenerate themselves from leaves or pieces of leaf.
The ideal time. Propagate in spring or early summer if possible. It is then that the young plants will have plentiful light to grow and develop better. In some plants, tip cuttings become available only in the spring anyhow as a result of cutting back, and you can then use these to

increase your plants. Other plants can be divided when they are repotted. By early summer the mother plants are already strong enough to stand having cuttings taken. Cuttings of woody plants can also be taken in summer. Naturally you always wait until after the spring-flowering plants have bloomed to divide them or take cuttings. Tubers are divided at the end of the rest period.

Propagation from Seed
This method is only a quick one with annual plants (that is, those that develop completely and flower in one year). They usually go from seed to flower in eight to twelve weeks. With other plants it often takes months for the seeds to sprout (palms) and then months and years until the plants are large and ready to flower. Propagation by seed offers those who like to experiment a full palette of species that are not obtainable as plants. Meanwhile, the plant dealers and mail order specialists offer seeds of countless flowering and green plants, palms, and cactus. Not to be forgotten are the seeds of exotic fruits (see pages 63–65), which are left over, as it were, after the fruit is eaten.
When seeds sprout, they take up water and swell. In the process the seed coat splits and the growth enzymes are activated. At first the root begins to grow, then the shoot, after which come the simply structured seed-leaves, and finally the true leaves. The seed-leaves wither and the stem extends itself, developing more and more leaves as the plant grows.
The ideal time for seeding generally is also spring. If you want to use plant lights, you can sow all year long and further cultivate the young plants that grow in fall and winter under artificial light.

What You Need to Know Before You Propagate
Some plants contain poisons that are released when they are cut and will irritate the skin or mucous membranes (warning notes in the specific plant portraits), and you can receive injury from cactus spines. Therefore, while working, wear gloves, do not rub your eyes, and make sure the plant juice does not get into open wounds. Hold the

Propagation—child's play. Herbaceous tip and stem cuttings root easily in water.

cut surfaces of plants that "bleed" (spurges, for instance) under water to stop the milky flow.

What You Need for Propagating

- Germinating or transplanting soil.
- Propagating tray with a cover or a heatable propagating bed (alternative: mini greenhouse or heating mat for plants that need warmer soil temperatures).
- Transplanting pots of pressed peat or plastic.
- Thinning out stick.
- Plant labels.
- Waterproof pencil for labeling.
- Sharp kitchen or craft knife.
- Root hormone powder.
- Charcoal powder or pieces.

The Right Propagating Medium

Almost all plants sprout and root well in a potting medium that is poor in nutrients and permeable to water and air but also retentive of both of them.

Basic prerequisites: Potting medium must be free of harmful microorganisms. Suitable are a mixture of two parts unfertilized peat and one part quartz sand or commercial transplanting or germinating soils and soilless mixes, as well as Jiffy peat pellets, which are usually made of slightly fertilized peat.

For cacti a commercial cactus mix or a mix of fine pumice, coarse quartz sand, and some fine peat is used. To kill sprouts and fungus spores, the material is sterilized in the oven for two hours at 350°F (170°C) and allowed to stand for two days.

For succulents or other cuttings that need a particularly air-permeable medium you can use quartz sand or perlite for rooting. Do not use builders' sand.

Hydrocultivated young plants are raised in expanded clay granules—which are generally .08 to .16 in. (2–4 mm) in size and are sold as a propagation set with mesh pots and transplanting pots by some garden dealers —or in plastic cubes.

Easily rooted in water are aglaonema (*Aglaonema*), begonia (*Begonia*), croton (*Codiaeum*), flame nettle (*Coleus*), pothos (*Epipremnum*), creeping fig (*Ficus pumila*), wax vine (*Hoya*), fern-leaf aralia (*Polyscias*), African violets (*Saintpaulia*), spiderwort (*Tradescantia*), and others.

Propagation from offsets and cuttings

Brood plants like air plant (*Kalanchoe pinnata*) and devil's-backbone (*Kalanchoe daigremontiana*) or mother spleenwort (*Asplenium bulbiferum*) produce already-rooted plantlets that need only be potted up.

Brood bulbs develop on some flowering bulbs, for instance on amaryllis. They are removed when they reach a diameter of about 2½ in. (6 cm) and are potted up. It can take one to three years until first flowering.

Offsets or stolons develop in bromeliads right next to the mother rosette. When they are half as large as the parent, they are separated and potted up. The more roots a particular offset has, the more easily it will grow. The time until flowering varies from species to species.

Stolons Root Easily
Spider plants form young plants on long shoots, which then can be cut off and potted.

Types of Cuttings
1 Tip cuttings are taken from flowerless annual growth tips. They should have two to four pairs of leaves and if from woody plants, be semi-wooded. Always cut just under a leaf bud and remove lower leaves.
2 Stem cuttings are taken from the middle and lower part of the stem. Cut and treat like tip cuttings.
3 Leaf cuttings are single leaves plus the base of the stem.
4 Leaf-section cuttings are especially good for rooting begonias and sansevierias (see drawing, page 60).

Propagating From Offsets
Offset is the overall term for mature young plants. They can form on the stem, leaves, or roots of the mother plant. They may already possess roots or will root without difficulty at their first contact with soil. Among them are:
• Brood plants like *Kalanchoe pinnata* (air plant) and *Kalanchoe daigremontiana* (devil's-backbone), and *Asplenium bulbiferum* (mother spleenwort), piggyback plant (see photograph, page 189), and *Begonia hispida var. cucullifera*, whose offsets arise on the leaves of the mother plant and are called plantlets (see drawing, left).
• Plants with brood bulbs like the blood lily or the amaryllis (see drawing, left).
• The offsets of the bromeliads (see drawing, left).
• Stolons of the spider plant (see drawing, Stolons), strawberry begonia, clivia, ferns, devil's tongue, various cacti and succulents.
• Offsets of orchids, for example of *Phalaenopsis* or *Dendrobium*.
The developed young plants are separated, when they have roots, and simply potted in good growing soil or stuck in water. Brood bulbs should be half as large as the mother bulb. With bromeliads the offset should already have formed its own cup. Orchid offsets are cut off with a piece of stem and are stapled onto the substrate surface.

Propagating From Cuttings

Cuttings are plant parts taken for the purpose of propagation.

Tip cuttings (see drawing 1, Types of Cuttings) are cut from annual shoots, flowerless if possible. These also include leaf crowns (see drawing 1, Crown and Stem Propagation), for example of dracaena and the umbrella of the umbrella sedge (see drawing, page 60).

With leaf crowns it's advisable to thin them a little beforehand or to remove several rosettes from a very dense crown. Cut segments with a sharp knife and disinfect with charcoal powder. Then pot.

Stem cuttings (see drawing 2, Types of Cuttings) describe cuttings with leaves from not-yet-hardened stems without the growth tip.

Both types of cuttings may be herbaceous, woody, or half-woody. Herbaceous cuttings are the most delicate but root most easily. Woody cuttings don't damp off so easily but are very slow to develop roots. Cuts are made just below a leaf node. The cutting should be about 2 to 4 in. (5–10 cm) long and have two to four leaf pairs. Remove the lower leaves, because contact with the soil promotes damping off.

Leaf cuttings (see drawing 3, Types of Cuttings) consist of a leaf with a little piece of stem. Plants that can be successfully reproduced this way are African violets, various kinds of sedums, peperomias, and begonias. If you are rooting leaf cuttings in water, you should put a little piece of charcoal in with it. This disinfects the water.

Leaf-section cuttings (see drawing 4, Types of Cuttings) are pieces of leaves, which will develop roots along the central vein. With begonias, the leaves are cut straight across and the leaf pieces stuck in the soil in the direction of growth. With *Streptocarpus* you can also cut out the central vein and stick the leaf halves in the soil horizontally.

Stalk cuttings are fleshy, not-too-woody shoots. Every piece should have at least one eye (budding place). You can plant them horizontally or upright (see drawings 2–4, Crown and Stem Propagation). Suitable for this method are *Dieffenbachia, Philodendron, Dracaena,* or *Yucca.*

Important: The direction of growth must be the same as it was, because the eye must point toward the light.

The Plastic Bag Trick

This method promotes rooting. A slip (cutting) is tied in a transparent plastic bag. As in a greenhouse, humid air develops there. This keeps the still rootless slip from evaporating too much water from the leaves. You can also cover large, shallow trays of cuttings with transparent plastic wrap. Other tricks for successful rooting: Warming the soil and planting in small pots.

Rooting Leaf Cuttings in Water

1 Cut off a leaf with its stem. Fill a glass with water and a piece of charcoal. Cover with plastic film. Poke holes in it and stick the leaf stems through.
2 Pot up the rooted young plants.

Propagating from Crown and Stem

1 Cut off the crown of a Dracaena or Yucca and root it in soil, as with cuttings.
2 Cut the stem in pieces and dust the cut ends with charcoal powder.
3 Pot the stem pieces vertically.
4 Alternatively, press the stem pieces into the potting medium horizontally with the eye facing upward. Then cover as described in step 3. Cover airtightly with plastic film. As soon as growth shows, remove the film.

Rooting Leaf Cuttings in Potting Medium

1 Cut off leaf with stem.
2 Dip cut end in rooting hormone.
3 Stick cutting in dampened potting medium and gently press soil down.
4 Tie in a plastic bag. Place a warming mat underneath. As soon as new growth appears, remove the plastic bag.

Propagation from seed and other methods

Root division. Pull plant apart carefully but bravely. First cut apart a matted root ball with a sharp knife, untangle twisted roots. Shake out as much of the old potting medium as possible and repot both halves in new earth.

Rooting an umbrella. The "umbrellas" of the umbrella sedge can be stuck in water head down or right side up. They will root in any case.

Layering can be done with plants that develop long shoots (ivy, etc.). Lay the young shoot on the soil of a small pot, make a scratch in the underside of a leaf node, and fasten it down with wire. As soon as it is well rooted, separate the shoot from the mother plant.

Simple Propagation Methods

Root division (see drawing, left). Wildly growing, bushy plants can also be reproduced in this manner.

Division of tubers. Tubers are first forced to the point that the sprouting points become visible, and they are then cut into pieces, each with an eye. Important: Disinfect the relatively large pieces with charcoal powder.

Rhizome division. Rhizomes are divided so that each piece has at least two eyes (leaf buds).

Rooting umbrellas (see drawing, left) are a feature of the sedges. Cut off the upper leaf crown with a two-inch (5 cm) stub, shorten the leaves by one-third with scissors, and stick the umbrella in tepid water or in damp sand. The new leaves appear in the middle of the umbrella.

Layering (see drawing, left) is the term used for tip cuttings that are not separated from the mother plant.

Propagating from Seed

Species and hybrids of many indoor plants can also be raised from seed. The fresher the seed is, the more likely it is to sprout. Many seed firms therefore sell them in a protective seed packet that must be opened before you sow. Furthermore you should follow the instructions given on the seed packet exactly. These instructions will note whether the seeds should be covered with soil (dark germinators) or not (light germinators), whether they must be soaked in lukewarm water before sowing or be scratched, as well as the specific germination temperature, which can be around 64° F (18° C) at the minimum and at the maximum between 77° to 82° F (25°–28° C). Large seeds are sown in peat pots or Jiffy pots, whichever is suitable; small, fine seeds are sown in flats.

Propagating from Seed

Even beginners succeed in growing plants from seed with the use of compressed pots. They are soon thoroughly permeated with the roots of the seedling and keep the root ball together when being transplanted to a larger container.

Propagating from Pieces of Leaf

Possible with begonias, streptocarpus, and sansevierias (above).

1 Cut off a healthy leaf from a sturdy mother plant.

2 Cut straight across into large pieces 2 to 3 in. (5–8 cm) long. Allow the cut pieces to dry somewhat.

3 Stick the pieces shallowly in sandy soil in the direction of growth.

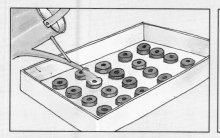
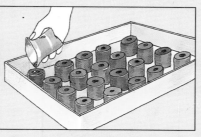
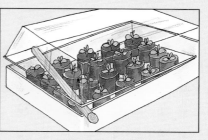

Seeding in Compressed Peat Pots

1 Lay the peat tablets in the tray of a mini-greenhouse, water with lukewarm water until they are swollen to full size.

<u>And this is how it's done:</u>
Sow seed in Jiffy pots or in a propagating flat. The propagating flat contains a finger-thick layer of expanded clay pellets or pebbles underneath and is then filled with seed-starting soil up to within 1 in. (3 cm) of the edge. Smooth the soil and make furrows for the seeds. Spread the seeds along the furrows. For dark germinators sift potting mix over them and press lightly. The layer should be double the thickness of the seed. Sprinkle the soil with soft, lukewarm water until it is damp all the way through. Cover the flat with a cover, film, or glass plate.

My Tip: Very fine seeds are easier to spread along the furrow if they are first mixed with fine sand and then sown.

Special Case: Grafting Cactus

Grafting is limited in use as a propagating method, but with the slow-growing cactus (see drawing, Cactus Grafting), it quickly produces plants ready to bloom. Having the correct stock is important for success. *Echinopsis* species, *Eriocereus jusbertii*, *Hylocereus* hybrids, and *Selenicereus* and *Trichocereus* species have proved especially suitable. Ideal time: April to September. The scion must be kept slightly damp, warm, and bright constantly but it must not stand in the sun.

Air Layering

Air layering is a way to propagate plants that are hard to reproduce from cuttings or to rejuvenate plants having very large, old branches that are bare at the bottom. It involves rooting from the leafy area and is a suitable process for rubber trees, dracaenas, philodendron, windowleaf, false aralia, cordyline, schefflera, fatsia, croton. Ideal time: Spring; for the rubber trees, June/July.

2 Press a seed into each peat pot ³⁄₈ in. (1 cm) deep. Cover with germinating soil. Close the cover. Place the mini-greenhouse in a bright—but not sunny—warm place.

3 After sprouting occurs, aerate often so that the condensed water can escape and the young plants do not damp off. Separate growing plants from each other!

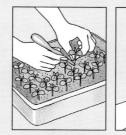  

Thinning Out

Thin out when the seedlings have two seed and two real leaves.
1 Loosen the seedling from the earth with a slender stick.
2 Shorten the root tip somewhat.
3 Bore a hole in the soil of the flower pot.
4 Plant the seedling up to the leaves, press lightly.

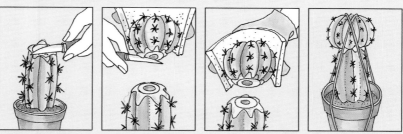

Cactus Grafting

1 Cut across the base under the growth tip, bevel the edges of the cut area with a sharp knife.
2 Cut off the scion and also bevel the cut place at a steep angle.
3 Before putting the two pieces together, cut away another thin slice from each of the cut areas.
4 Put the conducting channels together exactly and fasten the graft with a rubber band.

 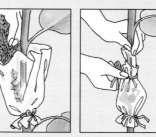 

Air Layering a Plant that Has Become Too Large

1 Make a cut in the stem. Dust the cut place with rooting hormone.
2 Fasten a plastic bag below the cut. Fill with dampened, coarsely shredded peat.
3 Fasten the bag above so that the peat doesn't dry out.
4 After thoroughly rooted, remove the bag, cut off the stem, and pot.

Further Care of the Seedlings

Until germination, which is what gardeners call sprouting, you must be sure that the potting medium never dries out and stays warm at all times.

Germination times vary greatly. Some plants have sprouted after several days, others (like palms) need months. Large seeds need an especially long time. Don't give up if they don't do anything at first.

Successful germination is evident, depending on the plant species, by one or two seed-leaves that look different from the characteristic true leaves. Now is the time to lift the covering for them to get air for several hours and for the plants to harden off slowly.

Thinning out is the term for the next step, when the first two true leaves or leaf pairs have formed and you must pull out the weakest plants to allow the strong seedlings more growing room. Or the young plants can be separated and put in individual pots, as shown in the drawings, Thinning Out, page 61.

For further development it's very important to have much light. But be careful—no sun. With too little light the tiny plants grow leggy and develop unnaturally long intervals between leaves. You might try placing a sheet of white Styrofoam behind the young plants. This will reflect the light.

Don't fertilize yet; the nutrients in the growing medium are enough to last for the first weeks. Only the fast-growing annuals may be fertilized for the first time after four weeks with a weak dosage.

Exotic Ambiance

Perfect in itself, like a work of art. A beautifully growing palm needs a solitary spot in the home. Any other plants will diminish the elegant effect.

A Chapter in Itself: Plants from the Seeds of Exotic Fruits

It's a shame to throw away the seeds or plant parts of exotic fruits. Anyone who likes to experiment can get attractive plants from them, and ones that not everyone has. Further advantage: Seeds from fruits are superfresh; for many tropical plants freshness is a prerequisite for successful germination. The mother plants of tropical fruits come from the same regions as our houseplants. The only difference is that for the most part they aren't cultivated and therefore we can't obtain them as houseplants. Thus the reports on experience with them and instructions for caring for them are incomplete.

From the tropics come such plants as papaya, star apple, mango, guava, mangosteen, pineapple, coconut, and ginger. This means that you are dealing with plants that need warmth; therefore in winter they will not stand it cooler than 59° F (15° C).

From the tropical highlands we get Andes berries and cherimoya. These plants need much light, warmth in summer and cooler temperatures in fall and winter.

Subtropical or Mediterranean regions are the habitat of the avocado, Japanese persimmon, date, pomegranate, orange, lemon, lichee, fig, and passion fruit. Plants from these regions like to be outside for the summer and during the winter want a situation around 50° F (10° C).

Collecting Seeds

It depends when the fruit is available in the market. Here is a brief overview of the main sales months:

All year round you can find: Avocados (see pages 64–65), tree tomatoes, dates (see pages 64–65), guavas, star apple, coconut, mango, passion fruit (see pages 64–65), and most citrus fruit (see pages 64–65).

Available only at certain seasons are: Pineapple (September to December), cherimoya (September to February, see pages 64–65), pineapple-guava (March to July), pomegranates (June to December), Andes berries (January to June), lichee (January to March and May to December), rambutan (January

to February, June to October, and in December).

The best time for seeding and vegetative reproduction of pineapple crowns or ginger rhizomes (page 65) is spring.

Therefore you need to be aware that:

• Seeds from fruit bought in winter may have encountered frost and then will not germinate.

• Injured (cut through) seeds are not going to germinate.

• Seeds from fruit that was half-ripe when harvested are also half-ripe and will not germinate. You recognize such fruit by color comparison with ripe fruit, faded taste, and still-green seeds.

Sowing

You can do this immediately after collecting the seed or several days later. Fruit seeds that we don't eat are "garbage" anyway; with others you must remove them from the flesh before the fruit is eaten. After washing, dry the seeds with paper towels and let them dry in the air for several hours. Then you can sow them, preferably in a heated propagation bed.

Germination Times

The times for germination vary widely. Plants that in their native habitats grow as trees normally germinate more slowly than herbaceous plants such as the *Passiflora* (see page 64). Some seeds don't germinate at all because they are "sterile." Palm seeds often take months. Don't throw in the towel if you don't have success immediately and keep on trying.

Flowers and Fruits

You can only expect flowers or fruits from a very few of the exotic plants you raise from seeds yourself. You mustn't forget that most of them are trees in their habitats and always remain juvenile plants in pots. But some plants will surprise you with flowers at a certain age, even in a pot or a tub. If they do form fruit, as a rule it will not taste very much like the fruit purchased at the market.

Caring for Popular Exotics

The following notes give specifics of breeding, location, and care for some popular exotic plants.

Fortunella margarita, Kumquat

Sow seed in a heated propagation bed (68° to 72° F [20°–22° C]). Plants raised from seed will bloom after eight to ten years.

Passion fruit

Kumquats

Location and care: Put young plants in a bright spot at first, later in full sun, preferably outdoors from the middle of May. Water plant well in summer and fertilize it lightly every 14 days. Beginning in September, keep it drier; bring it into the house, placing it in a bright, cool location (50° F [10° C]). Repot young plants yearly in spring in all-purpose potting soil with Styrofoam flakes in it.

Passiflora edulis, Passion Fruit

Wash and dry seeds, then sow. Do not cover them—light germinators. Sprouting takes 12 to 14 weeks.
Location and care: See *Plassiflora,* page 124.

Persea americana, Avocado

Remove pit from flesh of fruit and stick the broad end ¾ to 1 in. (2–3 cm) deep into potting soil. Location and care: Keep plant in a bright place all year long, in summer warm, in winter cool (59° F [15° C]). Keep it uniformly damp all year long.

Carica papaya, Papaya

Wash seed and sow. Cover it lightly with soil. Invert a plastic bag over pot. The seed will germinate after several days. Location and care: Keep plant warm, bright, and humid all year long. Only water it moderately.

Phoenix dactylifera, Date palm

Soak date pits from packaged dates in warm water for two or three days. Push pits about ¾ in. (2 cm) deep into propagating soil. The seeds sprout after two to six months.
Location and care: Keep plant in a light to sunny spot all year long and warm in summer, but in winter, around 50° F (10°C). Water it moderately.

Papaya

Dates

Lemon

Ginger
rhizome

Avocado

Zingiber officinale, Ginger

Lay the rhizome flat on the soil (don't use germinating soil) with the eye pointing upward and just cover lightly. Put in a shady, warm place. The first shoots appear after two months.

Location and care: Keep plant bright, warm, and always slightly damp from spring till fall. In fall let it die back. Winter over the rhizome in its pot at room temperature and force it again in the spring.

65

Green Living—Beautiful Living

More and more homeowners are building greenhouses and making them into green living rooms or into a gathering place for green and flowering rarities. Here the plants receive light from all sides, which is better than ordinary window light. Important: Ventilation flaps and adjustable jalousies or shades are needed to avoid stagnant air and keep out the midday sun, especially in summer.

This beautiful plant grouping consists among other things of two silver-jade plants as sentries (in foreground), a ceiling-high fiddle-leaf fig (left), a light-hungry coconut palm and cut-leaved philodendron (right). In the background is a fruiting dwarf orange, a vigorously growing passionflower, and a quartet of unassuming aspidistras. In front of them is a delicately flowered oleander.

67

A

Absorption scales
Water-absorbing scales which are found on the gray tillandsias. Therefore these plants can be provided with water and nutrients through sprays and dipping.

Acaricide
A specific agent that kills mites (for example spider mites/red spider). But there are also insecticides that are effective against different varieties of mites.

Acclimation
See HARDENING OFF.

Adventitious roots
Roots that form on stems and leaves. They do not arise during the ordinary course of root development but spontaneously through injury and isolation (in cuttings), or after treatment with growth hormones. Adventitious roots occur mainly in monocotyledonous plants and ferns. AERIAL ROOTS are adventitious roots.

Aerial roots
Special roots that some plants form to hold onto tree trunks, walls, or themselves. This type of root is found in tropical plants particularly. Aerial roots can take up air, water, and nutrients. When they encounter the ground, they take root there and become strong prop roots (for example, as in the windowleaf). In orchids the aerial roots are covered with a silvery membrane called the velamen. Important: Never cut off the aerial roots.

Air layering
A plant propagation or rejuvenation method in which a cut is made in a plant stem to promote root development. The cut is then wrapped, first with dampened peat and then with a plastic covering to retain moisture (see drawings, page 61).

Air plants
Designation for plants (also called EPIPHYTES) that in their tropical habitat seek out the crown or branch fork of trees and shrubs to live in. Most form AERIAL ROOTS to hold on with and for the uptake of nutrients and humidity, since they can't reach the ground. Air plants are not parasites.

Alkaline
Other terms are *basic* or *sweet* (in contrast to *acidic* or *sour*). In plant culture a SUBSTRATE (soil) is alkaline when it contains a lot of lime and has a PH VALUE over 7. Alkaline soils develop primarily from watering with hard water containing lime salts and are bad for almost all houseplants. In soil testing, a soil is designated slightly alkaline if it has a pH value of 7.1 to 8.

Alkaloids
Nitrogenous plant compounds that affect the human nervous system. Examples of alkaloid plants: dumb cane, gloriosa lily, as well as all plants of the nightshade family. Alkaloids can often be lethal even in very small doses.

Alternating
Arrangement along a stem in which the leaves do not grow directly opposite each other but are spaced at intervals.

Annual plants (Annuals)
Plants that flower, fruit, and then die within one year of sowing. (See PERENNIAL PLANTS.)

Aphids
Also called plant lice. See First Aid for Your Plants, pages 50–55.

Areoles
Woolly cushions on the ends of cactus tubercles or on the edges of the ribs, from which the thorns arise and which usually also produce the flowers and buds. Every cactus species has its own typical form of areole.

Assimilation

Process by which plants convert foreign substances into their own bodily substances. A distinction is made between carbon dioxide assimilation (also called PHOTO-SYNTHESIS), by which sugar is produced, and nitrogen assimilation, by which protein is produced.

Azalea pot

A flowerpot that is lower than the standard container with the same diameter (also called a three-quarter pot). Ideal for plants that are shallow-rooted like azaleas.

B

Bacteria

The oldest single-celled organisms, which are present practically everywhere. They decompose and disintegrate organic substances, thus bringing about composting and mineralization. Certain species have particular significance for the nitrogenous nourishment of plants. Others cause serious plant illnesses that are indicated by wilting or damp rot and for the most part cannot be treated.

Ball

Term for soil thoroughly grown through with roots (*root ball, earth ball*) or for a compacted quantity of peat (*peat ball*).

Ball dryness

Lack of moisture in the root ball of a pot plant, recognizable when the soil draws away from the edge of the flowerpot. Most plants tolerate ball dryness for a very short period only. First aid treatment: A soaking (see drawing, page 42).

Bastard

Product of a crossing of plants of different varieties, subspecies, species, or genera. Bastards are also called HYBRIDS.

Beneficial insects

Insects that kill pests. They are a biological form of insect control. You can get them from garden suppliers.

Biennial plants

Plants that only form leaves the first year and in the second year bloom, fruit, and then die, for example the German violet (*Exacum affine*).

Biological insect control

Plant protection without chemicals. This includes the use of BENEFICIAL INSECTS as well as treatment with solutions made from plants. In the broadest sense, it also includes prevention through optimal care and treatment with plant tonics, as for example aromatic sprays (see page 52) or plant brews.

Biotechnical insect control

Control of insects by natural, chemical, or physical stimuli, for example by yellow-painted, water-filled saucers, YELLOW STICKY BOARDS (for aphids, whiteflies, and fungus gnats), attractants, and decoys. Mechanical controls such as picking off or washing insects from the leaves could also be included.

Bleeding

If plants such as rubber plant or poinsettia are injured by cutting or breakage, the milky juice contained in the stalk and shoots will run out. This is called bleeding.

Bonsai

Term for the Japanese art of forming miniature trees on the model of the large ones and for the miniature tree itself. From *bon* = pot and *sai* = tree.

Botanical name

Internationally used scientific descriptive name for a plant. The botanical name consists of two parts: (1) the genus name, for example *Ficus;* (2) the species name, for example *elastica*. Additionally, the variety or cultivar name is added, enclosed in single quotation marks, when there is one, for example 'Decora'. The complete name is thus *Ficus elastica* 'Decora'. An *x* mark is placed before the genus or species name to indicate either a bigeneric hybrid or one derived from two species, respectively.

Bracts

Modified leaves that are situated higher than the true foliage leaves and function to protect the flower and lure insects. Some bracts are splendidly colored and substitute for the petals, as in the poinsettia, for example, and the bougainvillea, flamingo flower, and spathe flower.

Breeding

Attempts through crossing and selection to develop new varieties that enjoy particular characteristics. Some breeding goals are, among others, larger flowers, more double flowers, new flower colors, as well as resistance to disease and climate.

Brood buds

Small tubers or bulbs, also called bulblets or bulbils, that form in leaf axils, at leaf edges, or in place of flowers. They are adapted for propagation. Some plants also develop perfect little plants (brood plantlets), like the devil's-backbone (*Kalanchoe daigremontiana*), for example.

Budders

Collective term for plants that reproduce vegetatively. Propagation methods include RUNNERS, OFFSETS, and extend to air layering (see drawings, page 61) or DIVIDING.

Buds

Plant organs from which stems, leaves, flowers, or entire plants develop. A distinction is made between terminal buds at the end of a shoot, axillary buds in the leaf axils, and adventitious buds, which are produced from MERISTEM tissue. Dormant buds (sleeping eyes) can remain in the bud stage all year and only begin to grow under special circumstances. Flower and leaf buds develop into the respective organs; whole plants develop from BROOD BUDS.

Bulbs

From the Latin *bulbus*, for "onion," bulbs are composed of thickened leaf bases, or scales. Not to be confused with PSEUDO-BULB or false bulbs of orchids, which are thickened branch internodes. The bulb serves as a food reserve and an organ for wintering over. Example: amaryllis.

Bush

Plants with woody shoots in which several equivalent branches grow out of the ground.

C

Cactus fertilizer

Nitrogen-poor complete fertilizer that is formulated for the particular requirements of cacti and other succulents but not for epiphytic species. Commercially available.

Calcium (Ca)

A white metal that is an essential building material during the entire life span of a plant and is one of the principal nutrients. It increases the resistance of plant tissue, promotes ASSIMILATION, and binds acids produced in the plant.

Callus

Wound-healing tissue that a plant forms after injury. Cuttings can only produce roots after callus tissue has formed.

Calyx

Bell-shaped, rounded, tube-shaped, or funnel-shaped flower structure that consists of the SEPALS.

Capillary action

Process by which water in thin tubes is "induced" to move over shorter or longer distances. In practice capillary action is used in arrangements for watering while one is on vacation (see drawings, page 43).

Carbon Dioxide (CO$_2$)

Colorless and odorless gas that occurs in the air and in the soil. A very important compound for plant life, since it is the basic building unit for manufacture of carbohydrates through photosynthesis.

Carnivorous plants

See INSECTIVOROUS PLANTS.

Chelate

Chemical ring structure that enables iron (or other metals) to dissolve better and thus be available to the plants. The hobby gardener thus uses, for example iron chelate or chelated iron. The brown-red powder is dissolved in water and used to treat CHLOROSIS.

Chemical control methods

Control and prevention of insects with chemical agents, which with misuse or carelessness can endanger humans and other animals. Therefore, chemical pesticides are classified according to the severity of their toxicity into various poison classifications or as nontoxic. The products are labeled with appropriate symbols. Among other things, chemical controls include such agents to combat diseases and pests as INSECTICIDES, FUNGICIDES, ACARACIDES, nematode killers (see Control Procedures, page 54), as well as snail poisons.

Chemical fertilizer

Inorganic fertilizers whose nutrients are compounded in salts and are thus readily available to plants. Danger: Overdosage. Contrast: ORGANIC FERTILIZERS in which the nutrients must first be released by microorganisms and be processed suitably for plants, taking somewhat longer.

Chlorine (Cl)

Gaseous element that is added to the public water supply as a disinfectant. Chlorine, which is injurious to plants, evaporates when water is allowed to stand overnight. In the form of chloride ions it serves as a micronutrient and is available primarily in inorganic fertilizers.

Chlorophyll

Green pigment without which PHOTOSYNTHESIS cannot take place. Is also called leaf green and its structure is similar to that of hemoglobin. In chlorophyll magnesium takes the place assumed by iron in human blood.

Chlorosis

A plant disease caused by iron deficiency. (See drawing, page 54.)

Cistern

The bromeliads' reservoir or apparatus for catching water and nutrients. (See CUP.)

Clay granules

Extremely water-retentive substrate that gives up moisture to roots as needed so that they develop superbly well in it. Ideal way to water during short vacations. Plants with the entire root ball can be repotted into this substrate at any time of year. Clay granules are available in various sizes at garden centers.

Climbers

Term for plants that climb on other branches, tree trunks, limbs, or can be espaliered, using organs that they have developed for just this purpose, for example with adhesive disks, aerial roots, hooking tendrils or leaves, barblike side shoots, spines, thorns, or by winding on themselves.

Cold frame

An unheated glass frame used to protect plants from severe winter weather.

Cold house

Term for a greenhouse whose temperature in winter does not run to more than 36° to 54° F (2°–12° C). Plants that need cool over wintering are called cold-house plants.

Commercial potting soil

Industrially mixed potting soil that is prepared for and sold at retail. Soil mixtures are formulated to meet a variety of specific plant requirements.

Common English name

English but also popular name for a plant. Often an Anglicized version of the scientific name—like wooly kohleria, *Kohleria lanata*. But there are also many plants that do not have English names.

Complete fertilizer

Fertilizer that contains all the principal nutrients essential to plant life and often also trace elements (see FERTILIZER).

Contact poison

Plant pesticide that affects insects when they come into contact with it. Respiratory and food poisons and SYSTEMIC CONTROL AGENTS have other modes of action.

Contact stimulus

Many plants react sensitively to external contacts. These stimuli can be light, temperature, chemical agents, mechanical movement, or injury. The most striking reaction is shown by the sensitive plant (*Mimosa pudica*). Its leaf stalks and leaflet stems have hinges that snap together at the slightest touch and furthermore, they do so one after the other, right down to the leaf stalk. In many plants (oxalis, for instance), the change from day to night produces sleep motions, with the leaves or flowers opening with light and closing with darkness.

Container

Plant pot, usually of plastic, with solid or openwork walls (basket).

Corky growth (Suberization)

Development of suberin, which is deposited in the cell walls and is largely impermeable to air and water. In some plants it can develop into real tumors. The causes are too high a moisture content in soil and air combined with too dark a location. In clivia too much fertilizing will induce cork spots. Especially striking suberizations are displayed in some members of the spurge family during light-poor seasons. Corky surfaces can no longer assimilate but do not injure the plant. They are merely blemishes, which can also appear in begonias, rubber trees, cacti, orchids, geraniums, and peperomias. For treatment of corky spots, see First Aid for Your Plants, pages 50–55.

Creeping plants

Plants with horizontally growing rooted RUNNERS or creeping branches. Suitable for ground covers. Examples: Strawberry begonia and creeping fig.

Crown

Point at which root merges with the upper part of the plant (stem). Extremely sensitive in some plants!

Culm

Stem of grasses. It is either round and then usually hollow (notably in corn and sugar cane) or triangular and filled with marrow. Giant grasses like the bamboos possess the strongest, thickest, and longest culms.

Cup

Term for the CISTERN of bromeliads, which are therefore also called cup bromeliads. The cup is produced by the rosettelike arrangement of the leaves and serves the plant in nature as the "catch basin" for water, dew, and the rotting material that provides nutrients.

Cutting back

Necessary measure for plant shaping, rejuvenation, and producing new growth, bushy growth, and good branching (see page 44).

Cuttings

Plant sections that can be put in soil or water to root. A cutting can be a tip cutting, a piece of stem, a leaf, or a piece of a leaf (see pages 58–60).

Cyme

Form of INFLORESCENCE. See drawing, page 15.

D

Damping off

Disease of seedlings and cuttings that is caused—especially under crowded conditions—by fungus in the potting medium and results in injury to root tissue. It causes the plantlets to break off.

Dark germinators

Plants whose seeds will only sprout in absolute darkness. The sown seeds must thus always be covered until germination so that no light can reach them.

Daughter bulbs

A kind of offset development in flowering bulbs, for example in the amaryllis (*Hippeastrum* hybrids).

Deficiency diseases

Disease symptoms that appear with wrong or neglected fertilization (see First Aid for Your Plants, pages 50–55).

Dicotyledonous

Plants with two seed-leaves situated side by side. The main root is a taproot, the leaves are variable and are furnished with a network of veins.

Dioecious

When a species has male and female flowers growing on different plants, it is termed dioecious and further defined as male or female. Familiar examples of this property are the domestic willow, or in the houseplant category, the chenille plant (*Acalypha hispida*) and many palms. Contrast: MONOECIOUS.

Dividing

Propagation method suitable for plants with many shoots. Examples: Bromeliads, baby's tears, zebra plants, coral moss.

Dormancy

See REST PERIOD.

Dosage

Proper, precise measurement of herbicides, pesticides, fertilizer, or water.

Double flowers

Flowers with many petals. These are missing the stamens, which have been converted—usually through cross-breeding—into petals. Contrast: SINGLE FLOWERS.

Downy mildew

See MILDEW and First Aid for Your Plants, pages 50–55. Also called *false mildew* and *gray mildew*.

Drainage

Measures for removal and direction of water. It is required for plants to avoid injurious standing water. Should not be overlooked, particularly with larger pots or tubs. For this purpose gravel, sand, expanded clay balls, or large fragments of Styrofoam should be placed in the bottom of the pot for drainage. To keep drainage material from mixing with the potting medium, lay a piece of screening between the drainage and the soil layers.

E

Efflorescence

Deposits of lime and fertilizer salts on the outer walls of a clay pot. They occur when watering has been done with hard water or fertilizing done too often. Efflorescences can be removed with a vinegar-water solution and a scrub brush.

Enclosed plant window

Window of generous proportions that is closed off like a greenhouse and can be furnished with humidifiers, heating, aeration, and other technical equipment. Ideal for tropical plants, which need warmth and high humidity.

Epidermis

Outermost tissue layer of the entire plant body. In many plants the epidermis contains calcium or silica for better tissue strength.

Epiphyte boards/supports

Artificially created "perches" used in the home culture of epiphytes. Regular tree trunks or branches are used, but tubes with holes punched in them or moss stakes are also suitable.

Epiphytes

See drawing, page 40. Plants that in their natural habitats do not grow on the ground but in tree branchings, as for example many ferns, bromeliads, and orchids. Therefore, epiphytes are also called air plants (see AIR PLANTS).

Ethylene

Gaseous plant hormone that is given off during the ripening phase of fruits (such as apples, citrus). Promotes flowering in bromeliads; on the other hand, orchids and hibiscus react to the fragrance of apple and citrus by dropping flowers and buds.

Evaporative cooling

Coolness that arises as a result of evaporation or from TRANSPIRATION from plant leaves; it can also be produced by damp soil or clay pots.

Evergreens

Plants that don't shed their leaves in the fall. Of course these plants renew their leaves, too. But this is not apparent because it doesn't happen at a particular time of year.

Evolution

The process of development and change through time. Like all other living organisms, plants have gone from simple structures to ever more specialized life forms in the course of their developmental history. As organisms bound to their locations, they must continually adapt to their environment throughout millions of years to avoid extinction.

Expanded clay

Classic planting medium for water culture. Expanded clay is obtained by firing selected clays at a temperature of 2192° F (1200° C). The water contained in the clay is vaporized and gives it a porous structure and hard skin, which takes up very little water. It is produced as balls, pellets, and granules. It is stable in structure, which means that it will not decay. It is not possible for it to compact, sour, or putrify as soil may. Its porous nature allows the best possible air and water exchange. Furthermore, roots find an extraordinarily good foothold in this potting medium.

F

False mildew

See MILDEW and First Aid for Your Plants, pages 50–55. Also called *downy mildew* and *gray mildew*.

Family

Group of genera with certain specific characteristics in common. The largest plant family may be that of the orchids. It represents almost 10 percent of all flowering plants.

Family name

Indicates membership in a particular family. Thus for example, the lady's slipper belongs to the family of orchids (Orchidaceae), the African violet to the family of gesneriads (Gesneriaceae), the rubber plant to the mulberry family (Moraceae).

Fasciation

Abnormal, chicken-comb-like growth form of stems of cacti and other succulents. The vegetative cone broadens to linear or band shape, forming misshapen structures.

Fertile

Technical term for seed and fruit production. The opposite of sterile. Flowers with sex organs (that is with stamens and pistil) are fertile; flowers without these organs are sterile, for example the enlarged marginal flowers of the climbing hydrangea.

Fertilization

Merging of a male nucleus of a pollen grain with a female egg cell.

Fertilizer

Plant nutrients that are provided for plants by humans. The most important nutrients are: nitrogen (N), phosphorus (P), and potassium (K). A distinction is made between chemical, organic, and chemical-organic fertilizers.

Flower

See drawing, page 15.

Flowering plants

The most highly developed class of plants. In technical language they are called angiosperms. Older and less highly developed are the gymnosperms, which include the palm ferns, ginkgo, and conifers; still older are ferns, mosses, lichens, fungi, algae, and bacteria.

Forcing

Advancing the blooming time by regulation of light and warmth. Is especially common practice with flowering bulbs. For instance, you can force crocuses, hyacinths, or tulips as early as late fall in a warm room so that they are blooming at Christmas.

Frond

Popular term for palm or fern leaves.

Frosting
Silver-gray waxy deposit looking like hoar-frost that appears on foliage or buds of some plants, such as succulents (like *Cotyledon*, *Sedum*) or cacti (like *Cereus peruvianus*). Frosting serves as a protection against light and transpiration.

Fruiting
Growth stage after flowering. Usually the fruit encloses a seed or seeds.

Fungicide
Chemical agent for controlling fungal diseases (see First Aid for Your Plants, pages 50–55).

Fungus
Plants in one of the lower groups whose bodies consist of threadlike hyphae (mycelium) and contain no chlorophyll. They serve as "garbage eaters" because they can digest cellulose and wood pulp. They are either decay dwellers, parasites (causes of disease in humans, animals, and plants) or live in symbiosis with other plants, for instance orchids and lichens. Some produce important substances for human beings (penicillin) or cause certain processes (such as fermentation). Dampness and specific temperatures are prerequisites for their viability but the pH value and concentrations of oxygen and carbon dioxide in their environment are also determining factors.

Fungus diseases
See First Aid for Your Plants, pages 50–55.

Fungus gnats
See First Aid for Your Plants, pages 50–55.

G

Generative reproduction
Sexual reproduction of a plant through seeds. The seeds contain the plant embryo, which develops after the sex cells combine. The offspring need not resemble the mother plant. Contrast: VEGETATIVE REPRODUCTION.

Genus
Term for plant species that have certain characteristics in common within a family.

Genus hybrids
The name for a plant resulting from the cross between plants of different genera.

Genus name
First part of the botanical name of a plant, which is always capitalized and italicized. Examples: *Aeschynanthus, Saintpaulia, Ficus.*

Grafting
Method of propagation in which a scion or an eye of a desired plant is bonded to another plant. Both grow together so closely that the stock plant takes over the supply of water and nutrients, while the scion or eye produces the new growth that conforms to the appearance of the scion. It is practiced particularly with *Citrus* species, whose seedlings often fail to bloom.

Granulate
Plant pesticide or fertilizer or potting medium in form of small granules.

Gray mildew
See MILDEW and First Aid for Your Plants, pages 50–55. Also called *false mildew* and *downy mildew.*

Greening
Reaction of colored leaves to light deficiency. The plants can only afford chlorophyll-free areas in bright locations. In dark locations they must become green all over in order to gain enough assimilation area.

Growth period
See VEGETATIVE PERIOD.

Growth point
See VEGETATIVE CONE.

Growth regulators
Materials that the gardener sprays or waters in to inhibit growth and to encourage development of side shoots, thus achieving compact, bushy plants. As soon as the growth regulators are metabolized, the plant resumes its normal pattern of growth. Some of these agents can also initiate or precipitate flower development.

H

Habit
Botanical term for the form of a plant, the plant's appearance.

Half-shrub
Plants whose lower parts remain firm and woody but whose upper parts are herbaceous. Examples: *Columnea, Pelargonium* species, *Pentas lanceolata.*

Hanging plants
Plants with trailing or creeping stems that look particularly attractive in a hanging container.

Hardening off
Carefully accommodating the plant to changed temperature and light conditions. Also called *acclimation.*

Honeydew
Sticky excretion of aphids and scale that one finds not only on plant leaves but also on windowsills, floors, and furniture. Honeydew attracts ants but also sooty mold, which can dirty the leaves terribly. Wash off immediately!

Hormone
Substance produced by plants that can, even in small amounts, stimulate or inhibit growth and development. Also called phytohormones.

Hothouse (Warmhouse)
Term for the greenhouses in the botanical garden in which average temperatures of 68° to 77° F (20°–25° C) are maintained and where tropical plants, so-called hothouse plants, are housed.

Humidity
Fraction, expressed as percentage, of water vapor in the air: 0% = absolutely dry; 100% = saturated with water vapor, or mist. Houseplants need between 50% and 70% humidity, depending on where they come from. Artificially heated air is invariably too dry. You can use various measures (see drawings, page 43) to increase the humidity.

Humus

Nutrient-rich substrate that consists of decayed and decaying organic material.

Hybrid

Result of a crossing of plants of different varieties, species, or genera (see BASTARD). Most hybrids are plants that have arisen from crossings of different species of the same genus. Orchid hybrids are particularly common.

Hydroculture (Hydroponics)

Plant culture without soil. The plants stand in a special substrate that gives them support (for example gravel) and are supplied with a nutrient solution.

Hygrometer

Instrument for measuring humidity.

I

Inflorescence

See drawing, page 15. The arrangement of the flowers on a plant.

Insecticide

A material used to control insects.

Insectivorous plants

Insect-eating plants like the venus's-flytrap and the pitcher plant (see page 173), sundew, or butterworts. They are also called carnivorous plants.

Internodes

Intervals along a stem between leaf nodes, from Latin *inter* = between, *nodus* = node.

Ion exchanger

Slow-release fertilizer consisting of golden-brown, sparkling, shining synthetic resin particles that slowly release nutrients. In exchange the synthetic resin binds the ions that the plant cannot use and may produce alkalinity, such as chlorine and calcium. Ion exchangers facilitate hydroponic culture. If you use them you must be sure to soften any extremely hard tap water.

Iron (Fe)

Important trace element that is necessary for plant growth and for making chlorophyll and protein. In alkaline soil or in the presence of hard water iron can be bonded to calcium and is then no longer available to the plants, resulting in symptoms of deficiency (see First Aid for Your Plants, pages 50–55). The plants can actually starve because they lack the iron necessary for synthesizing chlorophyll.

J

Jiffy Pots

Peat disks, which swell when they are soaked in water. They are excellent for seeding and growing young plants. In time the roots of the young plants grow all through the "nursery pot" and can then be planted in a larger container (see page 61).

K

Keiki

Term for OFFSETS from orchids.

L

Labellum

The middle and lower, most conspicuous petal of an orchid flower. It is formed into a lip and serves as a "landing area" for pollinating insects.

Lava gravel/sand

Porous mineral pebbles of volcanic origin, which are used to make cactus soil water permeable and can also be used in water culture. Lava gravel is obtainable in garden centers. In pet shops it is sold under the name Lavalite.

Layers

Term for one- or two-year-old plant shoots that are bent down, laid in humus-rich soil, fastened firmly, and covered with earth. Root development is promoted by scratching or cutting into the branch at the bending point.

Leaf

Important plant organ that assists in nutrition (see PHOTOSYNTHESIS), provides the plant with oxygen (see RESPIRATION), and regulates the water supply (see TRANSPIRATION). The foliage leaf consists of base, petiole, and blade. It can be flat, paper thin, fat and fleshy, but also in the shape of a needle or a tube.

Leaf eelworms

See First Aid for Your Plants, pages 50–55.

Leaf spot fungus

See First Aid for Your Plants, pages 50–55.

Leaf veins

Conducting pathways or vascular bundles of leaves, also called nerves. They serve to provide water and nutrients.

Legginess

Gardeners' term for the development of long, weak, pale shoots with large intervals between the leaf nodes and no leaves. Cause: Too little light and too high a temperature.

Lianas

Plants rooted in the ground with ropelike, woody stems that work their way toward the light by climbing, looping, or aerial roots. Examples: Windowleaf, philodendron, pothos.

Light

Essential to life for the plant. Light is necessary for PHOTOSYNTHESIS, regulates growth, flower development, sprouting, leaf coloring, and leaf drop.

Light deficiency

Bad for all plants because PHOTOSYNTHESIS will be disrupted by lack of light. Light deficiency is a cause of LEGGINESS, GREENING, of colored leaves, failure to grow, and leaf drop.

Light germinators
Plants whose seeds need light to sprout. Their seeds should not be sowed too thickly and should never be covered with soil.

Light mark
See drawing, page 45. Marking on pot that enables one to replace the pot exactly as it was before it was moved for cleaning a window or for watering.

Lightmeter
See drawing, page 45. Instrument for measuring light. Obtainable in garden and photography supply stores.

Lime-hating plants
Plants that either will not tolerate lime in water and substrate or that tolerate it badly. For instance, azaleas, camellias, and miniature orange trees prefer a low lime content.

Lithophyte
Plants that live on rocks and stones (from Greek: *lithos* = stone, *phyton* = plant).

Long-day plants
Plants that need daily long light periods and short dark periods to set flowers. Contrast: SHORT-DAY PLANTS.

Loss of leaves
Loss of a plant's lower leaves because of poor care or too dark a location. This loss is normal in some plant species. For example, the lower leaves may be shed in order to develop a trunk as in *Dracaena marginata* or *Yucca*.

M

Magnesium (Mg)
Important building material for plant cells and principal nutrient. Necessary for synthesis of chlorophyll.

Mealybugs
See First Aid for Your Plants, pages 50–55.

Meranti
Orchid plant material that is derived from the wood of the tropical tree *Shorea*. Meranti is used primarily in window culture. Why orchids root so well in meranti wood chips is not clear as of this writing.

Meristem
Young plant tissue consisting of cells that are still capable of division (growth). It is located in tips of stems and roots but also is produced in the callus and root development of cuttings.

Metabolism
Conversion and processing of nutrients and elimination of byproducts.

Microclimate
Climates in immediate vicinity of one or several plants. Can be affected by other plants, walls, heating units, or humidifiers (see drawings, page 43).

Micronutrients
Another word for the trace elements boron, iron, copper, manganese, molybdenum, zinc, and others. Although plants need them in only tiny amounts, lack of them can lead to disease and poor growth.

Mildew
A fungus that attacks plants. There are several types, among them: true mildew and false mildew, which is also called downy or gray mildew. See First Aid for Your Plants, pages 50–55.

Milky sap
Milky, sometimes poisonous fluid that some plants excrete if they are injured, for example spurge plants like poinsettia and other euphorbia species.

Mimicry
Perfect imitation and adaptation to the environment or milieu. Serves plants for deception, reproduction, and as protection from being eaten by animals.

Minimum-maximum thermometer
Measuring instrument that establishes the highest and lowest temperature so that one can determine the temperature differences between day and night. Important for orchid culture, in which a lower night temperature is essential for flower development.

Minis (Miniature plants)
Plants kept small by means of breeding, small amount of potting medium, and sometimes by use of growth-inhibiting hormones. They are good for creating dish gardens, bottle gardens, or for window greenhouses.

Mites
See First Aid for Your Plants, pages 50–55.

Mixed fertilizers
Fertilizers that contain various organic and inorganic nutrients.

Monocotyledonous
Plants that have only one seed leaf, for example palms and grasses. The group of monocotyledonous plants is called the *Monocotyledonae*.

Monoecious
When male and female flowers appear on the same plant, it is termed monoecious. Contrast: DIOECIOUS.

Monopodial
Growth of a single axis. Monopodial growth is recognizable by an unbranching, vertical main stem, from which side branches are produced (for example, Norfolk Island pine). Compare: SYMPODIAL.

Moss build-up
Is caused by compacted soil and excess dampness. Can injure plants that poorly tolerate dampness around the stem area, and it inhibits aeration of the soil. Therefore, carefully loosen the top layer of soil with a fork. Be careful not to injure roots and plant. Remove mossy layer.

Moss stake
See drawing, page 44. Term for a moisture retentive support for plants with air roots, for example *Philodendron* and *Syngonium* species.

Mother plant

Plant that is still nurturing its offsets and from which cuttings are taken. Or that which is a female partner in hybridizing.

Multigeneric hybrids

Crossing of three or more different genera—especially common with orchids. To avoid gigantic words when more than three genera are involved, a completely new name is invented for the hybrid. Example: *Potinara*, developed from *Brassovola*, *Laelia*, *Cattleya*, and *Sophronitis*.

Mutation

Change in a plant's genes that appears spontaneously or can be artificially induced by irradiation (ultraviolet, röentgen, or radioactive rays) or chemicals (for instance the poison colchicine from the autumn crocus), which are employed during hybridization.

Mycelium

Fungus network that consists of fine filaments (*hypae*).

N

Necrosis

Dead tissue, an injury, which can be caused by various things such as incorrect use of fertilizers, too much sun, too much or too little water, too low a humidity, as well as disease or parasites.

Nematodes

See First Aid for Your Plants, page 50–55.

New growth

Arising of new shoots in a plant. A signal that the vegetative phase is beginning again, as in the spring. A plant that shows good new growth is healthy and vigorous.

Nighttime temperature

The cool temperature of the dark period. Important requirement for orchids to set flowers.

Nitrogen (N)

One of the three most important primary nutrients, which is contained in every complete fertilizer. It is used mainly for synthesis of protein compounds and is responsible for leaf and shoot development.

Nodes

Point of origin of leaves on the stem. Some plants (for example those of the carnation family) have prominently thickened nodes.

NPK

Fertilizer formula indicating the three primary nutrients that a plant needs. N = nitrogen, P = phosphorus, K = potassium. The proportion of each nutrient contained in a specific fertilizer is expressed in numbers (for example, 14+7+14 or 14-7-14, which means: 14 percent nitrogen, 7 percent phosphorus, 14 percent potassium).

Nutrients

Specific elements that plants need for growth and good health. The principal nutrients consist of nitrogen (N), phosphorus (P), and potassium (K), and in addition calcium (Ca), magnesium (Mg), and sulfur (S). The MICRONUTRIENTS or trace elements are mainly heavy metals. The plants obtain nutrients from the fertilizers that we give them.

O

Offsets

See drawing, page 60. Young plantlets that are produced from the stem form roots; then, they are separated from the mother plant and can be planted. Examples: Agave, bromeliads, spider plant, and screw pine.

Opposite leaves

Plant leaves that are situated opposite each other at a leaf node.

Organic fertilizers

Fertilizers made from plant or animal products such as manure, dried blood, horn and hoof meal, stinging nettle broth, or guano. You can produce it yourself but it is also supplied commercially for use on garden and houseplants. Organic fertilizers must first be released by soil organisms so that the plants can take them up. Because this takes some time, they are slow to take effect. They are less useful for pot plants because the soil organisms in the confined area of a pot are greatly diminished.

Oxygen

A colorless, odorless gaseous chemical agent that is essential for all forms of plant and animal life. Plants take up oxygen in RESPIRATION and use it to break down organic materials. Through this process energy is released for growth and development. The oxygen content of air is 21 percent.

P

Palm pots

Containers that are made higher and narrower than ordinary ones. This is because palms develop roots more vertically than horizontally and the root ball is often forced above the pot. If you can't find palm pots, you can also use the equally tall, narrow rose containers.

Panicle

See drawing, page 15. Pyramidal inflorescence formed by multiple branches. Each branch is a RACEME.

Parasites

See First Aid for Your Plants, pages 50–55.

Peat

Soil from bogs, dug out after the bogs have been drained and then milled and packed in sacks. It is used for improving the soil in gardens and in the production of potting soil. To inhibit the depletion of this increasingly rare soil type, its place is being taken by fortified substitutes, such as bark or compost.

Peat pots

Small pots of compressed peat. Best suited for seeding and growing young plants. Later the plants can be set out, pot and all, in a larger container.

Perennial plants (Perennials)

Plants that survive for several years, usually with new growth from the woody parts. (See ANNUAL PLANTS.)

Perlite

Volcanic, industrially fabricated "pebbles" that, like pumice, provide good drainage and aeration, do not rot, and retain few nutrients. Perlite is used for potting mediums for orchids and cactus, as well as for propagation.

Petals

See drawing on page 15.

Phosphorus (P)

One of the three chief nutrients for plants. Phosphorus plays a large role in the energy economy of the plant and in its development of roots, flowers, and fruits. It also promotes the processes of maturation.

Photoperiodism

Plants' dependency on light. Plant developmental processes, like setting flowers or the development of storage organs (tubers and bulbs), are controlled by the length of daily light and dark periods (that is, by the length of the day). Photoperiodism is used by growers to control the development of flowers, for example with chrysanthemums and poinsettias. (See SHORT-DAY PLANTS and LONG-DAY PLANTS.)

Photosynthesis

Manufacture of organic substances from inorganic substances with the help of light (Greek: *photos* = light, *synthesis* = putting together). Through their microscopic stomata, leaves take carbon dioxide from the air, change it with the aid of light, chlorophyll, and water into carbohydrate (sugar), and give off oxygen. Without plants and their ability to use light as a source of energy, life on our earth would be impossible. (See ASSIMILATION.)

Phototropism

Bending of plant organs according to the influence of light. As a rule, stems turn toward the light, roots show no reaction or turn away from light.

Physiological injury

Diseases that are induced by mistakes in culture or poor location of plants (see First Aid for Your Plants, pages 50–55).

pH value

The pH value (Latin: *potentia hydrogenii*) indicates the hydrogen concentration and is expressed in numbers that range from 1 to 14. In this scale, 7 is neutral. Anything below 7 indicates an acid reaction, anything above it, an alkaline one. Almost all houseplants thrive best with a pH value of 5.5 to 6.5. The pH can easily be measured with indicator sticks (available in garden and pet stores).

Pinching out (Pinching back)

See drawing, page 44. Breaking off the soft ends of shoots with the thumb and forefinger. It leads to better branching and thus to bushier growth.

Pinnate

Term for leaves that consist of several leaflets, arranged along the leaf stalk or rachis.

Pistil

See drawing, page 15. Female organ of the flower. Consists of ovary, style, and stigma.

Poisonous plants

Plants containing more or less toxic substances that are lethal or injurious to humans or animals. Members of the following plant families are frequently poisonous: aralia, arum, dogbane, nightshade. Observe warning notes in individual plant descriptions.

Pollen

The pollen grain is the male sex cell. The word *pollen* may also refer to all the pollen grains contained in the anther.

Pollination

Transport of the pollen to the stigma by wind, water, insects, birds, or the human hand, as with a brush.

Pores

Another term for the openings (stomata) that are usually situated on the underside of the leaf. Pores provide for the gas exchange in PHOTOSYNTHESIS and RESPIRATION and give off water vapor; they evaporate water.

Potassium (K)

One of the three principal nutrients. It positively influences the water content of the cells and is important for various basic life processes: Potassium produces resistance to drought, frost, and certain plant diseases. Potassium is contained in every complete fertilizer. Potassium fertilizers can be given after flowering to all plants that need to enter winter with strong wood.

Propagation

See GENERATIVE REPRODUCTION and VEGETATIVE PROPAGATION.

Prop root

Air roots that branch when they touch the ground, as with window-leaf, for example.

Pruning

Regular removal of dead plant parts and wilted flowers. Good for plant health.

Pseudobulb

The thickened stem of an orchid that serves as a storage place for water and nutrients and helps the orchid to survive dry spells. Every year a new plump, smooth pseudobulb grows and develops two more leaves. The old one shrivels and loses its foliage but provides the younger one with nourishment.

Pumice

Large-pored, stable (that is to say, it will not rot) volcanic rock with very little water storage capacity. Ground pumice provides for good aeration of the potting medium and provides good drainage in orchid culture.

Pyrethrum

Natural insecticide from chrysanthemum species that is not harmful to bees and is quickly broken down. It is considered nontoxic to humans and mammals, since it is poorly absorbed by the stomach and a healthy skin. But according to the latest findings, it may be injurious if it gets into open wounds. It can reach the nervous system through the blood. Be careful with all wounds and skin ailments, especially those of allergies! Wear gloves when spraying and spray only when there is no wind. Still more questionable are insecticides with pyrethroid, which is a synthetic pyrethrum.

R

Raceme

See drawing, page 15. A form of inflorescence with several single flowers growing on individual small stems and along a larger main stem.

Raphides

Crystal needles of calcium oxalate that lie in close bundles. Raphides are found in most plants of the arum family, especially in *Dieffenbachia*, in spider plant, and in *Dracaena*. They are located in specialized cells that open swiftly at the slightest touch and catapult the crystal needles out. These can easily get into the mucous membranes of mouth and throat and can produce burns and irritation.

Repotting

The word for transplanting into larger containers with new, unused potting medium.

Resistance

Inherited or developed ability to withstand disease and insects (in plants) or chemical substances (in insects). It plays an important role in plant breeding, whose goal is to produce varieties that can resist pests and disease.

Respiration

Like us, plants breathe day and night with all their cells, taking in oxygen and giving off carbon dioxide and water. Thus energy is released, which is used in photosynthesis.

Rest period

Period in which a plant no longer grows—that is, does not put out new leaves or shoots. With many houseplants the rest period occurs in the fall and winter months, when the amount of light is also diminished. In this period these plants receive less water, no fertilizer, and a cooler location. Also referred to as *dormancy*.

Rhizome

Underground, horizontal stem axis that forms shoots on top and roots underneath. Rhizomes are also called root stalks or rootstocks and differ from roots in that they develop buds and scales. They occur in various *Gesneriaceae* species, for example, and in the arum lily.

Root ball

Term for the soil of a pot plant when it is completely laced with roots.

Root eelworms

See First Aid for Your Plants, pages 50–55.

Root hairs

The fine hairs on the sides near the tip of roots. Not very long, they take up water and nutrients.

Rooting hormones

Hormone preparations in powder, liquid, or paste form that promote rooting of cuttings.

Root rot

Disease caused by soil fungus. (See First Aid for Your Plants, pages 50–55.)

Roots

See drawing, page 14. In most plants they have the function of anchoring the plant in the ground and taking up water and nutrients which they store or send to the stem of the plant. Examples of specialized root forms are AERIAL ROOTS, PROP ROOTS, and ADVENTITIOUS ROOTS.

Rosette

A particularly dense arrangement of leaves, in which all the leaves appear to come from a single point on the stem. This impression is produced because the stem has extremely short internodes. Rosette plants are bromeliads, echeverias, bird's-nest ferns, and African violets.

Runners

Side shoots, above ground or underground, that can grow from the base of the stem, the flower rosette, the mother plant, or the root crown. Runners are also called stolons and appear on the strawberry begonia, for example, and the sword fern.

S

Salt burn

Arises from overfertilization or through concentration of fertilizer salts in "old" potting medium. Can be expressed in growth reduction, CHLOROSIS, or dying tissue. Remedy, see page 45.

Salt sensitivity

Many plants are sensitive to high concentrations of fertilizer salts. In the descriptions of species and variety these plants are especially noted. They should receive one-half to one-quarter of the prescribed quantity of fertilizer, at most, or an organic fertilizer.

Scale

See First Aid for Your Plants, pages 50–55.

Seed

Fertilized part of a flowering plant, which can sprout and bring forth a new plant. It is often provided with a food reserve and a protective coat.

Seed-leaves

The first leaves of a plant. As soon as they reach light, chlorophyll is formed in them, which enables the plant to begin to nourish itself through the process of photosynthesis. There are plants that produce only one seed-leaf (see MONOCOTYLEDONOUS) and those that produce two (see DICOTYLEDONOUS).

Seedling
New plants that have arisen from fertilized egg cells. The seedling consists of seed root, seed stem, seed bud, and seed-leaves. It is bipolar: The root system develops from the seed root at one end, while the stem and leaf system develop from the seed bud at the other end.

Selection
Plant breeders' term for the separating out of plants that do not display the characteristics that were desired in hybridization. Selection also occurs in nature.

Self-climbing plant
One that develops adhesive disks or adventitious aerial roots at the ends of the tendrils, as for example ivy.

Self-pollination
Method of pollination in which a stigma is dusted with the pollen of the same flower. Thus the hereditary factors of one and the same plant are continually passed on (inbreeding).

Sepals
A plant's protective enclosure, as a rule green enclosure for petals, stamens with pollen, and fruit leaves.

Shading
Measures to protect plants from sunburn, particularly in the middle of the day and in the spring when the plants are not yet accustomed to the high light intensity. Shading can be accomplished with curtains, jalousies, awnings, tissue paper, or with neighboring plants that offer shade.

Shallow-rooted plant
One that does not develop deep-reaching main roots or taproots but whose roots branch vigorously sideways, like azaleas.

Sharp sand
Lime-free river sand or quartz sand that is added to potting materials to make them water permeable and to disperse the fertilizer salts well. It is an important component of the soil used in propagation. Not recommended for houseplants are colored sands or builder's sand, which contain lime.

Shoot
Growth unit, as a rule consisting of stem, leaves, and terminal bud.

Short-day plants
Plants that, for a particular period of time, need a short day to set flowers—that is, short periods of light and long periods of darkness. Examples: chrysanthemums, poinsettias. Contrast: LONG-DAY PLANTS.

Silicon (Si)
Chemical element that constitutes 80 percent of the earth's surface. In plants it occurs primarily in horsetails and grasses. The silicon compound silicic acid strengthens the cell walls of plants and makes them resistant to attacks of fungus and bacteria. Broths or teas made from horsetails (see recipe, page 52) are thus outstanding plant tonics. Silica soil and diatomaceous earth work just as well.

Single flowers
Possessing as a rule substantially fewer petals than double flowers. Usually the stamens are visible in single flowers.

Slow-release fertilizers
Fertilizers in which the nutrients are continually given up to the plants slowly and over a long period of time.

Snails/Slugs
See First Aid for Your Plants, pages 50–55.

Soaking
See drawing, page 42. First aid measure for a root ball that is completely dried out.

Soft scale
See First Aid for Your Plants, pages 50–55.

Soft-skinned mites
See First Aid for Your Plants, pages 50–55.

Soil warmth
A soil temperature on the order of 68° F (20° C) or more. Important for plants that are accustomed to high soil temperatures in their native locations and fail to thrive when their roots are cold. A requirement for germination for many tropical plants. Warm soil can be provided by warming mats or heatable propagation flats.

Sooty mold
See First Aid for Your Plants, pages 50–55.

Sori
Groups of spore cases (SPORANGIA) in ferns. Depending on the species, they are located in differently shaped little clumps on the undersides of the leaves. In some ferns, the spore cases are covered with a protective layer until maturity.

Spadix
A thick or fleshy, spikelike form of inflorescence (see drawing, page 15) in the arum family.

Spathe
BRACT of the arum lily, tailflowers, and other members of the arum family. Can often be strikingly colored and serves as an attractant for pollinators.

Species
Designation for a part of the botanical name of a plant, which as a rule tells something about its appearance, characteristics, or place of origin. Example: *Clivia miniata*. The species name *miniata* means that it is describing a fiery red *Clivia* (Latin: *miniatus* = minimum-colored, *minium* being red lead). All the plants in a particular species are alike in their essential features.

Sphagnum
Swamp and peat moss (*Sphagnum squarrosum* and *Sphagnum cuspidatum*). Formerly the classic component of orchid substrates but now, for environmental reasons, is more rarely used. Can be replaced by orchid chips, PERLITE, or glasswool.

Spider mites
Also red spider. (See First Aid for Your Plants, pages 50–55.)

Spike

See drawing, page 15. A form of inflorescence without stalks on individual flowers.

Sporangia

Cases in which spores are developed. They appear on ferns, for instance. They are arranged in bands or clusters (see SORI) on the undersides of fern fronds.

Spores

Single, asexual cells of ferns. They can remain in the SPORANGIA or are thrown out when they are ripe.

Springtails

See First Aid for Your Plants, pages 50–55.

Sprouting temperature

Optimum ground and air temperature for plants to begin to sprout. It can vary widely depending on the species. Some plants need warmth and others need coolness to be able to sprout.

ssp

Abbreviation for SUBSPECIES.

Stalk

Unbranching, leafless stem, which bears the flower or inflorescence and sometimes also bracts. Examples: *Amaryllis, Strelitzia,* arum lily.

Standard

See drawing, page 44. Form of training in which plant is limited to a desired height so that it branches to the sides. Thus the central stem is strengthened. (Also called *tree* form.)

Standing water (Sogginess)

With few exceptions, the death of any plant. Occurs when the water from irrigation cannot drain and the soil becomes soggy. If too much water expels the oxygen from the soil, the roots suffocate and rot. Therefore: always provide good DRAINAGE.

Stem

Herbaceous, branching or unbranching shoot with or without leaves.

Stem cutting

Piece of a stem, for example *Dieffenbachia, Dracaena,* or *Yucca* that can be used for PROPAGATION.

Stem joints

See INTERNODES.

Stem rot

General term for fungus infections. (See First Aid for Your Plants, pages 50–55.)

Sterile

Expression for unfruitful or germ free. The opposite of FERTILE.

Sterile leaves

Non-spore-bearing leaves of some ferns that may have an additional function. They may serve to collect humus and water and may not be removed. For example: brown leaves of the staghorn fern.

Sterilize

To make germ free, to disinfect. For potting soil accomplished by steaming in a special apparatus or with chemicals. It is important, especially for sowing or culture, because disease organisms can be transmitted through the soil. The commercially prepared propagating soils are germ free because they are treated.

Stigma

See drawing, page 15. The stigma is a part of the flower, specifically the upper part of the pistil and the real organ of pollen reception. To capture the male pollen, it is coated with a slippery or sticky layer.

Stolons

Another term for RUNNERS.

Storage organs

Plant organs that can stockpile water and nutrients, such as tubers, bulbs, pseudobulbs, and rhizomes.

Styrofoam

Pieces of nonbiodegradable plastic that are used to make potting soils for air permeable.

Suberization

See CORKY GROWTH.

Subspecies

Plants with only a few characteristics that are divergent from the species. Subspecies are designated by the addition of *ssp* (abbrev. for *subspecies*) to their botanical name.

Substrate

Technical term for potting material (from Latin *substratum* = undercovering).

Succulents

Plants with fleshy, juicy leaves or stems. Some examples of leaf succulents are agaves, aloes, and Livingstone daisies, whereas cacti, column euphorbias, or stapelias belong to the stem succulents.

Suckers

Young plant runners that grow out of the soil directly next to the mother plant.

Sulfur (S)

Chemical element that is one of the principal nutrients. It is needed by the plant for synthesis of protein, vitamin B[1], and pungent oils (garlic, horseradish, mustard) and is supplied in fertilizers in the form of sulphates of potassium, magnesium, ammonium, and calcium.

Summer oil

A mineral product (white oil) that destroys the waxy layer of the insect integument and clogs its respiratory organs. Used for SCALE.

Sunburn

See First Aid for Your Plants, pages 50–55.

Sympodial

Growth having several axes. Occurs when a shoot terminates its growth by withering of the terminal bud or by use of it for flower development. The bud in the axil of the uppermost leaves of the stem continues the stem system. Contrast: MONOPODIAL.

Systemic control agents

Chemicals that enter the leaves or roots of the plant and are transported throughout the plant by means of its vascular system.

T

Tendril
Climbing organ of plants. There are tendrils that arise from stems and those that arise from leaves. Stem tendrils are formed by the passion flower, for example, and grapes; leaf tendrils are found on peas and vetch.

Terminal cutting (Tip cutting)
See drawing, page 44. Cutting that contains a terminal bud.

Thinning out
After sprouting, the seedlings are usually so close together that they must be thinned out. The weakest are pulled out to give strong seedlings more room to grow. The plants also can be separated and potted individually.

Thrips
See First Aid for Your Plants, pages 50–55.

Tincture of green soap
Home remedy for control of scale and mealybugs (see recipe, page 52).

Trace elements
See MICRONUTRIENTS.

Transpiration
Giving off of water vapor by plants. All land plants give off water vapor, primarily through the PORES. At warmer temperatures, transpiration is increased. If the evaporated water is not replaced, the plant wilts. Transpiration produces EVAPORATIVE COOLING in the immediate vicinity of the leaves. This keeps the plant from suffering from heat shock.

Trapped air
Gardeners' expression for moist air, "trapped" by a plastic bag placed over a pot (see drawing, page 59) or by a piece of clear glass completely covering a propagation tray.

True mildew
See First Aid for Your Plants, pages 50–55.

Trunk
An old, generally woody, often very thick branching or unbranching stem that does not die in winter.

Tub plants
Plants that grow large relatively quickly and thus require large containers (tubs) and locations with plenty of space. Tub plants come mainly from the Mediterranean regions and thus thrive splendidly when they spend summer out of doors in a protected, sunny spot. The majority of them must be wintered over in a bright location at 41° to 50° F (5°–10° C). Some will also do well as houseplants (see pages 138, 139).

Tuber
See drawing, page 14. Thickened, more or less fleshy part of a stem. There are underground budding tubers, as with cyclamen and tuberous-rooted begonias, or above-ground ones, as with hearts-on-a-string. All tubers are storage organs for reserve food.

Tuberous roots
Tuberlike swollen roots that serve as storage areas, for example in terrestrial orchids.

Twiggy
Expression for an unbalanced growth form with long, relatively disorderly and widespreading slender shoots in woody plants.

U

Umbel
See drawing, page 15. A form of inflorescence.

V

Variegation
Term for leaves with white or yellow flecks and stripes. These light areas contain no chlorophyll and thus cannot assimilate. Variegated plants must be in as bright a location as possible but usually can't stand direct sunlight. In dark locations they may begin storing their chlorophyll again in order to develop enough of the assimilation areas that are necessary for their nutrition. Variegated leaves can also be produced by viruses—as in the flowering maple.

Variety
Often of hybrid origin of two plant species. The variety name, also called *cultivar*, is usually indicated by single quotation marks, for example: *Campanula isophylla* 'Mayi'. Abbreviation: *var.* = *varietas*.

Vascular bundles
Structures of the plant that transport up water and dissolved nutrients and deposit them, then transport processed nutrients down. They also transport systemic insecticides to every part of the plant. They are the circulatory system of the plant.

Vegetative cones
Growth points at the ends of shoots, roots, and buds.

Vegetative period
Also called growth period. Limited by our seasons, the vegetative period for us begins with the increase of light in late winter and spring and ends when the days become shorter. The beginning of the vegetative period is recognizable by the appearance of new growth.

Vegetative propagation
Asexual reproduction by plant division or by rooting of stems, leaves, or runners. The new plant thus obtained is identical to the MOTHER PLANT genetically and in appearance.

Ventilation

Necessary measures in houseplant culture, especially in winter. Stagnant, warm, dry air promotes disease and insect infestation. Therefore, ventilate often, but keep drafts and direct cold air from plants.

Virus

Disease-causing agent, see First Aid for Your Plants, pages 50–55.

Vitrine

A glass display case for plants that need high humidity. Can also be called an indoor greenhouse, terrarium, or Wardian case. Vitrines already existed in the last century. They were ingeniously made from cast iron (Wardian cases). Today they are technologically refined, with heating, humidifiers, and provision for sufficient light and ventilation. The frames are of aluminum or rot-resistant redwood and are obtainable in various sizes and shapes.

Volatile oils

Fragrant, as a rule, and strong smelling, easily dissipated materials that are concentrated in glandular cells or microscopically small oil reservoirs, for example in the petals of gardenia flowers, the leaves of fragrant geraniums, the roots of ginger, the bark of the cinnamon tree, in pepper seeds (peppercorns), and in the rind of the lemon.

W

Water

Necessity of life for humans, animals, and plants. It is an agent of transport for nutrients and an important factor in PHOTOSYNTHESIS. Without water the plants wilt, the stomata (pores) of the leaves close, and photosynthesis and TRANSPIRATION are interrupted. Many houseplants—because they come from other growth regions—are not adapted to our water, which often contains too much lime for them. In such cases the water should be softened (see drawing, page 42).

Water hardness

Measure for the limestone content of water, usually given in mg/L. Anyone who wants to know how hard the local water is can ascertain this value from your local waterworks. For houseplants, water over 13 mg/L should be softened (see drawing, page 42).

Watering space

See drawing, page 41. Must be allowed for when repotting. It prevents soil from washing over the edge of the pot when the plant is watered and permits a good soaking.

Water softening

See drawing, page 42.

Waxy coating

Extremely thin film or bloom with which some leaves protect themselves against evaporation of water.

Whiteflies

See First Aid for Your Plants, pages 50–55.

White oil

See SUMMER OIL.

Woody growth

A plant stem made stronger by lignin deposited in the cell wall.

X

Xerophytes

Plants that are able to withstand great dryness. Examples: cacti and other succulents like euphorbias, agaves, aloes, *Dorotheanthus,* and sedum.

Y

Yellow sticky boards

Plastic boards coated with sticky material and colored a particularly glaring yellow to serve as a lure for insects (see page 51).

PLANT PORTRAITS AND TIPS ON CULTURE

The passionflower is an
assiduous climber that
repays loving care with
flowers that are as
numerous as the
stars in the sky and as
beautiful as jeweled
ornaments.

84

Getting houseplants to grow and bloom and yes, even to fruit, is what makes indoor gardening so fascinating. In the following pages you will find out how to cultivate the most popular flowering and foliage plants, ferns, palms, orchids, and cacti correctly and thus successfully.

The Most Beautiful Houseplants and Their Culture

Learn to recognize the most common houseplants and know the requirements for cultivating them. Using these portraits, discover the particular growth form of each plant. The broad range of flower and leaf colors they provide is sure to give you many attractive decorating ideas.

Structured for Clarity and Easy Comparison

All the plant portraits are comprehensive and clear so that you can find out everything you need to know at a glance. All the descriptions follow the same format, so different plants can be easily compared with each other. And where will you find a particular houseplant? All varieties are arranged by category (see box on page 87) in correspondingly titled chapters, where they appear by their botanical names in alphabetical order. The English name is in large, easy-to-read type directly over the illustration. The name given is the one best known. However, if a plant has other names as well, they too are given.
The botanical name, placed above the English one, is used internationally and therefore determines the alphabetical order of the listings. When the botanical name of the genus appears over the name of a houseplant (for example *Echeveria*), the names of several species that are appropriate for indoor culture are given in the text. When a species name is used as the botanical name (for example, *Ardisia crenata*), the description refers only to this one particular species. This usually also means that no other species of this genus are cultivated as houseplants.

The Symbols and Their Meanings

Without your having to read through the text, the symbols give you information at once about the right location and such important procedures as watering and misting. They also indicate whether a plant is suitable for hydroculture or is poisonous.

☀ The plant tolerates full sun, also midday sun.

○ The plant needs a bright spot, near a window but not sunny.

◑ The plant will also thrive in semishade.

● The plant tolerates or prefers shade.

🪣 The plant needs abundant water. Water so much that there is considerable overflow in the saucer.

🪣 Keep the plant only moderately damp. Only a few drops should appear in the saucer.

🪣 Give little water. The saucer should remain dry.

🧴 Mist the plant often.

▦ The plant is suitable for hydroculture.

☠ The plant is poisonous.

Explanation of the Headings

The instructions for culture are arranged according to the following headings, which are in bold face.

Blooming Season: For the flowering plants, including orchids and cacti, this is the first item. This information is important if you want to acquire a flowering plant at the best time or want to know the right flowering time for the species when a plant you have simply doesn't bloom.
Family: Here you will find the botanical classification.
Origin: This gives the geographical origin.
Location: This is an important criterion for culture. Here you learn about the light and warmth requirements during the year.
Watering, Feeding: This tells you the optimum amounts of water and how often to fertilize. Important: Where "weak or low-dosage fertilizer" is advised, use only one-half to one-third of the manufacturer's recommended quantity to 1 qt (1 L) of water.
Further Culture: This informs you about individual humidity or warmth requirements, whether misting should be done, and when and in which potting medium a plant should be repotted.
Propagation: This describes the quickest propagation method for that particular houseplant. You can find out how to do it in the How To pages 58–61.
Pests, Diseases: Those to which the plant is particularly vulnerable are mentioned as are the chief potential causes of pest attack or disease. How you remedy them is described in the chapter First Aid for Your Plants (pages 50–55).
My Tip: Here the author gives more important information.
Warning: This appears for plants that are poisonous or cause skin irritation. Plants so designated can be harmful to susceptible adults, children, and pets; those with a skull and crossbones symbol may even be lethal if they are eaten or come into contact with the skin or the mucous membranes.

Caution—Other Things You Should Know About Plants

When choosing plants, keep in mind the following criteria if you have small children or housepets. Some plants are to be enjoyed with caution.
They can cause allergies. Classic examples of plant allergies are those caused by the chemical primin of the German primrose (also called poison primrose) and cases of contact dermatitis through phototoxic substances, for example in *Ficus* and *Citrus* species. Various members of the Compositae family are also allergenic, especially chrysanthemums.
They can cause injury, for example from spines, thorns, sharp leaf edges or leaf tips.
They can cause headaches. Here only plants with implicated fragrances in flowers and leaves are included.

Properly cared-for foliage plants are of such a lively green that one doesn't miss colored flowers.

They can contain toxic substances, which can be injurious to health for people and pets and can even be lethal if they are consumed. Small children put everything into their mouths and cats and many other pets love to nibble on some houseplants.

Mold fungus (*Aspergillus*) in the flowerpot can cause health problems in people with lowered resistance. Potted plants should be removed from areas occupied by patients at risk. In case of doubt, ask your doctor.

Warning, Poison!

Poisons appear in concentration in the following plant families:

Arum family (Araceae) contains a bitter plant juice and raphides—special cells, which contain fine needles of calcium oxalate—that enter the skin and inject their poison.

Lily family (Liliaceae) can contain saponins and alkaloids as well as skin-irritating substances.

Nightshade family (Solanaceae) plants are dangerous because of their strong, powerful alkaloids.

Dogbane family (Apocynaceae) produces two of the most powerful poison groups, alkaloids and glycosides.

Spurge family (Euphorbiaceae) is furnished with toxic protein materials. The bitter milky juice has a caustic effect externally as well as internally.

FLOWERING PLANTS

They fascinate with their multiplicity of color and form, some also with their infatuating fragrance. Some produce from a rather modest flower a gaily colored, decorative ornamental fruit. Many bloom every year and become old household friends that one would not wish to be without.

S ales figures prove it: Flowering plants are the most popular houseplants. Who can resist the cheerful array of spring-flowering primulas, the charm of the African violet, the elegance of the camellia or the gardenia? Flowering plants can set off a periodic display of localized color patterns against the quiet background of foliage plants.

On the following pages you will meet all the beauties the flowering plant market has to offer. Included are plants with decorative fruits, which in the last analysis are nothing more than the continuation of the flower. In addition, you will find an attractive choice of new or less common flowering plants as well as a small assortment of favorite tub plants, which in a manageable pot-plant stage are still easy to keep in the house. Many beauties like browallia, German violet, or pocketbook flower are so-called seasonal or throwaway plants. They are not cultivated after blooming because their lifetime is limited to one year. Some, like poinsettia, chrysanthemum, or cineraria are lasting, of course, but with time they either become less attractive or cannot be induced to bloom again without extraordinary measures. But there are still enough varieties left that with loving care grow larger and more beautiful from year to year and bloom punctually every year. Prime examples are clivia, azalea, cyclamen, gardenia, and camellia. The darlings of international breeders, flowering plants are continually being changed and improved. The goals are longer lasting flowers and blooming period, maxi or mini growth, new colors, more beautiful leaf forms, more abundant flowers, and above all, improved readiness to flower and suitability for houseplant culture.

What You Should Know About Flowering Plants

Most of our flowering houseplants come from tropical or subtropical regions. The first "flowering ancestors" arose in the tropical rain forests, which have a very even climate. So favored, tropical plants could develop the greatest variety of form and color in their flowers. The development of flowers is influenced by many factors, of which the most important is light. In general plants bloom again in every vegetative year. But there are exceptions, like the bromeliads; they bloom only once, provide for offspring that will flower, and then die. Also, there are plants that need a decade or even a century until the first flowering, like the bamboos or the century agave (century plant). Many flowers are regular jewels of fabled beauty. One need only think of the flower of the medinilla (see page 122) or the passionflower (see pages 84–85). The flowering season varies from species to species. With some plants the season can be changed (for example for Mother's Day or Christmas) through horticultural manipulation. But when they are left to themselves, they bloom again the second year just as they did before. But there are also cases where the flowers appear out of order, which can occur as a result of mistakes in culture, or a severe infestation of insects. Then the survival tactics of the plant are called into play and it tries to provide for descendants very quickly before it dies entirely.

Naturally, plants do not bloom for us. We are only beneficiaries of their gigantic effort to maintain the species. In order to make the flower as seductive as possible for the particular pollinator, nature played with the flower's color, form, and pattern; it invented marvelous fragrances and bestial odors, refined

Flowering plants live to be fertilized. Here is the perfect seduction: Long, curved flowers and abundant nectar attract hummingbirds to fertilize them.

falls and pleasant landing areas, for example, for insects.

The Right Culture

Buying plants in flower is not difficult—to nurse them back when they are fading and to bring them into flower again in the following year, on the other hand, demands some basic knowledge about plants and careful cultivation. The plant portraits and culture hints will be very helpful to you in this regard. Tropical plants from regions with uniform climate and light conditions all year long are easily brought to bloom again. If they receive enough humidity and sufficient light during the winter, they will flower again in the following vegetative year without much trouble. With others, observation of the rest period is most important. For the indoor gardener, this means mimicking as well as possible the living conditions such as periods of dryness or reduced light in the plant's place of origin.

In their native setting, poinsettias develop into thick, high hedges like our wild roses and offer birds places to perch.

FLOWERING PLANTS

Acalypha hispida
Chenille Plant

There are also varieties of *Acalypha* with white spikes.

The chenille plant grows wild as a bush in all tropical regions. Only the female plants of this dioecious species are offered as pot plants. It is also called red-hot cattail for its cattail-like flower spikes. On the market are other varieties with creamy white flowers, such as 'Alba', and attractive hanging forms, such as *Acalypha pendula,* which has smaller leaves with a more defined heart shape.

Blooming Season: April to October.

Family: Euphorbiaceae (spurge family).

Origin: Tropical regions worldwide.

Location: Bright, but not sunny. Warm all year long; in winter never below 61° F (16° C). Avoid drafts.

Watering, Feeding: Keep the root ball moderately damp with soft, room-temperature water. Water sparingly from No-

vember to January. From February to the end of August fertilize weekly.

Further Culture: Mist often. As necessary, repot *Acalypha* in spring in a larger pot with all-purpose potting soil. Cut back shoots beforehand. Pinch out the new growth often so that the plant will become bushy.

Propagation: In spring from cuttings. A soil temperature of over 68° F (20° C) and high humidity are required for successful rooting, so use a heatable propagation flat. Pinch back rooted young plants often.

Pests, Diseases: Spider mites, whitefly, aphids, and scale from dry air.

Note: Use exactly the same care for the colored-leaved *Acalypha* 'Wilksiana' hybrids with the descriptive name Jacob's Coat.

Warning: *Acalypha* species and varieties are poisonous in all parts.

Achimenes Hybrids
Monkey-faced Pansy

Achimenes hybrids bloom abundantly.

This luxuriantly blooming gesneriad, which is related to the African violet and gloxinia, is available in summer in white, yellow, pink, purple, and blue. Characteristic are the scaly rhizomes, which look like little fir cones. The leaves are green on the upper side, red tinged on the underside.

Blooming Season: July to September.

Family: Gesneriaceae (gesneriad family).

Origin: Central and South America. Only cultivated forms are available in trade.

Location: From spring to fall bright and warm (68° to 77° F [20°–25°C]). Avoid direct sun under any circumstances.

Watering, Feeding: Do not use cold water for watering. As long as the plant is growing and flowering, keep slightly damp. Fertilize 6 weeks after the growth of the

rhizome to the end of July. After that water little; from September on do not water at all, so the plant can wither.

Further Culture: Cut off withered parts and leave the rhizome in the pot until spring (or take it out and store it in peat or sand at 68° F [20° C]). In February place the rhizome in the pot so that it is covered with a scant inch (2 cm) of new soil. Place plant in a bright (not sunny), warm spot. Water with warm water and provide for indirect humidity (see page 43).

Propagation: By division of the rhizome in spring or tip cuttings in soil with a temperature over 68° F (20° C).

Pests, Diseases: Leaf spots from water that is too cold or splattering of leaves; rarely, aphids, mites, and viruses.

Note: Same care as for *Gloxinia sylvatica* (syn. *Seemannia sylvatica*).

Adenium
Desert Rose

Adenium obesum—grafted onto an oleander branch.

It probably owes its name to the port city of Aden in southwestern Arabia. Available commercially are *Adenium obesum* and *Adenium swazicum* (though rarely). The color of the flowers ranges from white pink to purple to lavender. That we even have this beautiful-flowered plant available to us and that it thrives is thanks to the gardeners who have grafted the succulent plant to its robust relative, the oleander. This is the reason the stem is so disproportionately thick.

Blooming Season: April to August.

Family: Apocynaceae (dogbane family).

Origin: Southern Arabia, Uganda, Kenya, Tanzania

Location: Full sun, warm all year long, in winter keep in a dark location and cooler (around 59° F [15° C]). In summer place outdoors in a wind-protected spot, as sunny as possible.

Watering, Feeding: Keep damp from April to October; November to March water just enough to keep the roots from dying back. During the growing season use flower and cactus fertilizer alternately every 14 days in the irrigation water.

Further Culture: Repot in spring as necessary in all-purpose potting soil with some loam. Plants that have become too leggy can be cut back.

Propagation: By tip cuttings, which are grafted to oleander stems of the same thickness. Difficult!

Pests, Diseases: Spider mites, mealy bugs, soft scale.

Warning: The milky juice of the desert rose is highly poisonous. When cutting or pruning the branches or when grafting, wear gloves. If you have children and pets, it's better to avoid this plant.

Aechmea
Living Vase

Aechmea fasciata has pink bracts.

The genus *Aechmea* consists of some 150 mostly epiphytic species. It's usually the pink *Aechmea fasciata* that's seen on the market, but other species like the striped *Aechmea chantinii* (with a red-gold inflorescence) are available also. Very beautiful too are *Aechmea fulgens,* with coral-pink flowers, or *Aechmea miniata,* in whose flowers both blue and red appear. The name Aechmea comes from the Greek (from *aichme* = lance tip) and refers to the pointed bracts. The leaves are arranged in a rosette, forming a cup, and are usually very spiny. And now an unspiny hybrid has been introduced; it is called 'Friderike'.

Blooming Season: May to October—but every leaf rosette blooms only once.

Family: Bromeliaceae (bromeliad family).

Origin: Brazil.

Location: Bright, but no sun. All year long not below 64° F (18° C). Tolerates centrally heated air.

Watering, Feeding: Always use soft water for watering. From April to October keep the root ball only moderately damp, but keep the cup well watered. From November to March reduce the amount of water. In spring and summer add a flower fertilizer to the water every 14 days.

Further Culture: On hot days mist plants often. Every 2 years repot in all-purpose potting soil. Remove spent rosettes.

Propagation: Through offsets (see drawing, page 58) or seeds.

Pests, Diseases: Brown leaves from rot and super-cooling. Scale, root lice.

My Tip: The offsets will only produce flowers if they are well cared for and sufficiently large. If they still won't bloom, the apple trick (see drawing, page 45) will help.

Aeschynanthus
Basket Plant

The basket plant astonishes with its cascades of flowers. Obtainable are *Aeschynanthus speciosus* (orange-red), *Aeschynanthus*

Aeschynanthus radicans may respond to uneven soil dampness by dropping its buds.

radicans (syn. *Aeschynanthus pulcher* [red]), *Aeschynanthus hildebrandii* (red), and *Aeschynanthus tricolor* (brown-red) as well as a host of attractive hybrids. All *Aeschynanthus* species and varieties make imposing hanging plants.

Blooming Season: Summer. Many plants will also start blooming even in spring.

Family: Gesneriaceae (gesneriad family).
Origin: Java, Borneo, from India and the Himalayas to New Guinea.
Location: All year long bright but not sunny, and warm, best over 68° F (20° C). In winter keep cooler for 4 weeks (around 59° F [15° C]) and almost dry. This promotes bud formation.
Watering, Feeding: Keep the root ball only slightly damp. The succulent leaves can store water, a signal that the plant needs only moderate watering. From March to the end of August feed every 2 weeks using a low dosage.
Further Culture: Mist often. Repot in February/March or after flowering in all-purpose potting soil with Styrofoam flakes.
Propagation: By soft cuttings in early summer. You can also simply lay shoots on the damp propagating medium. Roots will then form at the leaf nodes. Important: warm soil.
Pests, Diseases: Rarely aphids. Bud drop from change of location, temperature swings, too much or too little water.
My Tip: I hang my *Aeschynanthus* in a densely leaved tree in summer. Summer half-shade and damp humid air clearly do it good.

Allamanda cathartica
Golden Trumpet

An energetic climber—*Allamanda cathartica*.

The *Allamanda* develops shoots several yards long in a very short space of time. Then the large, dazzling yellow flower trumpets, which range from 3 to 4 1/2 in. (8–12 cm) in length, depending on the species, open one after another. Available commercially are *Allamanda cathartica* 'Hendersonii' (orange-yellow), 'Grandiflora' (lemon yellow), and the extremely vigorous grower 'Schottii' (yellow). They are sold trained over hoops, and in the house they need something to climb on.
Blooming Season: May to September, in suitable lighting conditions, even until Christmas.
Family: Apocynaceae (dogbane family).
Origin: Northeastern South America, mostly Brazil.
Location: Full sun. Warmth all year long, daytime temperature never below 64° F (18°

C). In winter rest period, nights 59° to 64° F (15°–18° C). The plants need ground warmth.
Watering, Feeding: From April to October give plenty of water and mist often. Then reduce both. In summer fertilize weekly, in winter only in a very bright location every 4 weeks.
Further Culture: In February/March repot in soil with nutrient-rich loam. After blooming in fall or spring before re-potting, the shoots may be cut back to 1/3 of their length. The flowers appear on new growth.
Propagation: By tip cuttings in spring or fall in a soil warmth of about 77° F (25° C).
Pests, Diseases: Yellowing of leaves from nutrient deficiency. Mealybugs and scale appear rarely.
Warning: All parts of the *Allamanda* are poisonous.

Anthurium
Tailflower, Flamingo Flower

Aphelandra
Zebra Plant

Anthurium-Scherzerianum hybrid.

Aphelandra squarrosa comes from Brazil.

The true flower of the tail-flower is not the colored spathe but the tail or spadix that rises out of it. On the market are *Anthurium-Scherzerianum* hybrids with smaller spathes of various colors, depending on the species, and a mostly orange-red, spirally shaped spadix. *Anthurium crystallinum* has beautifully marked leaves.

Blooming Season: *Anthurium-Scherzerianum* hybrids bloom all year long.

Family: Araceae (arum family).

Origin: Central and South America.

Location: All year around warm and very bright, but not sunny. In winter provide bottom heat and high humidity.

Watering, Fertilizing: During the growth period keep evenly damp. <u>Never use hard or cold water.</u> <u>Avoid sogginess.</u> From March to September, feed weekly, but use only half or a third of the dosage recommended on the package.

Further Culture: Mist often in spring and summer. When completely potbound can be repotted in spring. Suitable potting medium: all-purpose potting soil with Styrofoam particles mixed in.

Propagation: Through cuttings in spring or seeds.

Pests, Diseases: Curling leaves and spider mites in direct sun and air that is too dry. Also leaf spots, root rot, aphids, and scale.

My Tip: Cover the leaves when you are misting or they will develop ugly brown spots.

Warning: Anthuriums contain a substance that irritates mucous membranes.

Best-known representative of the genus is *Aphelandra squarrosa*, of which there are some hybrids available. It has compact growth, grows about 12 in. (30 cm) high, and has dark-green leaves with creamy-white veins. The striking sun-yellow flower spike consists of bracts that overlap like roof tiles and last for a long time and a tiny, short-lived, bright-yellow, tube-shaped flower. Anyone with a greenhouse or an enclosed flower window can also cultivate the red-flowered species.

Blooming Season: June to October (*for Aphelandra squarrosa*); but the blooming period can be altered so that the plants are available in flower at other times.

Family: Acanthaceae (acanthus family).

Origin: Central and South America.

Location: Bright all year, no sun. Warm, <u>and in winter not below 68° F (20° C)</u> (Exception: see My Tip). Provide humidity (see page 43).

Watering, Feeding: Use only soft, room-temperature water. Always keep soil slightly damp. From March to August fertilize every 14 days.

Further Culture: Mist often. After cutting back in spring, repot in all-purpose potting soil.

Propagation: By tip cuttings in a warm propagation flat.

Pests, Diseases: Aphids or scale in locations that are too warm and dry. Curling and dropping of leaves in dry air, drafts, or temperatures that are too cool.

My Tip: *Aphelandra* will bloom the next year only if you keep it cool (50° F [10° C]) in winter for 8 weeks and in a very bright spot, best under a plant light.

Ardisia crenata
Coralberry

Ardisia berries last for several months.

An attractive, evergreen small tree from Asia that is notable for its brilliant red berries. The white or pink flowers are rather insignificant. The plant grows to about 39 in. (1 m) high in its natural habitat. Botanically interesting are the seedlings that grow out of the berries. The coralberry is thus a true live-bearing plant (vivipary). A further peculiarity: Bacteria live in the node-shaped thickenings along the leaf margins. Tests have shown that seedlings from seed made bacteria-free do not survive.

Blooming Season: May and June. The red, pea-sized berries last for half a year but sometimes stay on even longer.

Family: Myrsinaceae (myrsine family).

Origin: Japan, Korea, Taiwan, China, northern India.

Location: Bright and warm all year long, but <u>no</u> full sun. In winter somewhat cooler. An east window is ideal.

Watering, Feeding: Keep root ball only moderately damp. From March to August use weak fertilizer weekly.

Further Culture: Provide bottom warmth and high humidity. Mist often! Repot in spring in all-purpose potting soil.

Propagation: From seed at soil temperatures over 77° F (25° C) or from cuttings, which do not root easily, however.

Pests, Diseases: Scale and mealybugs in dry centrally heated air.

My Tip: Provide high humidity during blooming season or the onset of new flowers and berries will be rather modest. A brush can be used to pollinate artificially, flower by flower, to promote fruiting.

Begonia x Hiemalis ('Elatior' Hybrids)
Winter-flowering Begonias

Elatior begonias—bouquets in pots.

An icon appears here.

Today, when we speak of winter-flowering begonias we are almost always referring to the so-called Elatior hybrids. In the hit parade of flowering plants they are near to the top. This is primarily due to the huge variety of colors they offer and the fact that they can be brought to bloom all year long and will flower uninterrupt-edly for almost a year. Especially beautiful varieties are: 'Alma' with pompom flowers in fiery orange, the red 'Ren-aissance', Rieger's famous 'Schwabenland', the pink-flowered 'Susi', and 'Goldstar', whose very double orange-yellow flowers resemble those of the hibiscus. Very popular also are the slightly trailing varieties in white, red, or pink from the 'Aphro-dite' series, which look superbly beautiful in hanging pots. As a rule, Elatior begonias are only grown as annuals.

Blooming Season: Almost all year long. Family: Begoniaceae (begonia family).

Origin: South America. All begonias in trade are from cultivated sources, however.

Location: Bright, but no sun. Room temperature all year long not below 64° F (18° C).

Watering, Feeding: Keep uniformly damp at all times. <u>Avoid sogginess or dryness of root ball</u>. Fertilize every 14 days.

Further Culture: Repotting is not needed, since further culture does not pay.

Propagation: In April/ May (but also possible at other times), from tip cuttings that should only be cut from perfect, healthy plants. Most successful in a heated propagating bed.

Pests, Diseases: The dreaded mildew arises principally from too much humidity.

Begonia
Bush Begonias

Begonia limmingheana blooms from March to May.

Bush begonias are half-shrubs or shrubs, which are suited for long-term cultivation, and some of them bloom profusely. Most species possess strikingly attractive leaves. The best-known representatives are:
- *Corallina hybrids*
- *Begonia limmingheiana*
- *Begonia serratipetala*
- *Begonia metallica*
- *Begonia egregia*
- *Begonia coccinea*

Blooming Season: Varies according to species and variety.
Family: Begoniaceae (begonia family).
Origin: Tropical America.
Location: Bright all year long. Smooth-leaved species tolerate more light and sun than species and varieties with hairy leaves. In summer 68° to 72° F (20°–22° C), in winter somewhat cooler (not below 59° F [15° C]).
Watering, Feeding: Always keep root ball evenly moist. Avoid sogginess, foot baths, or ball dryness. Fertilize every 8 to 14 days from March to August.
Further Culture: Can be repotted from March to July, and also at other times of year if needed. Best potting mediums: all-purpose soil with mixed-in Styrofoam flakes, or a mixture of peat moss and all-purpose soil in equal proportions. Cut back in spring before repotting, trim to shape in summer. Pinch back regularly so that plant does not get leggy.
Propagation: Tip cuttings root in water or soil.
Pests, Diseases: Mildew with ball dryness or too much dampness, leaf and flower drop possible.
My Tip: There are fascinating kinds of bush begonias. Ask for a listing of possible species and varieties from a specialty nursery.

Beloperone guttata (Justicia brandegeana)
Shrimp Plant

Beloperone also exists as a standard.

The shrimp plant is often considered a handsome throw-away plant for house and balcony. But this pretty half-shrub from Mexico can be a welcome houseguest for many years. Its leaves are oval and slightly hairy. The flower spikes are composed of yellow-orange bracts overlapping like roof tiles, and from them the real flower protrudes like a white tongue.

Blooming Season: The plant bears its bracts almost all year long. However, the white flower lasts only a few days.
Family: Acanthaceae (acanthus family).
Origin: Mexico.
Location: Outside or inside, very bright but no full sun. In summer warm, in fall/winter enjoys 54° to 61° F (12°–16° C) but will also tolerate room temperatures.
Watering, Feeding: In summer water well. From August on, somewhat less. In winter keep drier. From March to August fertilize weekly.
Further Culture: In spring, repot as necessary in all-purpose potting soil. Cut back by ²/₃ before repotting. This promotes the development of new shoots and compact, bushy growth. In summer trim back more often so that the plant will remain compact.
Propagation: From cuttings in spring in a warmed bed.
Pests, Diseases: Aphid attack after hot spells, leaf drop due to a winter location that is too dark and damp.
My Tip: Try making a tree form from a rooted cutting (see page 44).
Note: Similar care is required by the yellow shrimp plant, *Pachystachys lutea* (see photo, page 21), but it is more susceptible to cold.

Further culture is rewarding, for the shrimp plant is a vital half-shrub and not merely good for one season.

Billbergia nutans
Queen's Tears

Billbergia is beautiful and at the same time robust.

This bromeliad is one of the toughest houseplants we have, blooms tirelessly, and develops many offsets. Queen's tears develops rosettes of small, grasslike leaves, and nodding inflorescences (*nutans* = nodding) of green-purple flowers and deep-pink bracts. There are other hybrids with orange bracts and other *Billbergia* species on the market.

Blooming Season: With cool wintering over, in late summer; with warmer, in late winter.

Family: Bromeliaceae (bromeliad family).

Origin: Southern Brazil, Uruguay, Paraguay, northern Argentina.

Location: Very bright but not sunny. The plants may spend the summer outside in a protected place. Tolerate room temperature all year long. *Billbergia nutans* can also be cooler in winter. Hybrids and other varieties need warmth.

Watering, Feeding: In summer water well. In winter in a cool location, water less, in a warm location, water more. From May to August fertilize weekly.

Further Culture: In summer mist often and repot plants as necessary in larger shallow pots with all-purpose potting soil.

Propagation: From offsets.

Pests, Diseases: Rare.

My Tip: Queen's tears is a decorative beginner's plant that thrives despite dry centrally heated air and a not very bright location.

Browallia
Bush Violet

Browallia speciosa blooms all year long.

Of all six known species, *Browallia speciosa* is the most important as a houseplant. Grows to a half-shrub 12 to 20 in. (30–50 cm), has dark-green leaves and, arising from the leaf axils, many blue, lavender, and white single flowers that keep coming all year around. Also familiar are *Browallia viscosa* and *Browallia grandiflora*—both summer-flowering annuals used for bedding plants. Their blooming season depends on the time of sowing. If used as garden plants they are sown in February, for pot culture in August.

Blooming Season: *Browallia speciosa* all year long; *Browallia grandiflora* and *Browallia viscosa* from November to January.

Family: Solanaceae (nightshade family).

Origin: Tropical America.

Location: Bright to sunny and well ventilated. In full sun in summer between 11 and 15 hours of shade. Keep warm (over 68° F [20° C]) in summer, in winter somewhat cooler.

Watering, Feeding: In summer water plentifully, in winter only moderately (danger of rot). As long as the plant is growing, fertilize weekly.

Further Culture: No need to repot, since *Browallia* as a rule is cultivated as an annual.

Propagation: From cuttings or seeds. Sow in February in a bright window and do not cover seeds. Sprouting will take place at 68° to 77° F (20°–25° C) within 14 days. Place five to six young plants in a pot so that a good-looking bush will result.

Pests, Diseases: Whitefly when air is too dry.

Warning: Like all members of the nightshade family, *Browallia* is poisonous.

Brunfelsia
Yesterday, Today, and Tomorrow Plant

Brunfelsia pauciflora var. *calycina*.

Some 30 species of small trees and shrubs constitute the genus *Brunfelsia*. *Brunfelsia pauciflora* var. *calycina* has the greatest importance as a houseplant. It develops long, wide-spreading shoots that tend not to branch. The flowers of white, yellow, or light to dark purple, depending on the variety, are not very long-lived, but new ones open continually.

Blooming Season: January to August. There is also a winter-blooming variety with violet-blue flowers that have a white eye.

Family: Solanaceae (nightshade family).

Origin: Brazil.

Location: All year long bright to semishaded and warm. From November to January keep plants cool (50° to 54° F [10°–12° C]), which promotes setting of flowers.

Watering, Feeding: Water with soft, warm water. Keep plants well dampened from March to September and feed every 14 days. Then stop fertilizing and water less. Avoid dry centrally heated air at all costs. Mist often.

Further Culture: After the end of the main flowering period in early summer repot in a soilless mixture. Cut back long shoots.

Propagation: By tip or stem cuttings with ground temperature of 77° F (25° C). Difficult.

Pests, Diseases: Yellowing of leaves (chlorosis) from hard water, aphids.

Warning: Like all the nightshade family, *Brunfelsia* is poisonous.

Calceolaria Hybrids
Pocketbook Flower, Slipperwort

The "pocketbooks" are exotically leopard-spotted.

Calceolus is Latin and means small shoe. In the some 500 different species and the hybrids that have been derived from them, the inflated lower lip of the flower, which looks like a wide shoe, is the common characteristic. This lip, especially in the hybrids, may appear in one color, two colors, or spotted in brilliant yellow, red, or orange. One should not confuse these hybrids, which are offered in spring as houseplants and also are kept in conservatories as colorful eye-catchers, with the half-shrub *Calceolaria integrifolia*, the slipperwort for balcony tubs and flower beds, although both are grown as annuals and thrown away after flowering. Anyone with a cool mountain house can even grow such botanical treasures as *Calceolaria darwinii*.

Blooming Season: January to May.

Family: Scrophulariaceae (figwort family).

Origin: South America. Only cultivated forms in trade.

Location: Very bright but not full sun, as cool as possible (59°–68° F [15°–20° C]) and airy. A north window is ideal.

Watering, Feeding: Water plentifully but pour off excess water after half an hour. Fertilize weekly.

Further Culture: Repotting not necessary, since pocketbook plants are only kept as annuals.

Propagation: From seed in summer, sprouting temperature 64° F (18° C). Do not cover with soil. For the layperson, generally successful only when the young plants can get additional light from a plant light in fall and winter.

Pests, Diseases: Whitefly and aphids in air that is too warm and stagnant.

FLOWERING PLANTS

Camellia
Camellia

Tried and true—*Camellia japonica* 'Chandleri Elegans'.

Single flower—*Camellia japonica* 'Alba Simplex'.

○ 🪣 🌬️

Will it drop its buds or won't it? This anxious question is raised by everyone who has a camellia and has brought it along this far. Camellias have the reputation of reacting to the tiniest mistake in cultivation by dropping their buds. This isn't entirely true. If you provide high humidity and coolness and avoid its being near a heating unit, sudden temperature changes, and hard water, it will bring forth magnificent flowers every year. For the admirer, there are more than 10,000 varieties, with flowers ranging in color from pure white through countless shades of pink and salmon to pale and intense shades of red as well as bicolored varieties. There is also a great variation in flower size and doubleness. It would be going too far to attempt to list them all and describe them here, especially since the only variety nurseries usually offer is the trusty old 'Chandleri Elegans'.

Blooming Season: October to March.
Family: Theaceae (tea family).
Origin: East Asia.

Location: Airy, cool, and bright all year around. No direct sun. Overwinter at 43° to 46° F (6°–8° C), if possible not over 54° F (12° C). High temperatures are necessary (best 68° to 77° F [20°–25° C]) for setting buds; for maturing of the buds, however, temperatures should not exceed 59° F (15° C), since otherwise they will drop. In May, place outdoors in a semi-shady spot.

Watering, Feeding: Never use hard water. Keep root ball evenly damp. From beginning of new growth till end of July provide azalea fertilizer. After this, reduce water, which will promote setting of buds.

Further Culture: In winter mist leaves and buds daily, but avoid flowers. Repotting, if necessary, is done after blooming, at the latest at the end of July in all-purpose potting soil.

Propagation: With budless terminal cuttings in August. Olive-green shoots provide the best material. Rooting occurs after about eight weeks.

Pests, Diseases: Aphids, sooty mildew, leaf drop from too warm wintering over or incorrect summer care. Bud drop caused by too-high temperatures or turning the plant after the budding begins, too-dry soil, sogginess, or hard water.

My Tip: Varieties of *Camellia sasanqua* are best for houseplant culture. They grow slowly, develop elegant trailing branches, and begin blooming in October. But single varieties of *Camellia japonica* are good candidates, for example 'Apollo', 'Silver Waves', 'Apple Blossom', and 'Maiden's Blush'.

Showpiece of the Conservatory
The camellia hybrid 'Barbara Clark' is superb in form and blooms luxuriantly.

The varieties in the pictures:
Above: *Camellia japonica* 'Hatsu Warei'. Center: *Camellia japonica* 'Rubescens Major'. Right: *Camellia japonica* 'Oki no Numi'.

FLOWERING PLANTS

Campanula
Bellflower

Top favorite—*Campanula isophylla* 'Mayi'.

This plant is one that tolerates hard water—which is a rare occurrence. It is mainly *Campanula isophylla* that is offered as a pot plant, but both the white 'Alba' and the bluish-purple 'May' are available. Similar care is required by *Campanula fragilis* and *Campanula pyramidalis*.

Blooming Season: March to October.

Family: Campanulaceae (bellflower family).

Origin: Mediterranean region.

Location: Bright to sunny, but in summer protect from blazing midday sun. During the growth period in summer keep ventilated, best on a wind-protected balcony. In winter a cooler place around 50° F (10° C) is sufficient for "resting."

Watering, Feeding: From spring to fall always keep uniformly damp. On hot days water copiously, in winter very little. From May to August apply flower fertilizer every 14 days.

Further Culture: Cut back in fall after blooming, repot in new all-purpose soil in spring.

Propagation: From cuttings, which root easily in a soilless mix or in a blend of $\frac{1}{2}$ peat and $\frac{1}{2}$ sand.

Pests, Diseases: Spider mites in too warm a winter location and dry centrally heated air. Gray mold and leaf-spot disease in too-high humidity.

My Tip: The white milky sap that appears when you take cuttings can be stopped by dipping in lukewarm water.

The varieties in the pictures:
Above: *Campanula poscharskyana*.
Right: *Campanula isophylla* 'Alba'.

Capsicum annuum
Ornamental Pepper

A pretty ornament for the kitchen windowsill.

The ornamental pepper is primarily available in fall and at Christmas time. Depending on the variety, it has round, drum-shaped, or pointed oval fruits in brilliant violet, red, orange, or yellow. Many people don't know that it is closely related to the vegetable red pepper. The green parts of the plant are poisonous, but not its extremely hot fruits. They contain the skin-irritating alkaloid capsicin, which can be of varying strengths. As the botanical species name indicates, the plant is an annual. It is thrown away when the fruits shrivel.

Blooming Season: Spring and summer. The fruits are its true ornaments and these develop after flowering.

Family: Solanaceae (nightshade family).

Origin: East Asia and Central to South America.

Location: Bright to sunny and airy, if possible not over 68° F (20° C). Keep plants bought in winter cool, which will prolong their attractiveness.

Watering, Feeding: Keep uniformly damp but not wet. Fertilize weekly during the growing period.

Further Culture: Repotting not required, because plants are cultivated as annuals.

Propagation: From seed in spring (available where seeds are sold). Keep blooming plants in a very bright and protected spot outdoors to promote setting of fruit.

Pests, Diseases: Aphids and spider mites in too warm and dry a location and stagnant air.

Warning: Like the leaves of all the nightshade family the leaves of the ornamental pepper are poisonous. The non-toxic fruits are especially tempting to children, but because they are so hot they are immediately spit out.

Catharanthus roseus
Periwinkle

Chrysanthemum-Indicum Hybrids
Pot Chrysanthemum

Grows bushier year after year.

Chrysanthemums love a cool location.

The periwinkle is the exotic cousin of our blue-violet myrtle (*Vinca minor*) and was also formerly called *Vinca rosea*. A tropical cosmopolite that is really a shrub, it is offered as an annual pot plant and can be planted in a warm, well-protected place as well as in a flower bed. Its dark-green leaves, 1 to 3 in. (2.5–7 cm) long, are distinguished by a white central rib. The flowers, about 1 1/2 in. (3 cm) in size, are pink or white; the centers are red or yellow. The periwinkle has been in cultivation since 1757 and still enjoys great popularity.

Blooming Season: May to October.

Family: Apocynaceae (dogbane family).

Origin: Tropics.

Location: In the house, bright but not full sun and warm; with further culture in winter somewhat cooler (around 59° F [15° C]).

Outside, bright, protected, and warm. Does not thrive in cool, rainy regions.

Watering, Feeding: In summer water copiously, but <u>avoid sogginess</u>; in winter reduce water ration. From March to August fertilize every 14 days.

Further Culture: For further culture and after overwintering, repot every spring, using all-purpose potting soil.

Propagation: From cuttings in March or seeds in February in a heated propagation flat. Always put three young plants to a pot and trim them once so that they will branch.

Pests, Diseases: Rare.

My Tip: If you winter plants over you must take care that despite the cool winter location they don't get cold feet.

Warning: All parts of the periwinkle are very poisonous.

The most abundant supply of this shrub is available in the fall. Colors range from snow white through lemon yellow, golden yellow, bronze, pink, wine red and on to purple and light violet. There are varieties with double and single flowers, bushes, half-shrubs, and tree forms. Formerly, when rooms were still cool near the window, chrysanthemums were among the most popular plants.

Blooming Season: Originally July to December, today, through horticulture manipulation, all year long.

Family: Compositae (composite family).

Origin: China and Japan. Only cultivated are available in trade today.

Location: Bright and cool. Chrysanthemums will not last long in a warm room. Place wintered-over plants and new young plants out of doors in May.

Watering, Feeding: Always keep root ball slightly damp. With too little water the plant will wilt immediately. Fertilize newly acquired chrysanthemums weekly, as well as wintered-over or young plants during the spring to fall growth period.

Further Culture: After blooming cut back and winter over relatively dry at 37° to 41° F (3°–5° C). In March repot in all-purpose soil. Keep trimming new growth. Alternative to wintering over: Cut back and plant chrysanthemums in a bright, protected spot in the garden. Cover with evergreen branches before first frost. But even with winter protection the plant is not reliably frost hardy.

Propagation: In spring from cuttings.

Pests, Diseases: Aphids and spider mites in too warm a location.

Pot chrysanthemum as a tree.

Citrus
Miniature Orange, Dwarf Orange, Orange

Left, calamondin orange, right, kumquat.

Decorative, edible fruit; white, marvelously fragrant flowers; shiny, leathery, evergreen leaves—these qualities have made the citrus family a favorite indoor plant. Of course, for culture on a windowsill or a constricted area, only the miniature members of the citrus clan, which may grow to 39 in. (1 m) or at most 79 in. (2 m), can be considered: *Citrus microcarpa* (syn. *Citrus mitis*), *Fortunella japonica,* the Marumi kumquat or a cross between *Citrus* and *Fortunella,* the calamondin orange (*x citrofortunella mitis*).

Blooming Season: Flowers and fruits appear over the course of a year, often at the same time. The fruits last for weeks or months at a time.

Family: Rutaceae (rue family).

Origin: Southeast Asia.

Location: Very bright to sunny all year long. In summer warm and protected—best placed outdoors; in winter 59° to 64° F (15–18 C).

Watering, Feeding: From spring to fall water copiously. Never use hard water. In winter water sparingly. From March to August use weak fertilizer every week.

Further Culture: Mist often. When plant is completely potbound, repot in all-purpose soil. Cut back as little as possible.

Propagation: By means of cuttings in a heated propagation bed. Difficult.

Pests, Diseases: Scale, mealybugs, spider mites. Yellow leaves (chlorosis) from water that is too hard.

My Tip: For plants that don't go outside and therefore cannot be fertilized by insects, the pollen must be conveyed to the stigma by brush. Midday is the best time for effective pollination.

Clerodendrum
Glory-bower

The glory-bower is a strong climber.

Of the approximately 400 *Clerodendrum* species, only a few are under culture. The best known is *Clerodendrum thomsoniae* and is called "bleeding glory-bower" or "bleeding-heart vine," for its snow-white calyx leaves from which the intense red corolla peeps out. We are talking about a powerful climbing shrub, which in its African habitat climbs as high as 13 ft (4 m) by means of its twining stem. From March on the flowers appear in dense cymes and provide a breathtaking sight in gardens there.

Blooming Season: March to September.

Family: Verbenaceae (verbena family).

Origin: West Africa, Cameroon.

Location: Very bright but no direct sun. Warm and humid all year long.

Watering, Feeding: Use only softened, room-temperature water and keep plants slightly damp. Fertilize weekly from March to August.

Further Culture: Provide for high humidity, mist often. Repot in spring as necessary using all-purpose soil.

Propagation: From cuttings in May. Works only in a heated propagating bed.

Pests, Diseases: Flower and bud drop when air is too dry. Leaf spots with cold feet.

My Tip: Because the glory-bower does not tolerate heated air at all, I winter it over between the middle of December and the middle of February at a cool temperature around 54° F (12° C) and let it go through a kind of vegetative resting period. It then loses its leaves. In spring it is cut back, possibly repotted in new all-purpose soil, and placed in a warmer spot. Soon the new growth appears, and with it new flowers.

Clivia
Kaffir Lily

Clivia grows more beautiful with each year.

Clivia grows in damp, shady places between rocks or in the forest.
Blooming Season: February to May, with appropriate cool treatment, also at Christmas.
Family: Amaryllidaceae (amaryllis family).
Origin: Natal/Africa.
Location: From October to the end of February bright, cool (not over 54° F [12° C]) and not sunny. As soon as the flower stalk appears, half shady and warm—64° to 68° F (18°–20° C). The plant can spend the summer out of doors. Make a light mark (see page 45) on the pot.
Watering, Feeding: Water copiously in summer, but avoid sogginess. From October to the end of February maintain the resting period. Keep plants almost dry at 46° to 50° F (8°–10° C). From March to July fertilize every 14 days.

Further Culture: When new leaves grow and the flower shaft develops, mist. Dust the leaves occasionally with a damp wad of cotton. Repot young plants yearly in all-purpose potting soil, better to let older ones alone. Cut off dead flowers.
Propagation: In spring or summer from offsets. Separate carefully. It takes from 3 to 6 years for first flowering.
Pests, Diseases: Scale in too warm a winter location.
My Tip: If your *Clivia* does not bloom, it may be because the resting period has not been provided, the amount of water was increased too soon in the spring (the flower stalk should be at least 6 in. [15 cm] high), or watering was insufficient during the main growth phase of the flower stalk.
Warning: Clivia contains poisonous alkaloids.

Columnea
Columnea

No one can resist the cascade of fiery-red flowers of the columnea, which is probably one of the showiest of hanging plants. There are countless species and varieties under culture, such as *Columnea hirta, Columnea x banksii, Columnea gloriosa,* with the variety 'Purpurea', *Columnea microphylla,* of which there are also varieties with colored leaves, and species hybrids like 'Stavanger'.
Blooming Season: The red-orange to scarlet-red tube-shaped flowers appear at various times of year depending on the species and variety. The production of flowers is induced by a 30- to 40-day cooling period in winter at about 59° F (15° C).
Family: Gesneriaceae (gesneriad family).
Origin: Central America, mostly Costa Rica.
Location: Bright to semi-shady. Warm all year long except during the flower setting phase.
Watering, Feeding: During the growing period keep it uniformly slightly damp and fertilize weekly with a lowered dosage. Avoid hard water and alkaline fertilizers. During the winter period water only enough so that the plant does not dry out completely. As soon as buds are 1/4 in. (1/2 cm) long, give more water and put in a warmer spot.
Further Culture: Mist carefully, but not in sun and not on the flowers. Increase water as air temperature increases.

Magnificent hanging plant—*Columnea* hybrid 'Stavanger'.

After blooming, cut back and re-pot in shallow containers with an all-purpose soil mix.
Propagation: From terminal or stem cuttings at a bottom warmth of 77° F (25° C)
Pests, Diseases: Leaf drop from drafts. In dry room air, the stems lose their leaves.

Crassula coccinea
Rochea

Rochea flowers—bundles of fiery red rockets.

This was formerly classified under the botanical name *Rochea coccinea,* but today it is included in the genus *Crassula* (see page 155), which consists of some 300 species of succulents. The fiery-red rochea is a half-shrub (although one does not see this right away, since only the lower parts become woody), grows from 12 to 23 in. (30–60 cm) tall, and bears fragrant, brilliantly red flowers. The sturdy green branches are thickly furnished with opposite leaves, some ³/₄ in. (2 cm) long.

Blooming Season: May and June.

Family: Crassulaceae (orpine family).

Origin: South Africa.

Location: Very bright to sunny, and airy. No direct sun. May be summered over out of doors in a place protected from rain. In September bring in and place in a bright, cool spot (around 50° F [10° C])

until flower buds appear.

Watering, Feeding: In summer keep lightly damp, in winter almost dry. Apply cactus fertilizer every 14 days in summer.

Further Culture: After blooming cut the branches back about 4 in. (10 cm). This allows space for new growth and new flowering shoots. As necessary or every 2 years, repot in a blend of ²/₃ all-purpose soil and ¹/₃ perlite.

Propagation: From tips of stems in June in sandy soil. Let cut surfaces dry for a few days before planting.

Pests, Diseases: Aphids, soft scale, mealybugs, and leaf eelworms in too-warm and dark a winter location, which may also cause legginess. When humidity is too high, mildew is possible.

Crossandra infundibuliformis
Firecracker Flower

The world-famous hybrid 'Mona Wallhed'.

Of the some 50 species of the genus, only *Crossandra infundibuliformis* is available commercially. It reached Europe from India as early as 1817, but became popular over 30 years later, only after a Swedish gardener had bred out its "tropical demands." His variety 'Mona Wallhed' is still under cultivation today. Its size remains clearly smaller and it grows more compactly than the ancestral form, which in its native habitat can grow as high as 39 in. (1 m). The trumpet-shaped yellow, salmon, or orange flowers appear in spikes on long stems at the leaf axils.

Blooming Season: May to September.

Family: Acanthaceae (acanthus family).

Origin: India, Ceylon.

Location: Bright (especially in winter) to semishady, no sun. Warm all year long, in winter not below 64° F (18° C).

Watering, Feeding: During the growth and flowering periods water freely with soft, room-temperature water, from October to February more sparingly. From March to August use flower fertilizer in the water every 14 days.

Further Culture: Provide for high humidity, and so mist often, but do not wet the leaves while doing so. Repot in spring, using all-purpose potting soil with Styrofoam flakes.

Caution: Cold, wet feet are lethal for firecracker flower. Provide for bottom warmth.

Propagation: In February, from tip cuttings, which root well in a warmed propagating bed. Pinch back young plants frequently so they will become nicely bushy.

Pests, Diseases: Aphids, spider mites, leaf drop and curling leaves from dry, centrally heated air or cold, wet feet.

Cyclamen, Alpine violet

Specimen in the classic cyclamen color.

Variations like this are called "white with an eye."

Fresh, cool air and slight dampness are the culture secrets of the alpine violet or cyclamen, as we know it today. It originates in mountainous forest regions, where it grows in light shadow in alkaline soil, in scree, or in leaf-mold. Therefore, it would do better in a cool bedroom than in a heated living room. As for the soil, in this case you should certainly not imitate the native conditions. The Mediterranean locations of the original form are not only quite dry in summer but also offer the tuber only a compacted, alkaline soil.

The cyclamen is high on the list of favorite flowering plants. Annually over 20 million plants are under cultivation: varieties with flowers that are large or small, fringed or bordered, white, red, pink, salmon, or violet, and with green or marbled foliage—besides the so-called fragrant cyclamen and mini-cyclamen, whose charm is bewitching plant-lovers increasingly these days. The breeders extol the miniature version's willingness to bloom and its long-lastingness. The one important thing is, the small pot should never be allowed to dry out. It's too bad that cyclamens are usually regarded as throwaway plants, because they flower so regularly when they are cultivated over several years.

Blooming Season: September to April. Family: Primulaceae (primrose family).
Origin: Eastern Mediterranean region.
Location: Bright but not sunny. Airy all year long, but not too warm. Place outdoors in summer in a semishady spot; in winter the optimum temperature is around 59° F (15° C).
Watering, Feeding: Keep plants slightly damp in summer but never wet. Cyclamen are extraordinarily sensitive to wetness. Water the soil, <u>never water the tuber</u>. Feed weekly before and during blooming.
Further Culture: Repot in fall in all-purpose potting soil. Up to a third of the tuber must protrude from the soil. Only young seedlings may be deeper.
Propagation: Possible at any season from seeds in heated propagating bed at 64° to 68° F (18°–20° C). Cover seeds with soil (darkness germinator). Young plants need a great deal of light so that they will bush nicely and not develop too leggily. Therefore, it's better to sow in February so that the seedlings can grow in the months when light is plentiful.
Pests, Diseases: Browning of roots and rotting tubers from sogginess; aphids, spider mites, and other mites, especially when too warm. Gray mold with too much humidity.
My Tip: Pull out old leaves and flowers with a jerk, don't cut off, for the residue rots easily and contaminated soil can result. As a preventive, powder torn places with charcoal.

Miniature cyclamen tolerates room temperatures much better than large-flowered varieties and possess a special wild charm.

Dipladenia (also known as *Mandevilla*)
Dipladenia

The white-flowered *Dipladenia boliviensis*.

Dipteracanthus
Ruellia, Trailing Velvet Plant

Dipteracanthus have attractive leaves as well.

Dipladenia enchants with its purple-red, dark-pink, or white flowers, which appear all summer long on the thin branches. Various hybrids of *Dipladenia sanderi* and *Dipladenia splendens* are found under cultivation, for example the lushly blooming 'Rosea' (salmon pink) and 'Rubiniana' (strong rose red), which is not such a heavy bloomer, however. Entirely new is *Dipladenia boliviensis*, whose white flowers have an orange throat. *Dipladenia* needs a sturdy frame to climb on.

Blooming Season: May to October.

Family: Apocynaceae (dogbane family).

Origin: Tropical America.

Location: Very bright but not sunny all year around. Very warm and humid, especially during new growth. In winter 59° F (15° C) is enough.

Watering, Feeding: In principle, never use cold or hard tap water. From March to August water regularly and feed every 8 to 14 days. Reduce amount of water after blooming. Rest period from September/October to March.

Further Culture: Mist often or provide indirect humidity (see page 43). Transplant young plants every spring in all-purpose potting soil mixed with Styrofoam flakes. For older ones use a sturdier potting medium of all-purpose soil mix, adding a complete fertilizer.

Propagation: In spring from stem cuttings in a heated propagating bed.

Pests, Diseases: Curled leaves from air that's too dry, leaf and root damage from sogginess, scale, mealybugs, spider mites.

Warning: All parts of the dipladenia are very poisonous.

Of the 250 species the only ones seen in pot plant collections until now have been *Dipteracanthus devosianus* (syn. *Ruellia devosiana*) with white-and-violet-striped flowers, *Dipteracanthus makoyanus* (syn. *Ruellia makoyana*) with dark-pink flowers and *Dipteracanthus portellae* (syn. *Ruellia portellae*) with pink flowers. All have velvety leaves with light veins. They are good as ground covers for climate-controlled plant windows and as hanging plants.

Blooming Season: September to December.

Family: Acanthaceae (acanthus family).

Origin: Brazil.

Location: Bright to semishaded, no sun. All year long very warm and humid. Avoid dry centrally heated air and cold feet, which are the death of the plant.

Watering, Feeding: Use soft, room-temperature water. Always keep moderately damp and from March to August use a low dosage of fertilizer every 2 weeks.

Further Culture: Provide high humidity and warm ground. In winter insulate from cold stone window-sills with a heating mat or Styrofoam pad. Every year repot in a shallow container with either a soilless mixture or all-purpose potting soil mixed with some Styrofoam flakes.

Propagation: In spring from tip cuttings in a heatable propagating bed with a ground warmth of more than 72° F (22° C). After rooting has occurred, pinch back once or twice so the plant will branch better.

Pests, Diseases: Curled leaves in air too dry, growth disturbances and root rot from soil too cold and wet; whitefly.

Echeveria derenbergii from Mexico.

Echeveria pumila blooms from April to June.

The echeverias that remain small are decorative, easy-to-care-for collector's plants with minimal space requirements and members of an extraordinarily varied genus. There are about 100 species originating from Texas to South America. They almost all have in common the fleshy leaves arranged spirally in a rosette. Some grow stemless as heads, others form short-stemmed, branching half-shrubs or bushes. The orange-yellow or orange-red inflorescences always stand erect at the side. There are countless varieties and hybrids on the market, with green and brownish-red, often hairy or frosted leaves. The best known are:

• *Echeveria agavoides* has rust-red margined leaves. The variety 'Red Edge' is especially beautiful.

• *Echeveria carnicolor* is a flesh-colored species.

Grows less densely and puts out runners, so that you can use it well as a hanging plant.

• *Echeveria derenbergii* has glossy green leaves and orange flowers.

• *Echeveria gibbiflora* produces sand-purple rosettes on stems 11^1/$_2$ to 20 in. (30–50 cm) high. It blooms with bright-red, white-frosted flowers, which appear in fall in lofty cymes.

• *Echeveria harmsii* is a half-shrubby, decorative species, whose leaves are clustered in a tight rosette. The rust-red flowers appear in summer.

• *Echeveria nodulosa* presents interestingly marked leaves with a violet stripe pattern, is only 8 in. (20 cm) high, and blooms from March on with little red-brown flowers that have yellow tips.

• *Echeveria pulvinata* has, as its name says, leaves that look as though

they've been powdered. The white hairy covering shows that they are used to a great deal of light. The variety 'Ruby' is distinguished by red-tinged leaf margins, which disappear when the location is too dark.

• *Echeveria setosa,* the brushy echeveria, forms flat, stemless rosettes and blooms in the spring.

Blooming Season: Depending on kind of plant, in winter, spring, or summer. Flower development is dependent on the length of the day and the temperature.

Family: Crassulaceae (orpine or sedum family).

Origin: Southwestern US, Central and South America.

Location: Full sun year round, warm in summer, best outdoors in full sun. During resting time in winter, cool 41° to 50° F (5°–10° C), blooming plants warmer also.

Watering, Feeding: Little in summer; during the winter rest period give all nonblooming echeverias almost no water at all. Dampness kills them. From March to August during the growth period, give them some cactus fertilizer weekly.

Further Culture: Repot young plants yearly in cactus soil, older plants only as necessary.

Propagation: After blooming by removal of side rosettes or by leaf cuttings. Allow the cuttings to dry for a short time after cutting, stick in sandy soil, and then root at a ground temperature of 68° F (20° C).

Pests, Diseases: Root rot and mildew from too much water. Mealybugs and root lice, usually produced by too warm a winter location.

Note: The same care is given *Graptopetalum bellum,* which blooms from May to June.

Euphorbia milii
Crown-of-Thorns

The classic crown-of-thorns—*Euphorbia milii*.

White *Euphorbia milii* hybrid 'marathon'.

The crown-of-thorns is one of the most popular representatives of the over 2,000 species in the extensive genus *Euphorbia*. The various species are very different in their external appearances, the palette ranging from cactuslike succulents to herbs and bushes to trees. Common to all euphorbias are the rubbery, poisonous, caustic milky sap and the unisexual or simulated bisexual flowers that botanists term *cyathia*. The crown-of-thorns is an undemanding, persistently flowering houseplant, which is unfazed by dry, centrally heated air or blazing sun. In its own

habitat, in central and southern Madagascar, it grows on granite and gneiss heaps and there forms 40-inch (1-meter) high deciduous bushes. Formerly it went under the name of *Euphorbia splendens*. The crown-of-thorns develops long, thorny branches, about the thickness of a pencil, which can be trained over a hoop or espaliered. Newer varieties grow rather upright and compact and can get to be as high as 2 ft (60 cm). The flower colors vary according to the crosses between different red and rose tones as well as yellow and white. Also from Madagascar is the white- or pink-flowered *Euphorbia lophogona,* an evergreen, ever-blooming species that grows there in forests. Crosses of the two are particularly vigorous, good bloomers, and decorative and have almost replaced the pure species.

These so-called *Euphorbia-Lomi* hybrids (the name contains the first two letters of both parent species) flower almost all year long in yellow, pink, red, and violet, do not lose their leaves, and have a slightly higher need for dampness in the potting medium. They are somewhat susceptible to mildew, however.

Blooming Season: October to March.
Family: Euphorbiaceae (spurge family).
Origin: Madagascar.
Location: Very bright to full sun and warm all year long. Can be set outside in summer in a flower bed in a fully sunny, wind-protected place.
Watering, Feeding: Water moderately, especially in winter. After it has been flowering for 1 month, give only enough water so that the root ball does not dry out. From March to August water somewhat more and

use cactus fertilizer in the water every 2 weeks.
Further Culture: Repot young plants every 2 years in cactus soil with some all-purpose potting soil. The plant can be cut back or trimmed before the new shoots form in early summer.
Propagation: Use the cuttings left from pruning. Use pieces of older branches. Dip the cut surfaces in lukewarm water so that the flow of milky juice will stop, let dry for a day, and then stick in a peat and sand mixture.
Pests, Diseases: Leaf drop from too cool a location, too much water, or both.
Warning: All parts of the crown-of-thorns are poisonous. The milky juice contains skin and mucous membrane irritants. You can also receive injury from the sharp thorns.

About the pictures:
Above: Cream-colored hybrid.
Right: *Euphorbia keysii.*

Euphorbia pulcherrima
Poinsettia, Christmas Star

Poinsettias don't always have to be red, as this display of cultivars shows.

In its Mexican habitat the poinsettia grows as vigorously as the elder does here. It can reach a height of more than 10 ft (3 m) and during its "blooming season" in December it is the ornament of many a tropical garden. We know this magnificently colored member of the spurge family as a throw-away plant that is produced in quantity for sales at Christmas time. If ever you do not throw your plant away, it may come to look as though it's been done in by insects. Continued culture pays. Weedy-looking at first, the poinsettia gets woody and soon develops into a prettily branching bush. Like its cousin the crown-of-thorns (see page 108), its true flowers are insignificant. Instead it is the bracts that make a show in creamy white, yellow, salmon pink, and brilliant red. There are single-stemmed or bushy pot plants, hanging plants, and decorative tree forms on the market. The best-known poinsettia creations come from international breeders like Ecke, Hegg, Gro, and Gutbier. 'Gropom' is a French hybrid with apricot bracts. 'Regina' has creamy-white "stars" and looks very attractive when trained to tree form. 'Dorothea' grows bushy in width, bears pink bracts, and is sold as a hanging plant.

Blooming Season: November to January, but with light control (short-day plant) all year is possible.

Family: Euphorbiaceae (spurge family).

Origin: Tropical Mexico, Central America.

Location: Bright (no sun) and warm all year long. During blooming also somewhat cooler, so the flowers will last longer. Summering over outdoors is possible in a protected spot.

Watering, Feeding: Water freely before blooming from May to November. After blooming from February to May rather sparely. From June to October fertilize weekly.

Further Culture: For further culture cut back after the dropping of the true flowers (not the bracts). Pot plants and tree forms to 4 in. (10 cm), hanging plants to 2 in. (5 cm). After cutting keep warm at 64° to 68° F (18°–20° C) and almost dry. Repot only after the middle of May in all-purpose potting soil. Now water regularly again and fertilize. Trim the new growth, so that the plant will branch nicely.

Propagation: From tip cuttings in summer. Use discarded cuttings from pruning. Stop flow of milky juice by dipping the cut ends in lukewarm water. Stick cuttings shallowly and firmly in small pots.

Pests, Diseases: Mealybugs and scale as well as whitefly when air is too dry.

My Tip: To promote flower development and coloring of the bracts, the poinsettia must receive only 10 to 12 hours of light, depending on the species, from September for about 2 months. This light includes lamplight or the light from a street-light! It's best to put a bucket or a carton over the plant each night for 12 to 14 hours.

Warning: The milky juice can irritate skin and mucous membranes.

Eustoma grandiflorum
Prairie Gentian

Prairie gentians are only grown as annuals.

Until recently the prairie gentian (syn. *Lisianthus russelianus*) was only available as a cut flower. Today it has been recognized that this biennial plant, which in summer produces fragrant flower bells in cream, pink, and violet, is also an attractive, easy-to-care-for ornament to a room. Thus it is following the same path as the gerbera, from vase to pot. With the aid of growth inhibitors, the desirable cut-flower height of 35 in. (90 cm) has been checked. Pot plants are low and look very pretty in shallow pots. The prairie gentian has oval to oblong bluish-green leaves; it is not kept under cultivation after it flowers.

Blooming Season: July and August.

Family: Gentianaceae (gentian family).

Origin: Colorado, Nebraska, Texas, northern Mexico.

Location: Very bright, but not sunny, and warm.

Watering, Feeding: Keep moderately damp and feed weekly.

Further Culture: Repotting not necessary because of biennial culture.

Propagation: From seed. Difficult for layperson, but intriguing. Sow the very fine seeds in June/July in heatable propagation beds. Barely cover with fine soil. Keep seedlings bright and at 59° to 64° F (15° –18° C). Winter over at 50° F (10° C). Beginning March put three plants at a time in a 6- to 8-in. (15–20 cm) pot. Important: The leaf rosettes must have formed before winter! Flowering begins 10 to 12 months after sowing.

Pests, Diseases: Insignificant with culture as annual. The only danger is too much water, which can produce gray mold.

Exacum affine
German Violet, Persian Violet

The German violet—a unique bouquet of scents.

The German violet comes from the island of Socotra in the Gulf of Aden and is a biennial in its habitat. We know that the branching herbaceous plant grows as an annual 6 to 8 in. (15–20 cm) tall. It has small leaves and from summer to fall produces a wealth of fragrant light purple or white flowers, from which project the exquisite yellow anthers. The best-known varieties are called 'Atrocoeruleum' (dark purple) and 'Album' (white). The Persian violet is discarded after it flowers. If you winter the mother plant over at cool temperatures (at about 59° F [15° C]), you can take cuttings in the spring and carry on with them.

Blooming Season: July to September.

Family: Gentianaceae (gentian family).

Origin: Island of Socotra.

Location: Very bright, but not full sun. Average room temperature. Ideal: a rainproof hideaway under balcony or terrace, as the plant loves fresh air.

Watering, Feeding: Keep moderately damp all summer long. If the root ball dries out, the flowers will immediately begin to ebb. Feed every 14 days in summer.

Further Culture: None.

Propagation: From cuttings in spring or from seed. Sow on a windowsill in February. Do not cover seeds with earth (light germinator). Thin out seedlings and pot them in all-purpose potting soil.

Pests, Diseases: Insignificant because of annual culture.

Gardenia
Gardenia

Gardenia jasminoides and its double flowered varieties grow to more than 39 in. (1 m) and bloom with creamy-white, strongly fragrant flowers. The growth is shrubby, the leaves are evergreen and glossy like leather.

Blooming Season: July to October.

Family: Rubiaceae (madder family).

Origin: Ryukyu Islands, Japan, China.

Location: Very bright to sunny. Warm in summer, in winter from 59° to 64° F (15°–18° C), but with ground warmth.

Watering, Feeding: Never use hard, cold water. In summer, keep the root ball uniformly slightly damp. From March to August use a lime-free fertilizer every week. In winter water only moderately.

Further Culture: When the buds appear, provide high humidity (see page 43) and mist often. Stop spraying when plants bloom. In February repot in all-purpose soil mix. Older plants should be cut back first.

Propagation: In spring and late summer from cuttings in heatable propagation beds.

Pests, Diseases: Bud and flower drop because of temperature fluctuations or too much warmth. Growth disturbances and yellowing of the leaves from cold feet and hard irrigation water.

Fragrance and Elegance

Gardenias unite both and they are equally splendid as miniplants, in a pot, or as a tree form.

Gloriosa rothschildiana
Gloriosa Lily, Climbing Lily

The gloriosa lily is a sensational-looking vine with large, fiery-red flowers with red margins that may be as large as 4 in. (10 cm) in size.

Blooming Season: June to August.

Family: Liliaceae (lily family).

Origin: Tropical Asia, Africa, Madagascar.

Location: Very bright and warm for forcing and during the growing period.

Watering, Feeding: Water regularly from March to August and fertilize weekly. Then gradually cut back on watering and allow the plant to die back slowly.

Further Culture: Winter tubers over in the pot at about 59° F (15° C). In March place in pot with all-purpose potting soil, begin watering, and force at a ground temperature of 77° to 86° F (25° –30° C). Introduce a stake or a trellis. Mist often until buds form.

Propagation: In spring, from side tubers; however, each one possesses only one vegetative cone.

Pests, Diseases: Aphids and spider mites. Failure to bloom caused by too little light and warmth in the spring.

My Tip: When buying, make sure that the walnut-shaped tubers each show a little green point (bud).

Warning: The tubers contain colchicin, which is a poison.

Exotic Flowers on a Hoop
After a good rest period the gloriosa lily will bloom sumptuously like this.

Haemanthus
Blood Lily, African Blood Lily

The blood lily, *Haemanthus multiflorus*.

White-flowering *Haemanthus albiflos* is robust and undemanding. Red-blooming species are *Haemanthus katharinae* and *Haemanthus multiflorus*.

Blooming Season: *Haemanthus albiflos,* July to October; *Haemanthus multiflorus*, April to May; *Haemanthus katharinae,* July.

Family: Amaryllidaceae (amaryllis family).

Origin: South Africa, tropical East Africa.

Location: *Haemanthus albiflos* bright to full sun all year long. In summer warm, in winter cooler if possible—50° to 59° F (10° –15° C). *Haemanthus multiflorus* and *Haemanthus katharinae*, very bright but not sunny; in winter, not under 54° F (12° C).

Watering, Feeding: In summer, keep *Haemanthus albiflos* moderately damp and in winter, relatively dry, but only when at lower temperatures. Fertilize every 4 weeks and repot as necessary.

In summer, water *Haemanthus multiflorus* and *Haemanthus katharinae* copiously and fertilize weekly. Decrease water beginning in September so that the foliage can die back.

Further Culture: Remove dead leaves from the red varieties and winter the bulb over at 54° to 57° F (12° –14° C). Don't let the soil dry out completely. Renew the top layer of soil and force the plants.

Propagation: *Haemanthus albiflos* through offsets, *Haemanthus multiflorus* and *Haemanthus katharinae* from bulbs.

Pests, Diseases: Growth disturbances from sogginess.

Warning: The bulbs of the entire amaryllis family poisonous.

Hibiscus rosa-sinensis
Chinese Hibiscus

The hibiscus can grow 10 ft (3 m) tall in our region.

The trumpet-shaped flowers of this pink hibiscus can grow up to 6 in. (15 cm) across and have prominent golden-yellow stamens. They can be double or single in yellow, salmon, orange, pink, or red. The flowers of the pure species are rose red. Especially attractive is the variety 'Cooperi', which has small leaves dappled with white, and flowers in pink, carmine red, and deep-pink colors.

Blooming Season: March to October.

Family: Malvaceae (mallow family).

Origin: Tropical Asia, probably southern China.

Location: Very bright to full sun and warm. Cooler winter temperatures, around 59° F (15° C), help promote the development of flowers. Can be sunk in the garden from June on. First carefully acclimate it to the sun to avoid sunburn.

Watering, Feeding: Water copiously and regularly until September, less in winter. At the beginning of new growth until the middle of August, feed weekly with a high concentration; in a warm, bright winter location feed once a month. *Hibiscus* must be nourished; otherwise it will not bloom.

Further Culture: In heated rooms mist often or provide for indirect humidity. Repot young plants yearly, older plants as necessary; in spring, use all-purpose potting soil. First cut back any shoots that are too long.

Propagation: From semimature tip cuttings in May, in warm ground.

Pests, Diseases: Aphids, mealybugs, and spider mites with dry centrally heated air. Bud and flower drop with change of location, not enough light, dry root ball, or cold, wet feet.

Hippeastrum Hybrids
Amaryllis, Barbados Lily

The variety 'Trixi' develops a stem with 3 flowers.

'Apple Blossom' (left) and 'Fantastica' (right).

The fat bulbs of the amaryllis are on sale around Christmas time. Today there are countless varieties available, with colors ranging from snow-white through salmon, orange, and pink to all possible shades of red. In addition, there are white flowers with red margins, which look like piped ballet tutus, and hybrids with stripes of two and three colors. The most famous hybrids are the so-called Ludwig amaryllises from Holland, for example the red-and-white-striped 'Fantastica', the deep-rose 'Dutch Belle', the fire-red "Ludwig's Goliath', or the pink 'Fairyland'. Especially sought after are white varieties like 'Maria Goretti', 'Ludwig's Dazzler', 'Picoteé', and 'Early White'. An evergreen among the amaryllises is the sweet smelling 'Apple Blossom', in flower tones of pink and white. Mail order houses that specialize in bulbs stock these and other beautiful and exciting varieties. For those for whom the forcing of the bulb takes too long, there have recently appeared the so-called Pre-Pot-Amaryllis, prepared bulbs that come into bloom within 5 to 6 weeks.

Blooming Season:
January to April.
Family: Amaryllidaceae (amaryllis family).
Origin: Tropical and subtropical America. The only plants now in trade are cultivated forms.
Location: Put newly bought or wintered-over bulbs in a very bright, warm spot, after they have been planted in a roomy pot with all-purpose potting soil. (When planted, half the bulb must show above the soil.)
Watering, Feeding: At first, water scarcely at all. When the growth begins to show, give more water. As a rule the flower stalk appears before the leaves, but it can also be the other way around. After blooming has finished, cut off the stalk and feed weekly until August. There must be plentiful leaf development so that the bulb can store up new strength. Beginning in August, slowly decrease water and allow foliage to die back.
Further Culture:
Remove dry leaves and allow the bulb to rest for new growth at 59° F (15° C) in dry peat.
Propagation: From side bulbs, which should be the size of an apple before they are removed from the mother plant. Other possibilities: By cuttings from the bulb scales or by seeds, but both take considerable effort.
Pests, Diseases: Leak scorch, a fungus disease that specializes in amaryllis. It is promoted by a situation that is too cold and wet. If the fungus has not eaten too deeply into the tissue, the infected places can be cut out and dusted with charcoal. The bulb can often be saved this way.
My Tip: The same care can be used for *Hippeastralia*, a cross between *Hippeastrum* and *Sprekelia*, that produces daintier flowers and also does not grow as large.
Warning: The amaryllis contains poisonous substances.

Wax Vine, Porcelain Flower

Hoya bella blooms abundantly, whether on a trellis. . .

. . . bound to a hoop, or as a hanging plant.

The genus is named for Thomas Hoy, who from 1788 to 1809 was the head gardener to the Duke of Northnumberland (England). Of the 200 known species, the best known are *Hoya bella*, from southern Burma, and *Hoya carnosa*, which is found from Central China to Australia. *Hoya bella* grows without twining and remains altogether smaller and more delicate than *Hoya carnosa*, which is a vigorous climbing shrub with fleshy leaves. Both bloom in summer with sweet-smelling porcelain-white cymes that are purplish red in the center. *Hoya bella* grows best in an orchid basket or as a hanging plant in a climate-controlled, warm, and humid flower window. Also available today is a *Hoya carnosa* variety called 'Variegata' with yellow-and-green-striped leaves. It doesn't grow as vigorously as the pure species. Rarely seen in the market is *Hoya lacunosa*, with elliptical-lanceolate leaves and button-shaped, greenish-white flowers, which develop in umbels from March to June. This uncommon hanging plant prefers semishade and likes warmth all year around. An even rarer member of the genus is *Hoya linearis*, from the Himalayas, which is also warmth-loving. Its pencil-thin shoots and the white inflorescences are pendulous. The flowers of *Hoya multiflora* look like a fistful of lightning arrows about to be hurled. The hanging flowers of this species from Malaysia are dark-red in the center and yellow-green outside. Cultivate it just like *Hoya bella*.

Blooming Season: May to September.

Family: Asclepiadaceae (milkweed family).

Origin: Southern Burma, Central China to Australia.

Location: Very bright to full sun (no midday sun). Keep warm in summer—64° to 73° F (18°–23° C)—in winter, a few degrees cooler—57° to 64° F (14°–18° C). The warmer temperatures suffice for *Hoya bella*.

Watering, Feeding: In summer water moderately, in winter even less. During the growing season feed every 2 weeks. Fertilizing too well, however, will result in vigorous production of shoots and leaves at the expense of flower production. In plants that look too lush, increase the intervals between feedings or don't feed at all anymore. I have seen the most vigorously blooming hoyas with gardeners who do not do much in the way of care and never move the plants from one spot. The wax vine often responds to changed light intensity with flower and bud drop.

Further Culture: Both species tolerate dry indoor air. Nevertheless, mist regularly when new growth begins. In spring, repot as necessary in all-purpose potting soil. Mix in Styrofoam flakes or sand. Cut back shoots that are too long.

Propagation: Through tip or stem cuttings in a heated propagating flat.

Pests, Diseases: Aphids from too warm a winter location. Leaf drop and dying back of stems from too much water and cold feet. Flower drop from too dark a location or change of position. White specks on the leaves are species specific.

My Tip: With *Hoya carnosa* leave the short peduncle after the flower has finished blooming. The new flower will form on it.

Hydrangea macrophylla
French Hydrangea, Hortensia

There are also pot hortensias with shrubby growth.

The large, white, pink, red, or blue umbels of French hydrangea consist of vestigial sterile single flowers, whose real ornaments are the colored sepals. Recently French hortensia has enjoyed new popularity; its insignificant fertile single flowers are surrounded by a wreath of large sterile flowers. The blue color can be obtained from certain red and pink hortensias by watering the soil with aluminum sulfate or alum.

Blooming Season: French hydrangeas are sold in bloom from March to May, but the species' normal blooming season is in June and July.

Family: Saxifragaceae (saxifrage family).

Origin: Japan.

Location: Bright to semishade, no full sun. All year, not too warm, in summer best outside in the garden in a cool, shady place. In winter it is satisfied with 39° to 46° F (4°–8° C). Since the hortensia loses its leaves, the overwintering spot can be dark. In February put it in a warmer, bright place again.

Watering, Feeding: In spring, summer, and fall, water freely. (The translation of *hydrangea* is "swigger of water"!) In winter water only enough to keep the root ball from drying out. Never use alkaline water. In summer until the end of August, use rhododendron fertilizer in the water every 14 days.

Further Culture: After flowering it can be cut back. Transplant in spring. White, pink, and red varieties need moderately acid soil (azalea soil).

Propagation: From tip cuttings.

Pests, Diseases: Spider mites and aphids, from a location that is too warm and dry.

Hypocyrta
Nematanthus

Hypocyrta glabra begins to trail when it grows larger.

The orange flowers with puffy corona petals look like a mouth pursed for a kiss. The nematanthus is a low half-shrub that produces leathery, almost succulent leaves, which thus indicates that the plant can manage better in dry air than most of its tropical relatives. Besides *Hypocyrta glabra* you will also sometimes find the similar-looking *Hypocyrta strigillosa* in flower shops. Both are splendid hanging plants. *Hypocryta* has recently been added to the genus *Nematanthus*.

Blooming Season: The plants, which are very much in demand commercially, are offered in bloom from late summer till spring.

Family: Gesneriaceae (gesneriad family).

Origin: Brazil.

Location: Very bright, but not full sun. In summer can also hang in a tree with foliage that is not too dense. From December to February maintain at 54° to 59° F (12°–15° C), which promotes bud formation.

Watering, Feeding: From spring to fall keep only slightly damp, in winter keep almost dry. From March to August feed every 2 weeks with low dosage.

Further Culture: Repot in spring in all-purpose soil mix. After blooming, trim the plant somewhat, which will promote the growth of new shoots and bushier growth.

Propagation: By division and by tip cuttings in ground temperatures around 68° F (20° C). Works well in summer.

Pests, Diseases: Aphids from too warm a winter location.

Balsam, Busy Lizzy, Jewelweed, Snapweed, Touch-me-not

Magnificent in groupings—*Impatiens*-New Guinea hybrids in shades of pink.

Who does not know the touch-me-not from our forests? A relative of it is Busy Lizzy (*Impatiens walleriana*) from tropical East Africa, one of the most popular pot plants for houses, balconies, and gardens. It is available in white and countless color shades—delicate pink, salmon pink, orange, and scarlet red, as well as purple and lavender. Besides there are the light pink varieties with a white eye like 'Accent Bright Eyes' and white-and-red-striped ones like 'Star-bright' as well as the dwarf varieties 'Bab' or the Mini series, which grow only 6 in. (15 cm) tall and offer a wealth of color choices. Lately also the Impatiens-New Guinea hybrids have been established; these have *Impatiens hawkeri* in their ancestry. Attractive varieties include: the bronzy-green-leaved variety 'Exotica'. From

Ceylon comes *Impatiens repens*, a yellow-flowered creeping kind with reddish stems, which looks nice in a hanging pot.

Blooming Season: They all bloom in summer and fall.

Family: Balsaminaceae (balsam family).

Origin: Tropical East Africa, Ceylon, India, New Guinea. Mostly cultivars in commerce.

Location: Bright to semishade, New Guinea hybrids also sunny. Room temperature all year around. *Impatiens walleriana* even cooler in winter—54° to 59° F (12°–15° C). In darker locations, all species and varieties can stand cooler temperatures.

Watering, Feeding: Water regularly in summer, in winter less or the stems will rot. From March to August/September feed weekly, at best only half the usual dosage.

Further Culture: Clip Busy Lizzy now and again. They tend to straggle. In spring repot in all-purpose potting soil. Better: root cuttings and winter these over, since the mother plants quickly become unsightly.

Propagation: Very easy with tip cuttings. In spring, *Impatiens walleriana* also from seed, which is obtainable everywhere.

Pests, Diseases: Spider mites and aphids in too warm a winter location.

Impatiens walleriana 'Belizzy Rotstern'.

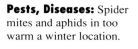

Above: *Impatiens walleriana* 'Belizzy Weiss'. Below: *Impatiens walleriana* 'Belizzy Lachspastell'.

Impatiens walleriana 'Orange'.

FLOWERING PLANTS

Ixora coccinea
Ixora, Flame-of-the-Woods

Ixora hybrid in warm salmon orange.

The Ixora is an evergreen, scarlet-red flowering bush, which is happiest in a humid flower window. It has leathery glossy leaves, 2 to 4 in. (5–10 cm) long. In summer the flowers are produced in lush racemes of umbels on the branches. With good culture the plant can grow to 39 in. (1 m) tall in a pot. Now there are also hybrids in other colors, for instance in dark orange, salmon red, and tinged with bright orange.

Blooming Season: May to September.

Family: Rubiaceae (madder family).

Origin: India.

Location: All year round bright to semishady, warm and humid. Important: requires ground warmth.

Watering, Feeding: The plant, like the coffee tree and the gardenia, which are related to it, <u>does not tolerate hard, cold water</u>. In summer keep evenly damp, in winter water more sparingly. From March to August feed with a low dosage every 2 weeks.

Further Culture: Mist the ixora often in the house. In fall, cut back the branches after blooming, and then don't do it again because the flowers form on the ends of shoots. As necessary, repot in spring with a mix of all-purpose potting soil.

Propagation: In spring, from tip cuttings at ground temperature of at least 77° F (25° C) and high humidity (doesn't always succeed). Trim young plants so they will branch nicely.

Pests, Diseases: Curled leaves in a sunny location. Blanched leaves (chlorosis) from water that is too hard or too cold and cold feet. Flower or leaf drop from abrupt changes in temperature or location. Scale from dry air.

Jacobinia
Jacobinia

Jacobinia carnea—a tropical beauty.

Of the 50 *Jacobinia* species the important pot plants are the greenhouse plant *Jacobinia carnea* and the conservatory plant *Jacobinia pauciflora*. *Jacobinia carnea* produces deep rose red flowers, which are clumped in dense longish-to-round heads. After several years of cultivation they can grow to over 39 in. (1 m) tall and are suitable for houseplant culture. The ideal jacobinia for the cool conservatory is *Jacobinia pauciflora*.

Blooming Season: *Jacobinia carnea*, from June to August; *Jacobinia pauciflora*, from December to February.

Family: Acanthaceae (acanthus family).

Origin: Brazil.

Location: *Jacobinia carnea*, all year long, bright, no sun. Warm in summer; in winter, not below 61° F (16° C). Loves high humidity and therefore is ideal in a climate controlled flower window. *Jacobinia pauciflora*, bright to sunny all year long; outside in summer; in winter, cool at 59° F (15°C).

Watering, Feeding: Keep both varieties moderately damp, but never let the root ball dry out. In winter water less. Feed every 14 days from March to August.

Further Culture: Cut back plants by half in spring and repot in all-purpose potting mix.

Propagation: By leafy cuttings in a heatable propagation flat at 68° to 72° F (20°–22° C). Pinch back two to three times.

Pests, Diseases: Spider mites and aphids; curled leaf tips from dry air, and leaf drop from dried-out root ball.

Note: The white-flowered *Whitfeldia,* which is a relative, is cultivated the same way as *Jacobinia carnea.*

Jasminum
Jasmine

Jasminum officinale—what a fragrance.

The best-known houseplant in this clan is *Jasminum officinale*, especially the large-flowered variety 'Grandiflorum'. *Jasminum polyanthum* has rose-tinged flowers. All species develop long, somewhat climbing shoots, which must be bound to a trellis or a hoop.

Blooming Season: June to September.

Family: Oleaceae (oleander family).

Origin: China, Iran to Kashmir, India, Ceylon.

Location: *Jasminum officinale* and *Jasminum polyanthum* all year long very bright, airy, and cool. In winter, below 50° F (10° C) if possible, otherwise no flower development.

Watering, Feeding: Never use cold or hard water. In summer water regularly, in winter keep slightly damp. In summer feed every 14 days.

Further Culture: Repot as needed in all-purpose potting soil. If lower stems lose their leaves, it can be cut back. It will form scarcely any flowers the year after being cut back.

Propagation: In spring and summer, from semiwoody tip or stem cuttings at 68° F (20° C); ground warmth. Pinch back young plants several times.

Pests, Diseases: Aphid attacks from a winter location that is too warm. Leaf drop with *Jasminum officinale* is species specific. In spring the plant will put out new growth.

My Tip: When winter temperatures are too warm, the jasmine will begin new growth too early and develop a very beautiful green color but no flowers. Therefore, air it regularly in the spring. This keeps the temperature low and the aphids away.

Warning: Flowers can cause headaches.

Jatropha podagrica
Tartogo, Bottle Plant

Jatropha—succulent with a bottle-shaped stem.

Coming from regions with periods of drought, the tartogo always has its water supply available. It's just the right plant for people who often forget to water. The unusual-looking succulent, 12 to 23 in. (30–60 cm) tall, is from Central America and has shield-shape, three- to five-lobed leaves about 8 in. (20 cm) across. The inflorescences are minimum red and often develop before the long-stemmed leaves but can also appear together with them in early summer.

Blooming Season: March to July, with good culture almost all year long.

Family: Euphorbiaceae (spurge family).

Origin: Nicaragua, Guatemala, Costa Rica.

Location: Full sun and warm the year around; in winter, not below 61° F (16° C).

Watering, Feeding: Water little. When leaves fall by themselves in the autumn—which is species specific—stop watering almost entirely. As soon as new flowers and leaves develop in early spring, slowly begin giving more water. In summer apply cactus fertilizer once a month.

Further Culture: Repot as needed in a mix of ²/₃ all-purpose soil and ¹/₃ lava gravel or in cactus soil.

Propagation: From fresh seeds that have been taken from blooming plants. However, for this purpose the flowers must have been artificially pollinated beforehand. Ideal sprouting temperature is 68° to 77° F (20°–25° C).

Pests, Diseases: Rare.

Warning: Although the name *Jatropha* freely translates as something like "medicine" (Greek: *iatros* = doctor, *trophe* = food), all the parts of this spurge are poisonous.

Don't worry if the leaves drop. The tartogo is signaling that it would like to be kept almost dry.

Kalanchoe
Palm-Beach Bells, Kalanchoe

Whether mini or maxi, kalanchoes glow most intensely in groups.

The kalanchoe (*Kalanchoe blossfeldiana*) is in first place on the scale of popularity for flowering plants. There are several million of them sold every year. Breeders are continually working on this easy-to-care-for plant so that now there is every possible color, from yellow, orange, through pink and red and on to violet. Moreover, these little plants with the succulent leaves are available in bloom all year around. Growers have learned to fool the plant with artificially dark short days and so make them flower at any desired time. The original form, which in its natural habitat in the mountains of northern Madagascar grows as a half-shrub to a height of 12 in. (30 cm), produces its minimum-red flowers in January. The tongue-twisting genus name *Kalanchoe* is supposed to be of Chinese origin. The species name goes back to a German seed dealer, Bloosfeld.

Of the more than 200 *Kalanchoe* species, the most unusual is the one with the flowers of rose-colored bells (see photographs, page 30 and below) descended from *Kalanchoe manginii*. Also familiar are the brood-leaf plants, *Kalanchoe pinnata*, *Kalanchoe daigre-*

Kalanchoe manginii— a peal of bells for the hanging basket.

montiana, and *Kalanchoe tubiflora*, which produce already-rooted plantlets on the leaves that fall off and grow anywhere a bit of soil exists.

Blooming Season: *Kalanchoe blossfeldiana*, February to May; *Kalanchoe manginii*, February to March.
Family: Crassulaceae (orpine family).
Origin: Madagascar.
Location: Bright and sunny. Warm in summer,

cooler in winter: *Kalanchoe blossfeldiana*, at least 59° F (15° C); the other species at 50° to 57° F (10°–14° C).
Watering, Feeding: In summer water only moderately; keep plants almost dry in winter. From March to August use cactus fertilizer every 4 weeks. Feed *kalanchoe blossfeldiana* every 14 days with a flower fertilizer.

Further Culture: Repot as necessary in a mixture of ⅓ clay granules or perlite and ⅔ all-purpose potting soil. All kalanchoes are short-day plants. The flowers develop when the plants receive only 8 to 10 hours of light daily for 4 to 6 weeks.
Propagation: In spring or summer, by cuttings or with brood plantlets.
Pests, Diseases: Aphids and mealybugs; mildew from too much warmth and dampness.

Leptospermum scoparium
Tea Tree, New Zealand Tea Tree, Manuka

The relationship to myrtle is unmistakable.

The tea tree is becoming more and more popular with us as indoor pot and tub plants. They are available either as bushy pot plants or as charming standard forms. In its homeland it grows both as a bush, 12 in. (30 cm) tall, and as a tree 33 ft (10 m) high. This shows how variable this species is; it begins blooming when still a young plant. The varieties offered today come with red, rose-colored, and carmine red single or double flowers. The evergreen leaves are green or bronze-red and likewise variable in form, but mostly narrow with sharp points.

Blooming Season: May and June.

Family: Myrtaceae (myrtle family).

Origin: Australia, New Zealand.

Location: Very bright to full sun all year long. In summer, warm; in winter, cool—39° to 50° F (4°–10° C).

Watering, Feeding: In summer, water freely with soft water. When the root ball dries out the needles drop. Like all the myrtle family it can't stand any lime! In winter, only water enough to keep the root ball from drying out. From March to August feed every 14 days.

Further Culture: In spring, repot in all-purpose potting soil. Cut back slightly after blooming, before wintering over, or in March so that the plant retains its shape and will grow bushier.

Propagation: From vegetative cuttings (use trimmed out branches), in spring; or from semi-woody cuttings in August. The cuttings will root in sand or in a sand-peat mixture in 4 to 6 weeks. Cover with plastic bag (see page 59).

Pests, Diseases: Rare.

Lotus berthelotii
Parrot's Beak, Winged Pea, Coral Gem

The parrot's beak will never forgive a dried-out root ball.

Parrot's beak is a splendid hanging plant that is often available in the spring. It is a shrub and in the ground it develops woody, creeping, or trailing branches with fine, silvery-haired leaves up to 1 in. (2 cm) long. The flowers occur in bunches on the stems, are a little more than 1 in. (3 cm) long, and are usually scarlet red (see photograph, page 31). The variety 'Gold Flush' has yellow flowers.

Blooming Season: March and April.

Family: Leguminosae (legume family).

Origin: Cape Verde and Canary Islands.

Location: Bright to sunny all year around. In summer, 68° F (20° C) and in winter not warmer than 50° F (10° C). From June, also in a protected spot outdoors. In fall, bring in before the first night frost.

Watering, Feeding: Keep evenly damp but never soggy. In winter water less. Leaves will drop immediately if root ball dries out. Feed every 14 days from February to October. The plants need many nutrients.

Further Culture: Repot in all-purpose potting soil after blooming. Can be cut back.

Propagation: From cuttings, which root easily at ground temperatures of 68° to 77° F (20°–25° C).

Pests, Diseases: Aphids when location too warm and not enough ventilation, especially in winter.

Nertera grandadensis
Bead Plant, Coral Moss

The medinilla is not only the most beautiful of a genus consisting of some 400 species but one of the most splendid of all flowering plants. It grows in the tropical forests of its native Philippines as a shrub over 79 in. (2 m) high with thick, squared branches and leathery, dark-green leaves up to 12 in. (30 cm) long. Its elegantly pendulous, rose-red panicles of flowers are composed of numerous single flowers covered over with bright pink bracts. They can be as long as 16 in. (40 cm). Since the medinilla is very difficult to propagate, it is one of the most expensive houseplants.

Blooming Season: April to July.

Family: Melastomataceae (melastome family).

Origin: Island of Luzon/Philippines.

Location: Bright but no sun. Warm, over 68° F (20°C). Best in a humid flower window. In winter keep cooler for 2 months— 61° F (16° C)—(rest period). This promotes development of flowers.

Watering, Feeding: Always keep evenly damp. Never use cold or hard water. During the rest period water very little. As soon as buds show, increase water and raise temperature. From March to August, feed weekly.

Further Culture: Mist often and provide indirect humidity (see page 43).

Exquisite Beauty
It is aptly named— *Medinilla magnifica*, the superb medinilla.

As necessary repot in spring in all-purpose soil mixed with Styrofoam flakes. Cut back twiggy-looking plants to old wood.

Propagation: By tip cuttings, at soil temperatures of 77° to 86° F (25°–30° C). Difficult.

Pests, Diseases: Failure to thrive because air too dry or cold feet.

My Tip: Do not move the medinilla once it has set buds.

Note: If you have a humid flower window or a vitrine, you can also keep two relatives of the medinilla: *Bertolonia* and *Sonerila*.
• Bertolonias are small, creeping herbs from South America, which are also useful as ground covers. For example *x Bertolonia houtteana* has choice leaf beauty. Its broadly oval, olive-green leaves are provided with purple-pink veins and spots. Bertolonias need year-long air temperatures of 68° F (20° C) and ground warmth, tolerate no hard or cold water, and do not like to be misted. The potting medium can be an all-purpose mix with Styrofoam flakes.
• *Sonerila* is its Asiatic counterpart. It's supposed to be a parent of the above-named *x Bertolonia houtteana. Sonerila magaritacea* 'Argentea', one of the several available cultivars, is a half-shrub that grows to 12 in. (30 cm) tall, with exuberant branching. The leaves are marked with silver-green on the upper side. The small flowers are pink and furnished with three sepals and three stamens. Culture like *Bertolonia*.

The berry ornaments of the *Nertera* last for months.

Nerteros, a Greek word, means something like "low." In fact, the coral moss stays close to the ground and spreads like a carpet of grass or moss. The most beautiful thing about this plant is its orange-red, pea-sized berries. They develop from rather insignificant, greenish star-shaped flowers. A perennial creeping plant, coral moss is thus not short-lived but can continue to be cultivated with success.

Blooming Season: Spring. The berries last from August into the winter.

Family: Rubiaceae (madder family).

Origin: Mountain regions of Central to South America. New Zealand and Tasmania.

Location: Bright but not sunny all year long. Keep as cool and fresh as possible. In winter, not below 54° F (12° C). From March on somewhat warmer.

Watering, Feeding: All summer keep uniformly damp, from fall to spring water less. From March to August fertilize every 4 weeks with a weak dosage. Otherwise the foliage will grow too lush and obscure the ornamental berries.

Further Culture: Except during the blooming season, mist now and again. Repot as necessary in all-purpose potting soil.

Propagation: By division after the fruits drop.

Pests, Diseases: Aphids in too warm a winter location or from drafts.

Passiflora
Passionflower

Passiflora caerulea needs cool wintering over.

Passiflora violacea needs more warmth.

From the more than 400 passionflower species the robust blue passionflower (*Passiflora caerulea*) is best known as a houseplant. In mild climates and with winter protection it can even be planted outdoors against a house wall. Needing more warmth are *Passiflora edulis, Passiflora racemosa, Passiflora violacea* and the giant granadilla, *Passiflora quadrangularis*. Common to all is the exquisite flower, whose parts are regarded as symbols for the passion of Christ. A botanical missionary in the seventeenth century wrote that the leaves ending with three points represent the lances; the runners, the lash; the three styles, the nails in the cross; the stigma, the sponge; the filaments on the flower, the crown of thorns; the central column, the stake to which Christ was bound during the flagellation. The Jesuits therefore named the genus *Passiflora* (from Latin: *passio* = suffering and *flos* = flower). All *Passiflora* species are assiduous climbers that develop yard-long (meter-long) shoots and grow best on a trellis or frame. The plants trained on hoops that are frequently offered commercially are usually susceptible to attacks of spider mites and whitefly because the leaves are crowded too closely together and no air can circulate between.

Blooming Season: *Passiflora caerulea* and *Passiflora edulis*, June to August/September; *Passiflora quadrangularis*, May to July; *Passiflora racemosa*, May to September; *Passiflora violacea*, August and September.

Family: Passifloraceae (passionflower family).

Origin: Tropical America.

Location: Bright to sunny all year long, and airy. In summer, warm; in winter cooler. *Passiflora caerulea* and *Passiflora edulis* around 50° F (10°C). This rest period promotes the development of flowers. *Passiflora racemosa* and *Passiflora quadrangularis* can be kept in a warm, humid flower window all year long. *Passiflora caerulea, Passiflora violacea*, and *Passiflora edulis* may also be summered over out of doors.

Watering, Feeding: Water copiously in summer, in winter only enough so that the root ball doesn't dry out. Feed weekly from March to August.

Further Culture: In spring, before repotting in all-purpose potting soil, cut back to two or three shoots. Repot older plants seldom, younger ones yearly.

Propagation: From slightly woody tip cuttings at a ground temperature of 72° F (22° C). In contrast to the mother plant, winter over the rooted cuttings the first year in a warm, bright location. Passionflowers can also be propagated very easily from seed, for example from market fruits of *Passiflora edulis* (see pages 64–65) or *Passiflora mollissima*.

Pests, Diseases: Failure to bloom from too cold a location or nutrient deficiency. Aphids when fresh air is lacking or there is too much heat in a winter location. Spider mites and thrips.

My Tip: Don't worry if your *Passiflora caerulea* loses its leaves in winter. In spring it will put out new growth.

Pelargonium-Grandiflorum Hybrids
Geranium

Pentas lanceolata
Star-Cluster, Egyptian Star-Cluster

There are geraniums (Pelargoniums) in bloom all year.

Star-cluster is available in pink, salmon, and red.

The single flowers of this hybrid geranium are exotically spotted or striped and can be up to 2 in. (5 cm) across. They appear in dense clusters in different colors from white, through pink and red down to a deep violet. The spring-green leaves are toothed along the margins and frequently larger than the balcony geraniums. Geraniums usually develop a single stalk, form woody stems, and grow to 16 in. (40 cm) tall. Recently varieties with a small growth habit and with daintier flowers have come on the market.

Blooming Season: From April to June. The blooming season is controlled by temperature and day length, so the plants can be bought in flower all year round.

Family: Geraniaceae (geranium family).

Origin: South Africa. Only hybrid forms are in trade, however.

Location: All year long very bright to full sun and airy. From June on a protected balcony outside. In summer, warm; in winter, cool—50° to 59° F (10°–15° C).

Watering, Feeding: From March to August water copiously, but absolutely avoid sogginess. Feed weekly. After this, reduce water and provide it only seldom in winter.

Further Culture: In spring, cut back shoots and repot in all-purpose soil mixed with sand. When new growth shows, put plants in a warmer place and increase water.

Propagation: From tip cuttings, best in August— in a peat-sand mixture. Repot young plants as soon as the root ball gets larger and pinch back.

Pests, Diseases: Whitefly and aphids. Gray mold and fungus infections from too damp and dark a location.

Of the 50 *Pentas* species, only *Pentas lanceolata* is under culture outside of Africa and Madagascar. It is a popular garden plant in tropical countries and has been raised in greenhouses for more than 100 years. The half-shrub that is seen in houseplant culture is 12 to 23 in. (30–60 cm) tall, has an upright to prone growth habit, and blooms with terminal cymes in white, salmon, pink, and carmine red. The small single flowers consist of 20 tubes about 1 in. (3 cm) long. The leaves are oval to linear-elliptical and hairy.

Blooming Season: September to January.

Family: Rubiaceae (madder family).

Origin: Tropical Africa, Arabia.

Location: Very bright but not sunny, all year long. In summer, warm and airy, even outside; in winter, cool—around 54° to 59° F (12°–15° C).

Watering, Feeding: Only use softened, room-temperature water. Rely on your instincts for watering. Avoid sogginess. After flowering keep drier until new growth shows. Feed with lowered dosage every 14 days.

Further Culture: In spring repot in all-purpose potting soil.

Propagation: From tip cuttings and in a heatable propagation flat. Keep pinching back young plants so they will branch nicely. Repot twice, and after the second repotting feed every 14 days.

Pests, Diseases: Yellow leaves caused by sogginess, cold feet, water that is too hard.

My Tip: The star-cluster is treated with growth inhibitors and retains its compact growth habit for a limited time only. Therefore, trim plants often, as long as no flower buds show.

Wet feet (roots) are poison for these warm-blooded beauties that ornament the gardens of Kilimanjaro, Arabia, and Abyssinia.

125

FLOWERING PLANTS

Primula
Primrose

Left, *Primula malacoides*; right, *Primula obconica*.

Of the some 500 primrose species the following have importance as houseplants:
• *Primula malacoides*, the fairy or baby primrose, is an annual.
• *Primula obconica*, the German or poison primrose. It grows to a height of 10 in. (25 cm), bears dense clusters of white, red, pink, or light violet flowers.
• *Primula vulgaris* (syn. *Primula acaulis*), the English primrose, is seen in trade in white, cream, yellow, orange, pink, red, purple, violet, and blue.
Blooming Season: Winter and spring. *Primula obconica*, all year.
Family: Primulaceae (primrose family).
Origin: *Primula vulgaris*, western and southern Europe; the other species come from China. Only hybrid forms are in trade, however.

Location: Bright but not sunny. Cool, especially before blooming season— 50° to 59° F (10°–15° C). The plants will only tolerate a heated room for a very short time.
Watering, Feeding: Always keep slightly damp, but avoid sogginess. During the blooming season fertilize weakly every 14 days.
Further Culture: Plant *Primula vulgaris* in the garden after it finishes blooming and it will flower there again the next spring. *Primula obconica* can be repotted after flowering.
Propagation: From seed, usually in summer. Difficult for the layperson.
Pests, Diseases: Brown roots and yellow leaves from too warm a location, too much fertilizer, dryness, sogginess, or hard water.
Warning: Contact with the German primula can produce allergies in sensitive people.

Reinwardtia indica
Yellow Flax

The yellow flax flowers in sunshine yellow in winter.

The yellow flax is among those new pot plants that are just conquering the market. As a winter-bloomer it is a wonderful addition to a rather cool conservatory. Trademarks of the attractive half-shrub, which grows some 39 in. (1 m) tall, are the brilliant golden-yellow flower trumpets, which appear in great numbers. They give the name to this tropical relative of our native blue flax, which owes its species name to the Dutch botanist Caspar Georg Carl Reinwardt.
Blooming Season: November to March.
Family: Linaceae (flax family).
Origin: Mountains of northern Indonesia.
Location: Very bright and airy, but not full sun. In summer can be outdoors as well, in a semishady spot. In winter keep under 50° to 54° F (10°–12° C).
Watering, Feeding: In summer, during the growing season, keep moderately damp and feed every 14 days with a weak dosage. In winter, water less.
Further Culture: In summer trim the shoots often so that the half-shrub develops a nice bushy growth and forms many shoots, on which the flowers will appear during the winter.
Propagation: From tip cuttings in spring. Root can be cool. No bottom warmth necessary.
Pests, Diseases: Aphid attacks when the winter location is too warm.

English primroses— a beautiful spring greeting.

Rhododendron simsii with single flowers.

Variety with very double flowers.

Of the more than 800 *Rhododendron* species, the only ones offered as houseplants are the large-flowered hybrids of *Rhododendron simsii*, the Indian azalea, and the small-flowered Japanese azalea (*Rhododendron obtusum*, var. *R. japonicum*).

Blooming Season: *Rhododendron-simsii* hybrids, winter to spring, depending on variety; *Rhododendron obtusum*, April, usually available in bloom at Christmas, however.

Family: Ericaceae (heath family).

Origin: Central China, Japan.

Location: Fresh, cool, and airy. Bright to semishady; no direct sun. From middle of May give it a semishady place outdoors. In fall and winter keep *Rhododendron-simsii* hybrids at 41° to 54° F (5°–12° C); *Rhodo-dendron obtusum*, at 41° F (5° C) (to ripen the buds). As soon as the buds begin to swell, place it in a warmer (around 64°F [18°C]) situation.

Watering, Feeding: Only use soft water. Azaleas do not tolerate any lime. <u>Never allow the root ball to dry out, but avoid sogginess at all costs</u>. In summer, water copiously. For bud formation in the fall, keep plant somewhat drier. After blooming until August feed with a lime-free flower fertilizer or rhododendron food in low concentrations every 14 days.

Further Culture: Regularly remove dead flowers and every 2 years repot in azalea soil or a mixture of 1/2 peat moss and 1/2 all-purpose soil. Trim branches in early summer several times. This promotes bushy growth. You should pinch out young shoots that develop before April or during the blooming period.

Propagation: By tip cuttings, at a ground temperature of 68° to 77° F (20°–25°C). Difficult, only done in specialty nurseries.

Pests, Diseases: Stunted leaves from soft-skinned mites or spider mites in too warm a location with dry air; out of doors, possible damage from snout weevils.

My Tip: Nonhardy azaleas are wonderfully suited for bonsai. In the nursery industry they are trimmed numerous times and are already well branched by the time they come to the market. The best for developing a bonsai is a potted azalea that has spent the summer in a shady, damp place in the garden and is trained in the fall and planted in a bonsai dish. One disad-vantage is that azalea wood is somewhat brittle. Bonsai fanciers recom-mend, therefore, that when bending the trunk you use both thumbs, spread out to brace it from behind. Find out from bonsai specialists in your area what is the best form for the growth of your particular azalea. Or buy a book that will give you step-by-step instructions on how one could, for example, make a simple potted azalea into a finished semicascade in 2 hours. The broom shape is also appropriate to the growth and requirements of the azalea. The azalea is not suitable for two of the classical bonsai forms: the root form and the cascade. The azalea roots and the sap flow to the branches are too weak so that the bonsai would not be sufficiently provided with water and nutrients.

Warning: Rhododendrons can contain poisonous chemicals.

FLOWERING PLANTS

Rosa chinensis
China Rose

Modern pot roses in mini and maxi forms.

So that rose lovers who do not garden may also have them, breeders have created numerous dwarf varieties. Best known are the descendants of the Chinese rose (*Rosa chinensis*) like 'Minima' (red-flowered). They grow 10 to 16 in. (25–40 cm) high and, depending on the hybrid, are double or single and in all the rose colors. Recognized varieties are: 'Zwergkönig' (pink) and 'Zwergkönigen' (pink), 'Baby Maskerade' (orange-yellow), 'Colibri' (red). Like all roses, the miniatures are summer flowering shrubs that lose their leaves in the fall and want to be wintered over cold.

Blooming Season: Summer and fall.
Family: Rosaceae (rose family).
Origin: China. Only hybrid forms exist in the trade.

Location: Very bright to sunny and airy. Best kept out of doors in summer in a bright spot, protected from full sun. Keep cool (not over 50° F [10° C]) in winter.
Watering, Feeding: From spring to fall keep evenly damp. In winter quarters, water only enough to keep the root ball from drying out. From March to the end of July feed every 14 days, then no more so that the wood can ripen.
Further Culture: Winter over in a cool but frost-free place. In spring repot in all-purpose soil and cut back; then still keep cool but in a brighter spot.
Propagation: From cuttings, seeds, or grafting. Difficult for the layperson.
Pests, Diseases: Aphids and spider mites; mildew.
My Tip: Regularly remove spent flowers, which will stimulate growth of new ones.

Saintpaulia-Ionantha Hybrids
African Violet

A dream in pastels—*Saintpaulia-Jonantha* hybrids.

There are African violets with single, double, wavy, or ruffled flowers in white and shades of pink, red, purple, and blue, with two-colored flowers and also miniatures.
Blooming Season: January to December, depending on the age of the plant. The plants bloom several times one after the other, interrupted by several weeks of rest.
Family: Gesneriaceae (gesneriad family).
Origin: Tanzania.
Location: Bright to semishady. No sun. Room temperature all year long—in summer, 68° F (20°C) or over; in winter, not under 64° F (18° C). Avoid cold feet.
Watering, Feeding: Always keep evenly damp with room-temperature, soft water. Never water from the top. Water that is too cold or too warm on leaves or flowers will produce ugly spots. Always pour off super-fluous water. When heat is turned up, provide for indirect humidity (see page 43). In spring and summer use weak fertilizer weekly.
Further Culture: Remove faded flowers. In spring repot in all-purpose or African violet potting soil.
Propagation: From leaf cuttings at a ground temperature of over 68° F (20° C).
Pests, Diseases: Aphids and mealybugs from dry air. Mites, thrips, and gray mold from cold damp feet. Mildew.

Single-flowered miniature Saint-paulias.

Schizanthus-Wisetonensis Hybrids
Butterfly Flower, Poor Man's Orchid

Scutellaria
Skullcap

You can sow annual butterfly flowers yourself.

Skullcap—a light-thirsty mountain beauty.

The flowers of the butterfly flower appear in lush bouquets. They are white, pink, yellow, salmon, carmine red, or violet and may be mottled or blazed, thereby allowing comparison with orchids. This plant is used as a balcony and garden plant because it blooms vigorously until fall, but it is also used as a pot plant for the windowsill. After flowering, the "poor man's orchid" is thrown away, for it is an annual and can easily be grown from seed (which is readily available).

Blooming Season: July to October.

Family: Solanaceae (nightshade family).

Origin: Chile. Only cultivars available in trade.

Location: Very bright, airy, and warm for blooming plants. For young plants, sunny in winter, plus airy and cool—around 50° F (10° C).

Watering, Feeding: Always keep evenly damp and feed weekly.

Further Culture: None.

Propagation: From seed, between November and April. Sprouting temperature is 61° to 64°F (16°–18°C). Plant several young plants to a 5-in. (12-cm) pot in all-purpose potting soil. Cultivate cool and bright.

Pests, Diseases: Rare. Negligible with annual culture. A location in full sun behind window glass can result in sunburn.

My Tip: If you sow in fall, you will have spring-flowering butterfly flowers. With May sowing, the young plants will not bloom until September.

Like the alpine skullcap (*Scutellaria alpina*), the tropical skullcap (*Scutellaria costaricana*) is also a mountain plant and accustomed to a great deal of light. To keep it from growing gangly reaching for the light on the windowsill, growers treat it with growth inhibitors. The attractive, somewhat woody plants grow some 20 in. (50 cm) high and in summer produce striking terminal spikes of fiery red, short-lipped flowers.

Blooming Season: May to July.

Family: Labiatae, also Lamiaceae (mint family).

Origin: Costa Rica.

Location: Very bright and airy all year long, but no sun. In summer, around 68° F (20° C); in winter, no cooler than 59° F (15° C). Important: The ground temperature should never fall below the air temperature.

Watering, Feeding: Keep evenly damp. From March to August feed weekly with a low-dose fertilizer.

Further Culture: Every 2 years, in fall, repot in all-purpose potting soil. Cut back first. Better: In fall produce new plants, which will then bloom the following year.

Propagation: By tip or stem cuttings in fall. They root quickly at ground temperatures of 68° to 77° F (20°–25° C). Put several plants into one pot, which will produce thicker clumps. Do not pinch back! The inflorescences form only at the ends of shoots.

Pests, Diseases: Spider mites in too warm and dry a winter location.

Light wanted: Indoors, tropical mountain plants like the skullcap change their typical habit and grow to the sky in their search for light.

FLOWERING PLANTS

Senecio-Cruentus Hybrids
Cineraria

Cinerarias are not really ashy—but they are very susceptible to plant lice.

With 2,000 to 3,000 species, the cinerarias are the largest and most varied genus of the composite family. The *Senecio-Cruentus* hybrids, with their simply inexhaustible wealth of colors, have become especially popular as pot plants. They are on sale in the spring and are thrown away when they finish blooming because further culture doesn't pay.

Blooming Season: March and April.

Family: Compositae (composite family).

Origin: Cool, damp mountain forests of the Canary Islands. Only hybrid forms are available in trade, however.

Location: Bright, airy, and cool—61° to 64° F (16°–18° C). Do not place plants close together.

Watering, Feeding: Water copiously. If possible, provide for indirect humidity (see page 43). Both practices promote longevity of flowering and hinder aphid invasions. Only fertilize if propagation is intended—from November to January every 14 days, weekly at other times.

Further Culture: Repotting is not necessary since the plants are bought only for their flowers.

Propagation: From seed in July/August. Winter over young plants in bright location. Keep them cool—48° to 54° F (9°–12° C).

Pests, Diseases: Aphids. As a precaution against

Blue cineraria with white ground.

aphid attack, stick an insecticide stake in the soil.

My Tip: In the cactus and succulent houses of many botanical gardens there are numerous *Senecio* species. Just look carefully sometime. It is surprising how varied this genus is and how little most of them resemble the cineraria, despite a close relationship. Here it can be observed—as it can with euphorbias and cacti—how two plants from completely different families have evolved the

same recipe for survival: *Senecio stapeliiformis* is similar enough in appearance to many stapelias to be confusing. The families differ in the flower, however. The bloom of *Senecio* is orange, a typical composite. On the hand, the species-typical flower on the stapelia is a simple, star-shaped flower that smells of carrion. A further example of this contemporaneously produced development, which botanists term convergence, is the Natal ivy, *Senecio macroglossus*, which differs from our ivy, *Hedera*, only by its thicker leaves. There are even white variegated forms, as with true ivy.

An elegant arrangement—single-flowered gloxinias in a jardiniere.

The *Sinningia* and its relatives live in South and Central America. There are some 50 different species there, which with the exception of two rhizomatous species all form tubers but have quite inconspicuous flowers. The ancestor of our modern *Sinningia* hybrids is *Sinningia speciosa*. It grows in southern Brazil on damp, rocky slopes and blooms there with dainty, violet-blue flower bells. In 1815 it was imported to England. The first large-flowered forms developed when *Sinningia regina* was used for hybridizing. This species, brought to Europe in 1903, was notable especially for its velvety, hairy, brown-red leaves with striking white veins. The nodding flowers are lavender and have a pale yellow, purple-spotted center stripe. From these two as well as other species like *Sinningia guttata,*

Sinningia helleri, and *Sinningia villosa* came numerous hybrids, among them the well-known dark-red 'Sonnenunter-gang' (which means "sunset"). It was the first *Sinningia* hybrid with smaller, softer leaves that no longer had ugly cracked places.

After a period of obscurity for the nostalgic gloxinia, breeders surprised us with a veritable color spectacle in these very plants. Besides the standard red, there are flowers in subdued rose and violet shades and two-colored flower bells. Each is, depending on its variety, fragrant, velvety, or silky. The double flowers look very much like old roses. When buying, you should be sure that the plant displays as many flower stems with buds as possible. With the modern lushly blooming varieties further culture does not pay, since the tubers are

too small for next year's growth and most die when wintered over.

Blooming Season: March to August.

Family: Gesneriaceae (gesneriad family).

Origin: The original home of the parents is Brazil. However, only hybrid forms are available in trade.

Location: Warm and humid; bright but not sunny.

Watering, Feeding: Keep slightly damp with soft, room-temperature water. If further culture is intended, fertilize weekly.

Further Culture: Do not mist; preferably provide for indirect humidity (see page 43). <u>Don't wet the leaves</u>! After flowers have stopped, allow the tuber to slowly go to rest. Remove dry leaves, let tuber dry out, and store in the old soil at a cool temperature—59° F (15° C). In spring repot in fresh all-purpose soil,

force in a warm, bright, humid situation.

Propagation: From seed. Expensive for the layperson because artificial light is necessary from November to February.

Pests, Diseases: Aphids from dry air can cause curling of leaves. Tipping of stem and rot result from cold, wet location and too deep a pot.

Note: The red-flowered *Sinningia cardinalis* (syn. *Rechsteineria cardinalis*) is cultivated exactly the same way. But here forcing the tuber is easier.

FLOWERING PLANTS

Solanum
Nightshades

Eggplant hybrid—*Solanum melongena*.

The coral bush, *Solanum pseudocapsicum*.

Three popular species of the genus *Solanum* thrive splendidly as houseplants and therefore enjoy great popularity: The Jerusalem cherry (*Solanum pseudocapsicum*); the eggplant (*Solanum melongena*), which is a white sport of the eggplant and like it an annual; as well as false Jerusalem cherry (*Solanum capsicastrum*), which also exists in a form with white leaves. The greenish-white flowers look very like potato flowers. The yellow, orange, or brilliant red berries of the Jerusalem cherry last, if one doesn't keep the pot too warm, from fall far into the winter. Many throw the plants away when the fruit decorations drop. That is too bad, for the evergreen, twiggy bushes can be cultivated further if you winter them correctly.

Blooming Season: May to June; the fruits keep from September to February.

Family: Solanaceae (nightshade family).

Origin: Madeira, Brazil, Uruguay.

Location: Bright to sunny and airy. In summer, out of doors as well. Winter over at 50° to 59 F° (10°–15°C).

Watering, Feeding: In spring and summer water freely, in fall and winter only enough to keep the root ball from drying out. From March to August feed every 14 days.

Further Culture: Mist often in a warm winter location—otherwise danger of plant lice! For further culture repot in spring, in a not-much-larger pot, using all-purpose potting soil. Decrease the size of the root ball slightly and cut the plant back.

Propagation: From self-harvested seeds. Remove flesh of fruit, let seeds dry, and sow in spring.

Trim young plants two times so that they will become bushy.

Pests, Diseases: Aphids, spider mites, and whitefly in a location that is too warm and too dry.

My Tip: Tub plant nurseries sometimes stock even more interesting Solanum species, for example:

• *Solanum aviculare*, the kangaroo apple, a bush from New Zealand and Australia that bears blue-violet flowers from August to September.

• *Solanum jasminoides*, the potato vine, is a fast-growing climber for the cool conservatory. It blooms from late winter on until almost summer with whitish-blue flowers and with good nourishment can produce shoots up to 39 in. (1 m) long.

• *Solanum laciniatum* is a lush half-shrub of the tropics that in a tub can attain a proud height of 10 ft (3 m). The wonderful violet flowers appear from spring to fall. Pigeon-egg-sized fruits are orange when they have ripened.

• *Solanum rantonnetii*, known as "blue potato bush," produces blue-violet single flowers 1 in. (2.5 cm) across from July to October (in perfect locations, flowers almost all year long). The shrub, which originates in South America, grows vigorously and can be trained into all sorts of forms.

• *Solanum wenlandii*, also called potato vine, is a warmth-loving evergreen vine with hooked thorns and is known as the most-beautiful climber in the family. The violet flowers, over 2 in. (6 cm) across, give pleasure from high summer until late fall. The leaves may be as long as 10 in. (25 cm).

Warning: All parts of the Jerusalem cherry and the *Solanum* species listed in "My Tip" are poisonous.

Spathiphyllum
Spathe Flower

There are many forms of spathe flower.

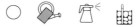

Of the some 40 species that grow primarily in tropical America, the most commonly used as houseplants are *Spathiphyllum floribundum*, 12 to 16 in. (30–40 cm) tall, and the altogether larger and taller *Spathiphyllum wallisii*. Of the latter there is even a fragrant variety, called 'Mauna Loa'. The spathe flower, incidentally one of the best plants for hydroculture, possesses evergreen, undivided, glossy leaves. They grow in tufts on a stem that scarcely sticks out of the ground. The flower develops in summer. It consists of the spikelike cream-colored spadix and the white or greenish-white bract.

Blooming Season: March to September.
Family: Araceae (arum family).
Origin: Colombia, Venezuela.
Location: Bright to semishady; astonishingly adaptable regarding light intensity. Room temperature, all year long, at 64° to 77° F (18°–25°C); in winter, not under 61° F (16° C).

Watering, Feeding: In spring and summer water moderately with softened, room-temperature water. During the rest period, from October to January, water less. From March to August, feed every week with weak dosage.

Further Culture: On warm days, mist or provide for indirect humidity (see page 43). In February/March, repot in all-purpose soil mixed with Styrofoam flakes.

Propagation: By seed or division at repotting.

Pests, Diseases: Scale and spider mites when air is too dry. Bag plants for 1 to 2 days (see page 50).

Warning: The spathe flower contains irritants to skin and mucous membranes.

Stephanotis floribunda
Madagascar Jasmine, Stephanotis

Stephanotis doesn't like to have its location changed.

In its native habitat the stephanotis grows as an evergreen climbing shrub with long runners. But it is also a popular houseplant. The leaves are dark green, glossy, and leathery. In summer it forms clusters of waxy, starlike, snow-white flowers, from which sometimes fruits develop. Anyone who doesn't have enough space can let the plant grow on a hoop. In a conservatory it can be trained on a trellis.

Blooming Season: June to September. With control of flowering through temperature and light intensity, it can also be induced to bloom in winter.
Family: Asclepiadaceae (milkweed family).
Origin: Madagascar.
Location: Very bright and airy, but not sunny. In summer, warm, at 68° to 77° F (20°–25 C); in winter, cool, at 54° to 57° F (12°–14°C). Does not tolerate change of position, especially after buds set, so make a light mark (see page 45).

Watering, Feeding: Water freely from March to August with soft, room-temperature water. The root ball must never dry out. Afterward, water more sparingly for maturing of shoots. From October to August, feed weekly.

Further Culture: Mist often in summer. Repot only as necessary, in spring, using all-purpose potting soil. Shorten bare shoots.

Propagation: From tip or stem cuttings. Cut these from spring to summer and root in a heatable propagation flat.

Pests, Diseases: Spider mites, aphids, and scale from too warm a winter location with dry air. Yellow leaves from hard water or lack of light. Bud and flower drop from draft or change of position.

Fragrant stars are the hallmark of stephanotis. They exude an intense perfume similar to that of the world-famous jasmine.

FLOWERING PLANTS

Streptocarpus
Cape Primrose

Like a fragrant bouquet—*Streptocarpus* hybrid.

Streptocarpus wendlandii has only one giant leaf, whose underside is purplish red.

In 1824 a botanist brought the first cape primrose to Europe. Since then innumerable hybrids have been developed with elegant orchidlike flowers in white, salmon, pink, red, violet, and blue, some of which have a striped throat or ruffled margins. Recently, small-flowered species also have become available, such as the bright-blue- to purple-flowered *Streptocarpus saxorum* (see photograph, page 30).

Blooming Season: May to September.
Family: Gesneriaceae (gesneriad family).
Origin: South Africa, tropical Africa, Burma and Thailand.
Location: Bright to semishady, but not sunny. Room temp- erature all year around. For the small- flowered hybrids the room tem- perature can go down to 59° F (15°C) in winter.

Watering, Feeding: Use soft, room-temperature water. Keep plants uniformly damp, in winter water somewhat less. From March to August feed every 14 days with a weak dosage but never fertilize a dry root ball.
Further Culture: Provide humidity. In spring, repot in all-purpose potting or African violet soil.
Propagation: The hybrids, by leaf cuttings (halves of leaves, or parts cut perpendicular to the center rib) at a ground temperature of 68° F (20°C) in a warmed propagation flat. Possible any time of the year but the best time is spring. The young plants form along the veins. The seeds are sown in spring.
Pests, Diseases: Aphids, spider mites, or thrips from air that is too dry. Brown leaf margins from too wet or too dry a culture.

Tillandsia
Tillandsia

Tillandsia cyanea is one of the green species.

With over 400 species, *Tillandsia* is the largest and richest genus in the family of bromeliads. Most tillandsias live epiphytically on trees, rocks, or other supports that are available. There are green and gray plants. With the gray ones the narrow, grasslike leaves are thick with silver-gray absorbent scales that can capture water vapor. Most tillandsias need relatively little space. Plants are sold appropriately bound to tree limbs. However, they also come stuck to stone or wood—an unnatural method of culture.

Blooming Season: Depending on species, spring or summer.
Family: Bromeliaceae (bromeliad family).
Origin: Tropical and subtropical America.
Location: Gray tillandsias, light all year. In summer, sunny and warm—best out of doors in the fresh air. In winter, 50° to 59° F (10°–15° C). Green tillandsias, warm and bright all year long, but not sunny. Ideal location: A warm, humid flower window.
Watering, Feeding: In summer, mist daily with lime-free water; in winter, one or two times weekly. In summer add a weak fertilizer to the spray water every 14 days.
Further Culture: Provide for indirect humidity (see page 43).
Propagation: By offsets, which are separated when they are half as large as the mother and then bound on a branch.
Pests, Diseases: Rarely, mealybugs or scale.
My Tip: Tillandsias are now severely endangered because of export from their native habitats by the containerloads. Therefore only buy plants that have been propagated under cultivation.

Vriesea splendens is the best-known species.

The calla only blooms when its rest period is observed.

The vrieseas offered as houseplants are mostly cultivated hybrids.

Best known is *Vriesea splendens*, the flaming sword. It forms rosettes of leaves about 20 in. (50 cm) tall, with striking brownish-red cross stripes and an orangey-red, flat flower spike. There are also green-leaved hybrids with dark red inflorescences or crosses of *Vriesea carinata*, lobsterclaws, and *Vriesea psittacina*, which means "parrot vriesea" and has flower spikes in several colors. Vrieseas can be cultivated bound to epiphyte supports or in not-very-large pots with loose soil.

Blooming Season: Vriesea hybrids are sold in bloom all year around and generally die after flowering.
Family: Bromeliaceae (bromeliad family).
Origin: Brazil.
Location: Bright to semishady. Warm and humid all year around. Best in a climate-controlled flower window. Important: Soil temperature over 64° F (18°C).
Watering, Feeding: Always keep slightly damp with soft, room-temperature water. Put water in the cup and on the root ball. In summer feed with a weak solution every 14 days.
Further Culture: Mist often and provide for indirect humidity (see page 43). Repotting not necessary since plants die after flowering.
Propagation: By offsets, which must be half as large as the mother plant. But *Vrieseas* do not develop these as easily as other bromeliads. Tie to supports or pot in small pots with all-purpose soil mixed with Styrofoam .
Pests, Diseases: Failure to grow and leaf damage from too much water and dry centrally heated air.

The most popular houseplant calla, *Zantedeschia aethiopica*, comes from South Africa's swampy regions, which dry out in summer. There it grows as a shrub and has either a partial or total rest period. The juicy, green, glossy leaves are carried on upright stems. The inflorescence consists of a white covering leaf (spathe) and a yellow spadix. Tubers of the pink-flowering *Zantedeschia rehmannii* and the yellow-flowered *Zantedeschia elliottiana* are also available.

Blooming Season: Spring to early summer.
Family: Araceae (arum family).
Origin: Tropical Africa, South Africa.
Location: Full sun to semishady. Warm in summer, cool in winter. Place outside from middle of May, bring inside in fall.
Watering, Feeding: Keep completely dry for 2 months after blooming (May and June) (conforming with the summer dry season in its native location). Afterward, shake out the root ball, repot, and slowly increase the amount of water. The plants need a great deal of humidity during the growing period. Before the new flowers develop, decrease the amount of water somewhat and water freely again when flower begins. From July till flowering, fertilize weekly.
Further Culture: None.
Propagation: By division of root stock after the rest period in the middle of July.
Pests, Diseases: Spider mites and aphids in too warm a winter location.
My Tip: In favorable climatic conditions and very protected spots the calla can also be planted outdoors in the garden.

RARITIES

Uncommon flowering plants: For fanciers, a small selection of attractive novelties, rarities, and, thus, plants with unusual flowers.

Pavonia multiflora
(*Triplochlamys multiflora*)
Pavonia

Small evergreen bush. The flowers have a purple-red cupule and a somewhat darker corolla; the stigma is pink, and the stamens are blue.

Blooming Season: Fall to spring. Family: Malvaceae (mallow family). Origin: Brazil. Location: All year around, bright and warm—in winter, not under 59° F (15° C). Watering, Feeding: Keep only moderately damp with soft water. From March to August feed weekly with a weak solution. Further Culture: The plants need high humidity. Mist often. In spring, repot in all-purpose potting soil. Cut back after flowering. Propagation: From tip cuttings. Difficult. Note: The same culture suits the singular *Goethea cauliflora,* whose scarlet flowers develop sideways from the stem from July to October.

Half-opened *pavonia* blossom with purple-red cupule, pink stigmas, and blue anthers.

Globba winitii
Globba

Gingerlike plants with tuber-shaped roots, large, oblong lanceolate leaves, and pendulous panicles of flowers. Approximately 100 species are recognized, some of which can be admired in botanical gardens. They are recognizable immediately by their unusual flowers, which in other species can also be cream-colored. In addition to *Globba winittii,* there are: *Globba atrosanguinea,* from Borneo; *Globba bulbifera,* which develops the brood buds; and *Globba marantina,* which comes from the South Sea islands. Blooming Season: July to November. Family: Zingiberaceae (ginger family). Origin: Thailand. Location: Very bright, but not full sun.

All year around 68° to 73° F (20°–23° C). Watering, Feeding: Water moderately. From March to August feed every week with weak solution. Further Culture: Provide high humidity. Leaves wilt in December/January, but do not let tubers dry out. In spring, repot in all-purpose soil and force again. Propagation: By brood tubers or division of old plants. My Tip: Anyone lucky enough to get hold of a curcuma, or hidden lily (*Curcuma roscoeana*) can cultivate it just like the globba.

Eranthemum pulchellum
Blue Sage

Small bush with dark green leaves and sturdy blue flower spikes. Is usually cultivated as an annual. Wonderful winter bloomer for the conservatory.

Blooming Season: December to February. Family: Acanthaceae (acanthus family). Origin: India. Location: Bright but not sunny. In summer, 64° to 73° F (18°–23° C). In winter, not below 61° F (16° C). Watering, Feeding: Keep moderately damp all year long. From March to April feed every three weeks. Further Culture: Repot in March in all-purpose potting soil. Propagation: From tip cuttings, after blooming, at ground temperature of 68° to 77° F (20°–25° C).

Oxalis adenophylla
Wood Sorrel/Oxalis

Bush with gray-green leaves that fold up in the evening as if going to sleep. The pink flowers are carried on long stems, some 2 in. (5 cm) long.

Blooming Season: April. Family: Oxalidaceae (oxalis family). Origin: Chile, Argentina. Location: Bright to full sun, but cool all year long. Watering, Feeding: Keep evenly damp during the growing season and fertilize weekly. Further Culture: Plants die back in fall and sprout again after a rest period. Propagation: By brood tubers.

Smithiantha hybrids
Temple-Bells

The temple-bells, whose genus is named after the English botanical artist Matilda Smith (around 1840), was formerly also known as *Naegelia multiflora*. The modern hybrids are descendants of *Smithiantha multiflora* and *Smithiantha zebrina*. They have soft, brown-patterned leaves and orange-red flowers. The small plants renew themselves from scaly rhizomes. Blooming Season: July to September. Family: Gesneriaceae (gesneriad family). Origin: Southern Mexico. Location: Bright and warm. Watering, Feeding: Keep slightly damp all the time with soft water from March to October. Feed every 14 days with weak solution. In winter keep plants completely dry. Further Culture: Provide indirect humidity (see page 43). Leaves wilt beginning in October. Dry the rhizome in the old pot and winter over at a cool temperature, around 54° F (12° C). In spring, repot in soilless mixture or African violet potting soil and resume watering. Force in plastic bag (see page 59). Propagation: From seed or division of the rhizome. My Tip: In the second year the plants you've raised from rhizomes are less governed by tropical conditions than the first store-bought ones that had grown up in a greenhouse.

Anigozanthos flavidus
Kangaroo-Paw

Bushy plant with lanceolate leaves, which in summer produces unusual, fuzzy, feltlike flowers.

Blooming Season: May to August. Family: Haemodoraceae (blood-wort family). Origin: Southern Australia. Location: Very bright all year around. In summer, warm (outside if possible); in winter, cool—50° to 59° C (10°–15 C). Watering, Feeding: Water copiously in summer. From March to August feed every week with low dosage. In winter, keep dry. Further Culture: As necessary, repot in spring in all-purpose soil. Propagation: By division of older plants, also from seed. My Tip: The kangaroo-paw needs an extraordinary amount of light and in a bad summer will scarcely bloom at all. Additionally, once in the home, especially in a dark spot, it loses the compact growth habit attained with growth inhibitors it received when it was raised for sale. Furthermore: If you cannot get already-grown plants of *Anigozanthos flavidus,* you can raise its relative, *Anigozanthos manglesii* from seed.

TUB PLANTS

Splendid flowering plants that soon outgrow the windowsill, love the fresh summer air out of doors, and need a cool location in winter.

Abutilon Hybrids
Flowering Maple, Parlor Maple

Shrub with green- or greenish-gold-flecked foliage.
<u>Blooming Season:</u> All year long.
<u>Family:</u> Malvaceae (mallow family).

<u>Origin:</u> Central and South America.
<u>Location:</u> In summer, out of doors—bright to semishady—bring into house in September and winter over in bright light and a cool temperature—54° to 57° F (12°–14° C). <u>Watering, Feeding:</u> Water freely from March to August and feed twice weekly. From September to February keep the root ball merely damp. <u>Further Culture:</u> In spring repot in all-purpose soil. Cut back by ²/₃ first.
<u>Propagation:</u> From tender cuttings in spring or half-woody ones in August.

Chamelaucium uncinatum
Geraldton Wax Flower

Small evergreen shrub with needle-fine leaves and small dark pink or white flowers.
<u>Blooming Season:</u> March to April.
<u>Family:</u> Myrtaceae (myrtle family).
<u>Origin:</u> Western Australia. <u>Location:</u> In summer, full sun; warm and airy. Winter over from September in bright light and cool temperature—around 50° F (10° C). <u>Watering, Feeding:</u> Keep moderately damp, still less in winter. Sogginess makes flowers drop! From March to August feed every 14 days. <u>Further Culture:</u> After blooming cut back shoots. Repot in spring as necessary, in all-purpose potting soil.
<u>Propagation:</u> From soft cuttings, at a soil temperature of 77° F (25° C).

Cystius x Racemosus
Broom

Evergreen shrub with small, three-part leaves and brilliant yellow racemes of flowers. Available commercially are bushy, tall pot plants that can broaden and grow as tall as 39 in. (1 m), and there are attractive tree forms as well. The broom, like the campanula (see page 100) is one of the few houseplants that does not require softened water.
<u>Blooming Season:</u> February to May.
<u>Family:</u> Leguminosae (legume family).
<u>Origin:</u> Canary Islands, Madeira.
<u>Location:</u> Outdoors in summer, in full sun to bright light, and warm. Bring indoors in September/October and winter over in bright light and cool temperature—46° to 50° F (8°–10° C) so that the flowers can develop. <u>Watering, Feeding:</u> Keep slightly damp constantly, all year long. In summer, water more; in winter, less. From March to August feed weekly; in winter, monthly. <u>Further Culture:</u> Repot young plants every year, after blooming, in all-purpose potting mix. Cutting back after blooming prevents loss of leaves. <u>My Tip:</u> Keep in bright, cool spot (but no full sun) while flowering. <u>Warning:</u> Broom, like other *Cystius* species, contains toxic materials.

Bougainvillea
Bougainvillea

Vines with strikingly colored bracts in cream-white, salmon, pink, red, or purple. Obtainable as a pot plant trained on a hoop, a bush, or a standard. Also found as such are *Bougainvillea glabra* and species like the vigorous grower *Bougainvillea spectabilis,* which has thorns and needs at least a conservatory for its need to spread.
<u>Blooming Season:</u> April to June.
<u>Family:</u> Nyctaginaceae (four-o'clock family). <u>Origin:</u> Brazil. <u>Location:</u> In summer, place outdoors in a sunny to very bright, warm, and protected spot. From September on, bring inside and keep bright and cool—57° to 68° F (10°–14° C). <u>Watering, Feeding:</u> From beginning of growth until August, water freely and feed weekly. Then keep drier. From November water little, and after foliage drop, do not water at all.
<u>Further Culture:</u> Cut back in March and repot in all-purpose soil. Mist on sunny days.
<u>Propagation:</u> Difficult.

Callistemon citrinus
Crimson Bottlebrush

Evergreen shrub with gray-green lanceolate leaves and long, bottlebrush-like flower spikes about 4 in. (10 cm) long, in which the red filaments of the stamens are especially prominent. The species most commonly available, *Callistemon citrinus,* grows to a height of about 10 ft (3 m) in its native habitat, and even here will become an impressive plant relatively quickly.
<u>Blooming Season:</u> June to July.
<u>Family:</u> Myrtaceae (myrtle family).
<u>Origin:</u> Southern Australia, New Caledonia. <u>Location:</u> Put outdoors in summer in full sun or in a very bright, warm spot. In September bring inside and winter over in bright light and at a cool temperature—43° to 46° F (6°– 8° C). <u>Watering, Feeding:</u> Water in summer with soft water and fertilize weekly. <u>Further Culture:</u> Repot in spring, in all-purpose soil, azalea mix, or ¹/₂ peat moss and ¹/₂ all-purpose soil.
<u>Propagation:</u> From tip cuttings, August to October at a ground temperature of 68° to 77° F (20° to 25° C). <u>Note:</u> The Christmas tree (*Metrosideros excelsa*) is cultivated just the same way.

Here the garden plant *Campanula poscharskyana* shows what an enchanting hanging plant it is.

Campanula poscharskyana
Campanula

About 6 in. (15 cm) high, this is a densely bushy, cushiony garden shrub. It generates thousands of sky-blue bells in short clusters and has heart-shaped leaves. Produces runners. Beautiful hanging plant.
<u>Blooming Season:</u> June/July and longer. <u>Family:</u> Campanulaceae (bellflower family). <u>Origin:</u> Dalmatia. <u>Location:</u> Semishade. <u>Watering, Feeding:</u> In summer, water freely. The plant loves very hard water. Feed weekly. <u>Further Culture:</u> After flowering, plant in the garden (the campanula will grow again in the spring) or winter over in a cool, bright spot with little water.
<u>Propagation:</u> From runners in the garden in summer.

FOLIAGE PLANTS

Foliage plants create the most natural background for the colorful display made by plants in flower.

Most green, or foliage, plants are actually flowering plants. In their native regions they regularly produce flowers and fruits (except Sago palm, Norfolk Island pine, and Monterey cypress). These plants are far older evolutionarily and had already been in existence for many millions of years when the so-called flowering plants evolved. The common division of plants into green and flowering ones has really occurred only on the basis of looks. Many regarded as green plants never bloom in our climate because in their native location they are very tall trees, and in pots they always remain in the juvenile form and never mature enough to flower.

Others are considered green plants because their leaves have a more decorative effect than the often modest or insignificant flowers they produce. The green plant parade on pages 142–191 will acquaint you with the most beautiful and best-known species and varieties, along with some bizarre rarities and interesting novelties in the marketplace. Ferns and palms, which really also belong in the green- or foliage-plant category, are consciously excluded here. They have their own chapters because they are very different botanically and in cultivation. Green plants are wonderfully suited for decorating living spaces because of their various growth forms and leaf sizes, structures, and colorations. They can cascade down from columns or pedestals, hang from the ceiling, climb on grillwork room dividers, or serve as a living curtain in a window. Especially eye catching are those plants that with good culture develop into stately indoor trees. Also not to be undervalued is the positive effect that green plants have on us. Green is the color human beings need most. Its nature is peaceful, it banishes depression, and it has a relaxing effect. This is not surprising when you know that the lenses of our eyes do not have to adjust for green as they do for other colors. The most popular "greens"

The giant leaves of the anthurium are regular light-traps. With its large leaf surfaces the plant tries to capture as much as possible of the scarce light that filters down through the foliage canopy of the rain forest.

are, according to statistics, the *Yucca* and the rubber plant, as well as the weeping fig, ivy, grape ivy, *Philodendron, Dracaena,* and dumb canes, not to mention the diverse houseplant grasses. Those who look for the unusual will certainly find pleasure in such uncommon plants as the string-of-beads, a succulent *Senecio* species (see page 193), or in the ornamental leaves of *Anthurium* (see photograph, above), or *Alocasia* (see photograph, left).

What You Should Know About Green Plants

Green plants come from all possible plant families. Certain families give us an especially large number of green representatives: the arum, begonia, aralia, bromeliad, grape, and maranta families (see photograph, page 33). The kaleidoscope of growth and vegetation forms is noteworthy. There are upright forms, creeping and climbing ones, herbaceous, shrubby, or treelike growers, evergreen and deciduous leaf plants, grasses, epiphytes, succulents, and carnivores (meat-eating plants). The leaf size varies from needle-fine to violin-sized. Depending on the species, the leaves can be thin or thick and fleshy, hard and leathery or velvety-soft, hairy, or waxy.

Exciting leaf patterns and colors document how inventive Nature is. But some leaf paintings, called variegations, are brought about by hybridizing.

The Right Culture

The leaves are the nerve of life for the plant, the place where photosynthesis and respiration take place. Keep your eye on them all the time. They are the first to indicate disease or insect attack. Consider while you are watering—apart from any individual care plans—that a lushly foliaged plant always needs more water than a thinly foliaged one because it has a larger evaporative area. You can read light tolerance and water requirements in the leaves of many green plants (see pages 16 and 26).

Who would recognize an indoor weeping fig in this plant? In its natural habitat the *Ficus benjamina* develops thick air roots, which it sends to the ground like powerful guy cables.

FOLIAGE PLANTS

Acorus gramineus
Grassy-leaved Sweet Flag

Yellow-striped sweet flag 'Argenteostriatus'.

The grassy-leaved sweet flag, a swamp plant, looks very much like grass (as its species name indicates—*gramineus* = grasslike). It belongs to the same family as the Swiss cheese plant (see page 172) or the philodendron (see pages 178–179) and is a very close relative of the sweet flag (*Acorus calamus*), an old healing herb. The nursery trade offers white- and yellow-striped varieties with sedgelike leaves about 20 in. (50 cm) long, like 'Argenteostriatus' and 'Aureovariegatus'. Especially pretty is the variety 'Pusillus', which is only 4 in. (10 cm) tall and is a true dwarf. All have a creeping root stock and are decorative plants for small or large water gardens in the house or conservatory.

Family: Araceae (arum family).

Origin: Japan, China, Thailand, India.

Location: Bright to semi-shady, not sunny, and airy. Cool (to 32° F [0° C]) in winter, if possible not warmer than 61°F (16° C). The plants love the fresh air of summer in a bright, cool, damp place in the garden, best in the swampy area of a garden pond. Sink the pot and take it out in fall.

Watering, Feeding: Water copiously. Being a swamp plant, the grassy-leaved sweet flag must never be allowed to dry out. It's best to stand the pot in a water-filled saucer. From spring to fall, feed every 14 days; in winter every 6 to 8 weeks.

Further Culture: Repot in spring, as needed, in all-purpose potting soil.

Propagation: By division of root stock in spring.

Pests, Diseases: Spider mites and thrips, poor growth and leaf damage in a winter location that is too warm and has dry air.

Aeonium
Aeonium

Aeonium arboreum, a "little rosette tree."

The name *Aeonium* (from Greek: *aionios* = eternal, outlasting) indicates that this plant is skilled at surviving thirst. In fact, in its native habitat, the *Aeonium* uses its juicy leaves as a water reservoir to survive in times of drought. The leaves are arranged in rosettes and in the best-known species, *Aeonium arboreum*, are carried on bare stems about 39 in. (1 m) high so that the plant looks like a little rosette tree. The variety 'Atropurpureum' has wine-red leaves in summer, but in winter these become green from lack of light. The effect made by *Aeonium tabuliforme* is very unusual. It develops plate-shaped rosettes, 6 to 12 in. (15-30 cm) wide, which rest on the ground and consist of 100 to 200 individual leaves. Aeoniums rarely bloom when cultivated as houseplants.

Family: Crassulaceae (orpine family).

Origin: Canary Islands, Morocco.

Location: Bright to full sun. For summer can be sunk in the garden in a spot protected from rain. In winter maintain at 50° to 61° F (10°– 16° C).

Watering, Feeding: Water sparingly, but never let the leaves shrivel with dryness. In winter, water very seldom. From May to September add cactus fertilizer to water every 14 days.

Further Culture: Repot in spring, as necessary, in cactus soil or a blend of $^2/_3$ all-purpose soil and $^1/_3$ perlite.

Propagation: By leaf rosettes or single leaves. Allow the cut surface to dry before planting. *Aeonium tabuliforme* by seed only.

Pests, Diseases: With too much water, sogginess, and too warm a winter location, mites, scales, or mealybug.

Aglaonema
Chinese Evergreen

The variety 'Silver King' is almost without chlorophyll.

The silver designs on the leaves mark the aglaonemas. The most common one is *Aglaonema commutatum* with silver-green striped, spotted, or dotted varieties like 'Silver King', 'Silver Queen', 'San Remo', and 'Pseudobracteatum'. The plants develop small trunks, 20 in. (50 cm) high, with herbaceous, broadly oval leaves; they can bloom, and after flowering they develop red berry fruits. *Aglaonema costatum* remains small. Its trunk branches bushily at the base.

Family: Araceae (arum family).

Origin: Southeast Asia.

Location: Shady to semishady. Warm all year long; in winter, not below 61° F (16° C).

Watering, Feeding: Water with soft, room-temperature water, in spring/summer more, in fall/winter somewhat less. From March to August feed every 14 days with lowered dosage.

Further Culture: Provide for soil warmth and indirect humidity (see page 43). Do not overmist, can cause leaf spots. Repot young plants every year, older ones only as necessary, in shallow containers with all-purpose potting soil. Mix Styrofoam flakes into soil.

Propagation: By division at repotting or in spring and summer by tip cuttings, in a heatable propagation flat (difficult).

Pests, Diseases: Spider mites, scale, mealybugs, and aphids from indoor air that is too dry. Growth disturbances and brown leaf margins from water that is too hard and cold, and cold feet.

Warning: The plants contain substances that irritate skin and mucous membranes. The berries are poisonous.

Alocasia
Elephant's-Ear Plant

Foliage beauty for the flower window—*Alocasia*.

The alocasia is valued as one of the most beautiful of all foliage plants. Only a few of the approximately 70 species in the genus are available to us. *Alocasia lowii* from Borneo has dark olive-green leaves up to 16 in. (40 cm) long with the large veins in white. In *Alocasia sanderiana*, from Mindanao (Philippines), the dark olive-green leaves gleam metallically and are decorated with silvery white veins and leaf margins. In the United States there are numerous hybrids from these magnificent exotics. They are best raised in a room greenhouse or an enclosed plant window, since they demand high temperature and humidity and need much space.

Family: Araceae (arum family).

Origin: Southeast Asia.

Location: Semishady to shady. All year long at more than 68° F (20° C) of warmth. In winter, somewhat cooler, but never below 63° F (17° C).

Watering, Feeding: Use only soft, room-temperature water. In spring, summer, and fall keep well dampened, but avoid sogginess. Water only sparingly in winter (rest period). From March to August feed with low dosage every 14 days.

Further Culture: Provide for high humidity. Repot every 2 years at the end of February, in all-purpose soil into which Styrofoam flakes have been mixed.

Propagation: By division of rhizomes at repotting. Protect cut surfaces from infections with charcoal powder. Grow in heatable propagation flats.

Pests, Diseases: Rotting of rhizomes in too cool a location.

Warning: The plants contain substances that irritate skin. The leaves of some species contain prussic acid.

Aloe
Aloe

Known and loved everywhere—*Aloe variegata.*

The tiger aloe, *Aloe variegata,* is a popular plant all over the world. It has white-spotted, succulent, triangular leaves, which are arranged overlapping each other like roof tiles. It grows to 12 in. (30 cm) tall at the most. The candelabra aloe (*Aloe arborescens*) is a well-known, problem-free indoor pot and tub plant. In the old days many a child's scraped knee was healed with its juices. It grows higher and more spreading than the tiger aloe, often developing a branching stem that is bare at the bottom, and has green leaves that are spiny at the edges. The *Aloe barbadensis* (syn. *Aloe vera*), the medicinal aloe, is also good for healing purposes. Today this species is marketed in pots as a "new" cosmetic plant. The juice of its succulent leaves is supposed to beautify and tighten the skin. All *Aloe* species bloom only when plants are older.

Family: Liliaceae (lily family).

Origin: South Africa.

Location: Full sun. In summer, warm; in winter, cool–43° to 50° F (6°–10° C). Loves a summer sojourn in a rain-protected, sunny spot out of doors.

Watering, Feeding: From spring to fall keep moderately damp, in winter water seldom. Avoid sogginess at all costs. During the summer feed every 2 to 3 weeks with a weak solution of cactus fertilizer in the irrigation water.

Further Culture: Repot in spring, as necessary, in cactus soil or soilless mix with sand.

Propagation: From side sprouts, which are separated, allowed to dry, and then stuck in sandy soil.

Pests, Diseases: Root lice and mealybugs.

Ampelopsis brevipedunculata
Ampelopsis

Ampelopsis loves the freshness of summer out of doors.

Nurseries sometimes call the ampelopsis *Vitis heterophylla variegata* because of its grapelike leaves. The correct botanical name is, nevertheless, *Ampelopsis brevipedunculata*. In garden centers you most often encounter the small-leaved hybrid form, *Ampelopsis brevipedunculata* var. *maximowiczii* 'Elegans'. It is a charming vine and hanging plant with red stems and green-, white-, or pink-marbled leaves, which it loses in fall if the location is too dark or the temperature too low. Bright conservatories are, therefore, the ideal locations for this viorously growing climbing shrub. There in a short time it will creep over walls, posts, and trellises.

Family: Vitaceae (grape family).

Origin: Eastern China.

Location: Bright (but not full sun) to semishady. In winter, as bright as possible. Only moderately warm all year around, preferably briskly cool. Winter over at about 41° to 54° F (5°–12° C). Loves a summer sojourn out of doors.

Watering, Feeding: Water freely in summer, less in winter. After the loss of leaves, keep almost dry during cool overwintering. From March to September feed every 14 days.

Further Culture: Repot plants, each spring, in all-purpose potting soil. In spring cut back hard.

Propagation: By tip or stem cuttings in summer.

Pests, Diseases: Spider mites and thrips after wintering over too warm.

Ananas
Pineapple

You need space for the ornamental pineapple.

Plants available are *Ananas comosus* var. *variegatus,* with green leaves striped in yellow and white; *Ananas comosus* var. *aureovariegatus,* with pink-tinged leaves; as well as *Ananas bracteatus,* which has a vivid red tuft of bracts over the fruit. They all form typical bromeliad rosettes of spiny toothed leaves up to 39 in. (1 m) long and, with a total diameter of 39 in. (1 m), need a great deal of space. On the other hand, the dwarf pineapple, *Ananas nanus,* develops rosettes that are only 8 in. (20 cm) across. Additionally, there are dwarf forms of *Ananas bracteatus* and varieties with smooth leaf margins. Important: Pineapple rosettes that have bloomed and fruited die out.
Family: Bromeliaceae (bromeliad family).
Origin: Tropical Central and South America.

Location: Bright; in winter, also sunny. Warm—over 68° F (20° C) all year long; in winter, not under 64° F (18° C).
Watering, Feeding: Water freely in summer with soft, room-temperature water; in winter, more sparingly. From May to September feed with weak concentration every 14 days.
Further Culture: The pineapple tolerates dry air. Every 2 years, in summer, repot in soilless mix or all-purpose potting soil.
Propagation: By offsets. Only separate when they are half as large as the mother plant. Or cut off the tuft of leaves at the top of the pineapple and root it in a soilless mix. Put a plastic bag over it (see page 59) and place it in a warm, bright spot.
Pests, Diseases: Rarely.
Warning: The leaf margins are dangerously sharp and pointed. Risk of cuts!

Araucaria heterophylla
Norfolk Island Pine

A very popular indoor tree—the Norfolk Island pine.

The discoverers of the Norfolk Island pine were the famous Captain Cook and the not less famous botanist Sir Joseph Banks. There are about 18 known species, but only this one is suitable for indoor culture. In its South Pacific home the Norfolk Island pine grows to a height of 197 ft (60 m).
Family: Araucariaceae (araucaria family).
Origin: Norfolk Island.
Location: Bright all around but not sunny. In the corner of a room it will grow slanting! In summer, at temperatures of 64° to 72° F (18°–22° C). Also put outdoors in a semi-shady spot with good air circulation. In winter keep cool, at least 41° F (5° C).
Watering, Feeding: Use only soft water. In spring, summer, and fall keep moderately damp; in winter water sparingly. From March to August feed with low concentration.
Further Culture: Provide high humidity with mist-ing. Repot every 2 to 3 years at most with a slightly acid potting medium, for example a blend of $2/3$ all-purpose soil with $1/3$ equal parts coarse sand and peat. Requires good drainage.
Propagation: By tip cuttings (cut from central leader), in December and January. Very difficult. Works only with rooting hormones and at very high soil temperatures.
Pests, Diseases: Drooping and degenerating branches as well as needle drop result from too warm a location that has poor air circulation. Same symptoms result from too much water in winter or too little water in the growing season. Since it cannot produce any new growth in the lower regions, the stem becomes bare all over.
My Tip: I have been very successful using rhodo-dendron food to fertilize my Norfolk Island pine.

The fresh, cool dampness of a sea breeze is the elixir of life for the Norfolk Island pine. Therefore you should mist it often and all over.

Asparagus
Asparagus

All of the some 300 *Asparagus* species are herbaceous or half-shrubs and are often very branching. What look like "leaves" or "needles" are false leaves (transformed side sprouts/phylloclads). The true leaves are usually changed into thorns.

Family: Liliaceae (lily family).

Origin: Africa, Asia.

Location: Very bright, but not sunny; the variety 'Sprengeri' also full sun. Room temperature year around at 68° F (20° C), in winter not under 50° F (10° C).

Watering, Feeding: Keep uniformly damp in summer, in winter water little. Feed weekly from March to August.

Further Culture: When completely potbound repot in all-purpose potting soil.

Propagation: By division or from seed in spring, at ground temperatures of 68° to 77° F (20°–25° C). When sowing, cover seeds with a thin layer of soil (dark germinators).

Pests, Diseases: Aphids, spider mites, and scale after overwintering in air that is too warm and too dry. Important: The plants are sensitive to insecticides.

Warning: The berries are poisonous.

Asparagus Collection
From top to bottom:
Asparagus setaceus 'Pyramidalis', *Asparagus acutifolius, Asparagus densiflorus* 'Meyeri', *Asparagus densiflorus, Asparagus falcatus.*

Aspidistra elatior
Barroom Plant, Cast-iron Plant

Beaucarnea recurvata
Ponytail Palm

The barroom plant grows and thrives everywhere.

The thickened stem serves as water storage.

Aspidistra elatior is very aptly called the cast-iron plant. For in fact this plant is extremely robust and manages even with the little light that staircases, hallways, and offices have to offer. It comes from the cool, shadowy mountain forests of Japan, grows to 39 in. (1 m) tall, and continually grows larger by means of its horizontally spreading rhizomes. The evergreen leaves become 28 to 31 in. (70–80 cm) long and 4 in. (10 cm) wide. They arise directly from the rhizome rolled up in a horn shape, and in the variety 'Variegata' they have yellow or white stripes. The insignificant flowers lie on the ground and are gray-violet.

Family: Liliaceae (lily family).

Origin: China, Japan.

Location: Bright to shady, never sunny. Fresh and cool all year long; in winter not under 50° F (10° C). However, the barroom plant also toler-ates warmer temperatures and dry indoor air. Keep colored-leaved varieties brighter and warmer over-all. The plants love a sum-mer sojourn out of doors.

Watering, Feeding: Keep moderately damp; in winter, almost dry. Avoid sogginess at all costs. From March to August feed every 2 weeks.

Further Culture: Repot in spring, but only when completely rootbound. Does well in all-purpose potting soil.

Propagation: By careful division of the rhizomes. Best time is March/April, when repotting.

Pests, Diseases: Root rot from standing water or leaf burn from blazing sunshine. Scale and spider mites in too warm a winter location.

My Tip: Fertilize the colored-leaved variety 'Variegata' less, because too much fertilizer causes the leaves to turn green.

Anyone who has seen the ponytail palm in its Mexican home is impress-ed. There it grows to a height of 26 to 33 ft (8–10 m), and is a many-branched shrub with down-curving, gray-green leaves almost 79 in. (2 m) long. But the most bizarre feature is the base of its stem. It can swell to a wide ball of 39 in. (1 m) in diameter and looks—as does the stem—scaly like the foot of an elephant. The extraordinary thick-ening serves the plant as a water reservoir against dry spells. Naturally, here the plant does not begin to reach the size it does in its home territory, but with good culture it can grow to 39 in. (1 m) tall in pot or tub and develop leaves that are 24 in. (60 cm) long.

Family: Agavaceae (agave family).

Origin: Mexico.

Location: Bright to full sun and good air circula-tion. In summer put out-side in a place protected from rain. In winter keep bright and cool, but not under 50° F (10° C).

Watering, Feeding: In summer, water moderate-ly; in winter keep nearly dry. Avoid standing water at all costs; it is lethal! From May to October fertilize every 4 weeks.

Further Culture: Repot every 2 to 3 years in all-purpose soil. Provide good drainage!

Propagation: By seed or side sprouts, which some-times appear.

Pests, Diseases: Spider mites and scale from too warm a winter location.

Begonia
Begonia, Leaf Begonia

Begonia masoniana 'Iron Cross', *Begonia boweri* hybrids, and *Begonia* 'Cleopatra' (from left to right).

The classic leaf begonias are the rex hybrids with their gigantic range of varieties. Their development goes back to the year 1858, when *Begonia rex* came to Europe and initiated a flurry of hybridizing that still persists today. *Begonia rex* could be crossed surprisingly well with other species, for instance with *Begonia diadema,* whose genes are still recognizable today. Rex begonias with diadema blood are identified by deeply lobed, toothed, longish leaves, whereas the classic rex begonias have almost completely smooth-edged, more rounded leaves. Bizarre oddities among the rex begonias are 'Comtesse Louise Erdody', with its snail-shaped rolled leaf base, as well as the purple-red-margined 'Bettina Rothschild', which attracts further attention with fire-red new growth. Frequently seen on the market, in addition to rex begonias, are the exotically spotted hybrids of *Begonia boweri,* Mexicross hybrids (which *Begonia boweri* and other leaf begonias have in their family tree), and *Begonia masoniana* 'Iron Cross', which bears a black marking resembling a cross on the spring-green leaves. These leaf begonias are also charming hanging plants. Anyone who wishes to collect them can order other hybrids or especially attractive rare botanical species from special begonia nurseries. Recommended are: *Begonia imperialis* 'Speculata' with green, irregular brown-bordered leaves; Begonia *heracleifolia* var. *nigricans* with hand-shaped, black-splotched leaves and light bristles on the undersides; then the red-black-leaved *Begonia* 'Halina'; the fern-leaved *Begonia foliosa;* as well as *Begonia goegoensis,* with shield-shaped, almost circular dark-green leaves and brilliant red leaf undersides. 'Sabi' enchants with its silver-washed foliage, as does the leaf begonia 'Trush' with pink pearls on the upper side of its leaves.

Family: Begoniaceae (begonia family).

Origin: Tropical and subtropical Asia, Americas, and Africa.

Location: Bright but not sunny. Warm all year long; winter temperature not under 61° F (16° C).

Watering, Feeding: Use only soft, room-temperature water. Keep moderately damp all year around, but never allow to dry out. Avoid sogginess and root ball dryness at all costs. Fertilize with low concentration every 14 days from March to September.

Further Culture: Provide for indirect humidity (see page 43). Never mist the leaves to avoid leaf spots. Repot only when thoroughly potbound, in spring, using all-purpose potting soil mixed with Styrofoam flakes. If necessary trim root ball; use shallow pot.

Propagation: From cuttings, leaf or root cuttings, or by division of rhizomes. Use a heatable propagation flat at a ground temperature of 75° F (24° C).

Pests, Diseases: Nematodes, true mildew, and root rot from bad location or errors in culture. Leaf drop in fall, as a rule, will be compensated for by new growth in spring.

My Tip: With rex begonias the leaves will become smaller if you don't pinch out the flowers.

Brachychiton rupestris
Queensland Bottle Tree

Gnarled like a bonsai—the Queensland bottle tree.

The bottle tree belongs to the same family as the cacao and cola trees. Of the 11 recognized species the best known is *Brachychiton rupestris* from Queensland. There, it grows to a height of 20 to 49 ft (6–15 m) and develops a striking bottle-shaped trunk, which in its habitat can have a diameter of more than 10 ft (3 m) at maturity. The gray-green leaves can be simple or compound on the same plant. In a pot, the effect of the thickened trunk base, which is often twisted, is interestingly bizarre. As in the *Beaucarnea* (see photograph, page 147), which shares the popular name of "bottle tree," the thickened trunk serves as a water reservoir for times of drought. *Brachychiton rupestris* is also sold as a bonsai.
Family: Sterculiaceae (sterculia family).
Origin: Eastern Australia.

Location: Very bright to full sun. In summer, at 64° to 68° F (18°–20° C), from June on also place outdoors in a spot that is protected from rain. In winter, no cooler than 50° F (10° C).
Watering, Feeding: Water little, keep rather dry. Avoid sogginess at all costs. From March to September feed with low concentration every 4 weeks.
Further Culture: Repot in spring when completely potbound, in all-purpose potting soil. Mixing sand in will improve water permeability.
Propagation: From tip cuttings and from seed.
Pests, Diseases: Spider mites and scale in too warm and dark a winter location. "Keeling over" of plant is caused by too much water.

Caladium
Mother-in-Law Plant, Caladium

There are also caladiums with red and pink variations.

The caladiums obtainable commercially are, generally speaking, crosses and are called *Caladium bicolor* or *Schomburgkii* hybrids. There are snow-white, pink, and red-flecked or marbled varieties. The colored-leaved marvels are often bought as tuberous root stocks from which the magnificent leaves will develop in the summer. In fall they die back. Only the tubers are wintered over.
Family: Araceae (arum family).
Origin: Tropical America, especially Brazil.
Location: Bright to semi-shade; no sun. Uniformly warm soil and air temperatures over 68° F (20° C).
Watering, Feeding: Keep plants that are leafed out uniformly damp from spring to August, then do not water any more so that the leaves can slowly dry out. From March to July feed weekly.
Further Culture: Provide for indirect humidity (see page 43). To winter over, leave tubers in the old soil until growth starts (or remove and place in peat) and store at 64° F (18° C). In January/February lay stored tubers in all-purpose potting soil. Keep the pot in a bright spot and keep damp and quite warm (air and soil temperatures at 77° to 79° F [25°–26° C]). Already developed plants are accustomed to 72° F (22° C).
Propagation: By separation of side tubers after development of some leaves. Or, with larger plants, by division of tuber after wintering over, as soon as they have developed sprouts 6 in. (15 cm) long.
Pests, Diseases: Aphids on new growth from indoor air that is too dry.
Warning: Contains irritants to skin and mucous membranes.

Divide only after new growth shows is the rule for anyone who wants to propagate the caladium. The reason: Before the new growth, the eyes on the tuber are very difficult to recognize, so you may cut into them.

Calathea
Calathea

Ceropegia woodii
Rosary Vine, Hearts-on-a-String

Calathea zebrina—one of the many recognized varieties.

The rosary vine is decorative and undemanding.

Enclosed flower windows, vitrines, or warm, humid greenhouses are favorite places for this inhabitant of the tropical rain forests. Thanks to horticultural art, however, there are also calatheas that get along very well in the house, especially *Calathea makoyana*. It has oval leaves that have olive-green spots on a cream-colored ground and grows to a height of 12 in. (30 cm). *Calathea lancifolia* has oblong leaves 12 in. (30 cm) long carried on stems 4 to 12 in. (10–30 cm) in length. Silver-white leaf blades with green margins decorate the foliage of *Calathea picturata* 'Argentea'; light double lines parallel to the side veins distinguish *Calathea ornata* 'Roseo-Lineata', while *Calathea zebrina* is marked with light green.

Family: Marantaceae (maranta family).

Origin: Tropical America.

Location: Bright to semi-shady all year around; no sun. Days, 68° F (20° C); nights, not under 61° F (16° C). When soil temperature is not warm enough, growth is impeded; in too dark a spot the leaf coloration is impaired.

Watering, Feeding: Keep moderately damp with soft, room-temperature water. Feed every 14 days with low concentration from March to August.

Further Culture: Provide high humidity with misting. Repot yearly in summer, using all-purpose potting soil. Mix Styrofoam flakes into the soil.

Propagation: By division of root stock at repotting.

Pests, Diseases: Spider mites and scale; rolled leaves from centrally heated air. Seen more often lately: *Calathea crocata*, a beauty in leaf and flower with saffron-yellow inflorescences.

Of 160 known species, only *Ceropegia woodii* plays a role as a house-plant. It is a succulent drought beater with fleshy leaves and a tuberous root stock. Its threadlike shoots, up to 79 in. (2 m) long, are furnished at intervals with small, heart-shaped leaves with silvery markings. This trailing growth makes it one of the prettiest hanging plants we have. In summer, there appear in the leaf axils little round tubers that quickly develop roots upon contact with the earth. The small flowers consist of a flesh-colored tubular corolla, which ends in five dark-brown points. These give the flower the appearance of a little umbrella or a lamp.

Family: Asclepiadaceae (milkweed family).

Origin: Rhodesia, Cape Colony.

Location: Very bright to full sun. In summer, warm; in winter, cooler, but not under 54° F (12° C). Average indoor temperatures are also tolerated.

Watering, Feeding: Keep slightly damp all year around; water only seldom in a cool winter location. From March to August feed with weak solution every 4 weeks.

Further Culture: Repot in spring every 2 to 3 years in all-purpose soil mixed with $^1/_3$ sand.

Propagation: From small tubers or stem cuttings. Allow cut surfaces to dry before planting.

Pests, Diseases: Rare.

My Tip: Several rosary plants hanging from the frame of a south window create a decorative "plant curtain" that needs minimum care.

Chlorophytum comosum

Spider Plant, Spider Ivy

○ 🪣 🫗 🧱

The spider plant, *Chlorophytum comosum,* forms thick clumps of rosettes, arching shoots with small white flowers, and many offsets. It thrives everywhere. The original form is green-leaved, but the striped varieties are better known.

Family: Liliaceae (lily family).

Origin: South Africa.

Location: Sunny, bright, or semishade. Room temperature all year around. In summer, place outdoors from June on.

Watering, Feeding: Keep uniformly damp all year long. Never allow the soil to dry out, but never overwater either. The roots rot easily. Feed weekly from March to August.

Further Culture: Mist plant now and then in warm and dry conditions. As soon as the roots rise above the edge of the pot, repot in all-purpose potting soil. Choose a roomy pot.

Propagation: Any time, from offsets.

Pests, Diseases: Aphids in too warm and dry a winter location. Brown leaf tips from too little or too much water. Cracked leaves from too warm a location without enough light.

From Runner to New Plant in No Time
Spider plants are easy to care for and are quickly surrounded by masses of offsets.

Cissus
Grape Ivy, Treebine

A beautiful variety—*Cissus antarctica* 'Ellen Danica'.

The following species have proved themselves for houseplant culture: *Cissus antarctica,* the kangaroo vine, which is a strong climber and produces shoots over 10 ft (3 m) long with firm, glossy-green simple leaves with saw-toothed edges. *Cissus rhombifolia,* the Venezuela treebine, is, as the botanical name suggests, furnished with diamond-shaped leaves. Its most beautiful variety, 'Ellen Danica', is distinguished by its coarsely serrated leaves, which sometimes have reddish hairs, and grows more compactly. Both species are outstanding vines and hanging plants and suitable for covering trellises and room dividers. *Cissus discolor* and *Cissus amazonica* are both suitable for warm, humid flower windows.

Family: Vitaceae (grape family).

Origin: Tropics.

Location: Bright to semishady; no sun. For *Cissus antarctica* and *Cissus rhombifolia,* year-round temperatures between 61° and 68° F (16°–20° C); in winter, even around 50° F (10° C) is suitable. For *Cissus discolor* and *Cissus amazonica,* over 68° F (20° C) all year around.

Watering, Feeding: Keep uniformly slightly damp. In cooler temperatures water less. Feed weekly from March to August.

Further Culture: Repot young plants every spring, mature ones only as necessary in all-purpose potting soil. Bare shoots can be cut back anytime.

Propagation: From tip and stem cuttings, in heatable propagation flats.

Pests, Diseases: Leaf drop or leaf spots from poor location and culture. Mildew and other fungus diseases from too wet a soil in winter.

Clusia rosea
Balsam apple

The Clusia is related to our St. John's wort.

The balsam apple belongs to a genus of epiphytic trees or shrubs and in its native habitat is found on and between rocks. The branches are thick, the twisted leaves evergreen and leathery, with lengths of 8 to 12 in. (20–30 cm) not a rarity. The rose-colored, fragrant blossoms resemble large camellias. They are filled with golden-yellow stamens, and the seed capsule that develops from them may be as large as a golf ball. Unfortunately these seldom appear in pot culture. But its attractive leaves alone make *Clusia,* which has many similarities to the rubber plant, a handsome green plant with great decorative value.

Family: Clusiaceae, formerly Guttiferae (garcinia family).

Origin: Tropical and subtropical America.

Location: Bright to semishady; no sun. Warm all year around, even in winter not below 64° F (18° C). From June can be set outdoors in a warm place protected from sun.

Watering, Feeding: Always keep moderately damp. Use soft, room-temperature water. During growing season feed with weak concentration every 14 days.

Further Culture: Mist often. As necessary, repot in spring in all-purpose potting soil.

Propagation: From tip cuttings, in a heatable propagation bed and at ground temperatures between 77° and 86° F (25°–30° C).

Pests, Diseases: Rare.

Codiaeum
Croton

The exuberantly colored leaves are hungry for light.

The croton is a well-known shrub from the Moluccas and colorful as a cheerful parrot among the leaf plants. There are countless variations of the only species under cultivation at present, *Codiaeum variegatum* var. *pictum*. The leathery leaves can be large, simple or lobed, small, straplike, and turned on themselves in addition. The color palette ranges from green through yellow, orange, red, to purple-red and almost black-green nuances. Among the color patterns there are spots, veining, mottling, or stripes. Since the leaves only begin to color when mature, you often see foliage of different colors on the same plant.

Family: Euphorbiaceae (spurge family).
Origin: Southeast Asia.
Location: Bright but not sunny. Without enough light, the strong colors fade. Warm all year round and as humid as possible. Avoid drafts, cold feet, and winter temperatures below 61° F (16° C).

Watering, Feeding: In spring and summer keep uniformly damp. From September to March water less. From March to August feed weekly with lowered concentration.

Further Culture: Mist often or provide for indirect humidity (see page 43). Repot young plants every 2 years, older ones only as necessary, in all-purpose potting soil mixed with Styrofoam flakes.

Propagation: From January to March, from tip and stem cuttings, at 77° to 86° F (25°–30° C). Dip cut ends in charcoal powder so that the white milky juice will not leak out. Air layering is another possibility.

Pests, Diseases: Scale or spider mites in air that is too dry. Leaf drop and bare stems from poor culture.

Warning: Poison plant.

Codonanthe crassifolia
Codonanthe

The milky juice is irritating to skin and mucous membranes. The codonanthe has trailing, woody, red-tinged shoots. The leaves are opposite, leathery, and slightly succulent, which the species' name, *Codonanthe crassifolia*, acknowledges. The trumpet-shaped flowers are white with red markings inside. The codonanthe is a pretty hanging plant, which does best in a climate-controlled flower window.

Family: Gesneriaceae (gesneriad family).
Origin: Tropical America.
Location: Very bright, but not sunny, all year around, and warm—preferably over 68°F (20° C). In winter keep cooler for 4 weeks—around 59°F (15°C)—and almost dry. This promotes bud development.

Watering, Feeding: Keep root ball only slightly damp. From March to end of August feed with low concentration every 2 weeks.

Further Culture: Mist frequently. Repot in February/March or after flowering, in African violet potting soil which has been mixed with Styrofoam flakes for better soil aeration.

Propagation: From not-yet-woody cuttings (with at least 3 pairs of leaves) in early summer. Simply stick the cuttings into the damp propagating medium. Important: Needs ground warmth. Large plants can also be divided.

Pests, Diseases: Aphids. Bud drop from change of location, temperature swings, or too much or too little water.

Codonanthe needs high humidity.

Coleus-Blumei Hybrids
Flame Nettle, Painted Leaves, Coleus

In a sunny spot the leaves flame like a fire.

The flame nettle is one of the most rewarding and colorful houseplants we know. All the plants available are cultivars and come in an astonishing multiplicity of colors. With white, cream, green, various shades of red, pink, and violet, the flame nettle paints bordered, veined, marbled, blazed, and striped leaf blades, each different from the next. The plant is a half-shrub, has a square stem like our stinging nettle, and grows about 20 in. (50 cm) tall. Its insignificant blue flowers resemble those of sage. The small-leaved *Coleus pumilus* is a particularly low-growing species. It trails and is a wonderful hanging plant with its red-white, green bordered leaves.

Family: Labiatae, also Lamiaceae (mint family).
Origin: Tropical Asia and Africa. Only hybrid forms are on the market.

Location: Full sun all year round, otherwise loses color and compact growth. In winter room temperature should never fall below 46° C (8° C).
Watering, Feeding: In summer water freely, otherwise the leaves wilt. In winter keep only moderately damp. Feed every 8 to 14 days from March to August.
Further Culture: Cut back hard in spring and repot in all-purpose potting soil.
Propagation: From tip cuttings (they root in water or potting medium), or by seed in a warmed bed. Trim young plants several times so that they will bush out nicely.
Pests, Diseases: Spider mites in too dry a winter location. Whitefly.
My Tip: Producing flowers costs the coleus strength and leads to smaller leaves. Therefore, pinch out buds when they first appear.

Cordyline
Ti Plant

Cordyline fruticosa develops a trunk in maturity.

Cordylines have white, club-shaped thickened roots. Well-known species are: *Cordyline fruticosa* and its varieties, with long-stemmed, broadly lanceolate, red variegated striped leaves, grows about 39 in. (1 m) high. *Cordyline australis* and *Cordyline indivisa* on the other hand have small leaves, which are red-striped in some varieties.
Family: Agavaceae (agave family).
Location: *Cordyline fruticosa*, bright but not sunny; warm and humid all year. An enclosed flower window is ideal. *Cordyline australis* and *Cordyline indivisa*, full sun. In summer place outside, in winter cool temperatures of 41° to 50° F (5°–10° C).
Watering, Feeding: Keep *Cordyline fruticosa* slightly damp all year around. Avoid sogginess, or the fleshy roots will rot. Water the other species moderately in summer; in winter, seldom. From March to August feed every 14 days with low concentration.
Further Culture: Mist plants often or provide for indirect humidity (see page 43). In spring repot as necessary in all-purpose potting soil.
Propagation: *Cordyline fruticosa*, mostly from tip cuttings with 6 to 10 leaves; also from stem pieces with 3 to 6 leaf scars laid horizontally on the potting medium; these can be divided after growth begins. *Cordyline australis* and *Cordyline indivisa*, from seed in January/February.
Pests, Diseases: Spider mites, scale, or thrips in dry, heated air; for the "cool" kinds, also from too warm a winter location.

Corynocarpus laevigatus
Corynocarpus

Like a rubber tree—*Corynocarpus.*

This evergreen shrub, with its rounded, oval, dark-green leaves, is a splendid decorative plant for bright, not too warm areas. Of the four or five species in the genus, *Corynocarpus laevigatus* is the only species under culture. Its botanical species name probably has to do with the smooth, rubber-plant-like character of the leaves (Latin: *laevigatus* = smooth). The genus name on the other hand refers to the form of the fruit (Greek: *koryne* = club, *karpos* = fruit). In nature the corynocarpus has oblong, orange stone fruit, whose pits are very poisonous. In our part of the world the flowers and fruits never appear, however.
Family: Corynocarpaceae (corynocarpus family).
Origin: New Zealand.
Location: All year around, very bright. In summer, around 68° F (20° C); in spring/winter, 41° to 50° F (5°–10° C).

The plant loves fresh air out of doors in summer.
Watering, Feeding: Keep moderately damp all year. Water less in cool winter location. From March to August feed every 14 days.
Further Culture: Repot as necessary, in spring, using all-purpose potting soil.
Propagation: In January/February or August/September, by stem or tip cuttings in ground temperatures around 68° F (20° C). Clip young plants often so that they will branch nicely.
Pests, Diseases: Scale and spider mites in too warm and dry a winter location.
Warning: The seeds of the corynocarpus are very poisonous.

Crassula arborescens
Silver Jade Plant

Crassula ovata is also good as a bonsai.

Of the more than 300 known *Crassula* species, *Crassula arborescens* and the very similar *Crassula ovata* have become the most familiar as houseplants. Both develop round to oval, succulent, silver-gray or glossy green leaves, grow bushy and treelike (arborescens), and soon develop into imposing, gnarled-looking plants of more than 39 in. (1 m) in height and breadth. The plants thus become quite heavy. The silver jade tree can, with good culture, grow very old and produces small red or white flowers, but seldom before 10 years.
Family: Crassulaceae (orpine family).
Origin: South Africa.
Location: Bright to full sun, but not directly in front of a window with full midday sun. Warm in summer—even outside in a bright (not sunny), and rain-protected spot. In winter, cool, if possible around 50° F (10° C).

When wintering too warm, leaf drop and ugly extended stems can be experienced.
Watering, Feeding: In summer keep moderately damp in the house, give somewhat more water outdoors. In winter keep almost dry. In summer months feed once a month with cactus fertilizer.
Further Culture: Repot as necessary in spring or summer in ²/₃ all-purpose potting soil mixed with ¹/₃ sand. Use heavy pots with good stability!
Propagation: From tip cuttings, which root easily in a peat-sand mixture or a soilless mix. Allow cut surfaces to dry for a few days.
Pests, Diseases: Mealybugs from too warm a winter situation. Root lice.
My Tip: The sickle plant, *Crassula falcata,* and other *Crassula* species are cared for the same way.

Pots for the silver jade plant must be stable and heavy when it gets older. In addition, place coarse gravel on the surface of the soil.

Cryptanthus
Earth Star

The earth star is a typical ground dweller.

The dry forests of Brazil are the home of the earth star. Accordingly, it is provided with tough leaves that dry air cannot injure too much. In contrast to most of the epiphytic bromeliads, it roots in the ground. Soil culture is therefore the correct way to cultivate the earth star, although it is sometimes offered for sale bound to an epiphyte support where it usually dries up. Best known are *Cryptanthus bivittatus,* with white- or pink-striped wavy leaves, and *Cryptanthus acaulis* with gray-scaled pink or brownish leaves, which can be as long as 3 to 8 in. (8–20 cm). The earth star forms flat, star-shaped rosettes, in whose center hides an insignificant white flower. This gives it the species name: from Greek, *kryptos* = hidden and *anthos* = flower.
Family: Bromeliaceae (bromeliad family).
Origin: Brazil.

Location: Bright to semi-shade; in winter, sunny too. Warm, all year long, between 68° to 72° F (20°–22° C). Ideal are flower windows, vitrines, bottle gardens, and terrariums.
Watering, Feeding: Keep uniformly damp. From March to August feed every 14 days with low concentration.
Further Culture: Provide high humidity. In a window in summer, mist daily; in winter, every 2 weeks. Repot as necessary in all-purpose potting soil.
Propagation: From offsets, which should be half as large as the mother plant before they are separated.
Warning: The earth star contains skin irritants.

Ctenanthe
Ctenanthe

Ctenanthe oppenheimiana 'Variegata'.

Of about 10 species in the genus, all of which are at home in the Brazilian rain forest, *Ctenanthe oppenheimiana* and *Ctenanthe lubbersiana* have proved to be the best as house-plants. Therefore, the best place for these members of the maranta family is the warm, humid flower window. Ctenanthes are foliage beauties and develop leaves up to 16 in. (40 cm) long, which are spotted or striped on the upper side. *Ctenanthe oppenheimiana,* as well as its varieties 'Variegata' and 'Tricolor' can be recognized by the red stems and red undersides of the leaves. All grow almost 39 in. (1 m) high and just as wide, since they send out runners. *Ctenanthe lubbersiana* is somewhat daintier and shorter—24 to 31 in. (60–80 cm).
Family: Marantaceae (maranta family).
Origin: Brazil.

Location: Very bright, but not full sun. In too dark a spot it loses its beautiful leaf markings. Warm all year around, more than 68° F (20° C)—even in winter, never under 64° F (18° C). Soil warmth is very important.
Watering, Feeding: Keep uniformly damp at all times with soft, room-temperature water. Feed every 14 days during the growing season with a low concentration.
Further Culture: Mist plants often and provide for indirect humidity (see page 43). In spring or early summer repot with all-purpose soil mixed with Styrofoam flakes.
Propagation: *Ctenanthe oppenheimiana,* by division; *Ctenanthe lubbersiana,* by cutting off the tuft of leaves at the end of the stem. Rooting only takes place in a warm soil and humid air.
Pests, Diseases: Rolled leaves from sun damage and air that is too dry.

Cupressus macrocarpa
Monterey Cypress

Cycas revoluta
Sago Palm, Japanese Sago Palm

The Monterey cypress grows very quickly.

Precious and expensive—a large *Cycas* specimen.

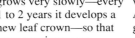

The Monterey cypress, a non-winter-hardy conifer from California, has quickly become popular as an indoor plant. Among other reasons, this is because one can trim the natural pyramid shape of this evergreen into such beautiful decorative miniature standards. Pruning back is unavoidable indoors anyway, since the cypress species grow very quickly and try as much as possible to attain their genetically programmed tree mass. The variety 'Goldcrest', which has attractive golden needles, is most often seen on the market.

Family: Cupressaceae (cypress family).

Origin: Southern California.

Location: Bright to semishady. In summer best outdoors in a bright but not sunny spot. Warm summer temperatures and cool winters—41° to 50°F (5°–10° C)—are ideal. A better location is an unheated conservatory.

Watering, Feeding: In summer keep uniformly damp. In winter, in lower temperature, water less; in warmth, water more. Avoid either dried-out root ball or sogginess. From March to September feed every 4 weeks at the most, otherwise the Monterey cypress will grow even faster.

Further Culture: Repot, as necessary, in spring or fall. Use all-purpose potting soil mixture.

Propagation: By tip cuttings in summer, in a heated propagation bed. Difficult.

Pests, Diseases: Spider mites in too warm a winter location.

The attractive sago palm is one of the oldest plants on earth and has only external appearances in common with the more recently evolved palms. It grows very slowly—every 1 to 2 years it develops a new leaf crown—so that large specimens are measured in inches (or centimeters) and can cost as much as a small car. The leathery fronds, which grow out of a central bromeliadlike stem, produce a very decorative effect. Plants in the market are exclusively young plants of *Cycas revoluta* (often also as bonsai).

Family: Cycadaceae (cycad family).

Origin: Southeast Asia, Japan.

Location: Bright but no sun. In summer keep warm; older specimens can go outdoors. In winter, cool—around 54° to 59° F (12°–15° C).

Watering, Feeding: Keep uniformly damp in summer; in winter water less. Allow soil to dry between waterings but never let it dry out completely. At all costs avoid sogginess. Fertilize with low dosage every week from March to August. Experts swear by guano or dried cow manure.

Further Culture: Repot every 2 to 5 years in all-purpose soil mixed with sand.

Propagation: From seed, at room temperatures of 86° F (30° C). Difficult and lengthy.

Pests, Diseases: Mealybugs in too warm a winter location with poor air circulation. Scale.

Warning: Highly toxic if consumed.

Umbrella Sedge, Galingale

Cyperus albostriatus doesn't like to stand in water.

Graceful culm of *Cyperus alternifolius.*

Umbrella sedges inhabit damp ground and swamps, and as houseplants, too, they like to have wet feet. The characteristic mark of most of the *Cyperus* species is an umbrellalike head of leaves. The insignificant little umbellate flowers appear almost all year long. There are some 600 species, of which *Cyperus alternifolius,* its white variety 'Variegatus', the subspecies ssp. *flabelliformis, Cyperus albostriatus, Cyperus gracilis,* and *Cyperus haspan* are important as houseplants.

• *Cyperus alternifolius* grows to more than 39 in. (1 m) tall and has finely grooved striped stems, on the end of which sits a dense head of leaves about 10 in. (25 cm) long, with an unremarkable brown flower in the middle. The white variety becomes green with increasing age and with too much nourishment.

• *Cyperus albostriatus* has shorter stems and broader leaves with rough edges. It is often sold under the incorrect name of *Cyperus diffusus.*

• *Cyperus gracilis* grows only 12 in. (30 cm) high.

• *Cyperus haspan* looks like a little papyrus plant and gets to be 12 to 20 in. (30–50 cm) tall.

• *Cyperus papyrus,* the true papyrus plant, provides a particularly exotic flair. It attains a height of more than 6 ft (2 m), develops an elegant head of loosely drooping, threadlike leaves, and a large, hundred-rayed umbellate flower. Now and then it is sold as a fully grown plant, but you can also raise it from seed yourself.

All are related to such prominent nut plants as the nut sedge (*Cyperus esculentus*).

Family: Cyperaceae (sedge family).

Origin: Tropics, subtropics, temperate regions.

Location: Bright to sunny, warm all year around. All, with the exception of *Cyperus albostriatus,* may be placed outdoors at the end of May. In winter keep somewhat cooler.

Watering, Feeding: Keep very wet in a warm, bright location. The saucer should be full constantly. Exception: *Cyperus albostriatus.* This broader-leaved species does not require foot baths. It is enough to keep the root ball uniformly damp. With the other species also remove foot baths at winter temperatures of 54° to 59° F (12°–15° C). For pot culture, feed every 1 to 2 weeks from April to August with a weak dosage.

Further Culture: In heated areas in winter, provide for indirect humidity and give the plants a shower often. If necessary, repot in the spring in ²/₃ all-purpose potting soil and ¹/₃ perlite and sand in equal proportions.

Propagation: By division of plants or by cutting of the "umbrella" with a 2-inch (5 cm) stem. Shorten leaves by ¹/₃ and root in room-temperature water (see drawing, page 60). Another way to propagate is by seed. Seeds are available for *Cyperus alternifolius, Cyperus esculentus,* and *Cyperus papyrus.* Do not cover seeds and put in a very light place—*Cyperus* are light germinators.

Pests, Diseases: Brown leaf tips from dry air or hard or acid water, torn leaves from too cool a situation. Spider mites and thrips also from dry air.

My Tip: Seldom fertilize specimens planted in water pools or aquariums and then only in very small amounts; otherwise, there is a danger of developing surplus salts in the water.

158

Dieffenbachia
Dumb Cane

One of the numerous *dieffenbachia* hybrids.

Best known varieties of dumb cane are the *Dieffenbachia-Amoena* hybrid 'Tropic Snow' with large, long 23 in. (60 cm), creamy-white-marbled leaves; *Dieffenbachia bowmannii* 'Camilla' with leaves 29 in. (75 cm) long that have light-green markings; or the less vigorous *Dieffenbachia maculata* with white-and-green spotted leaves.

Family: Araceae (arum family).

Origin: Tropical Central and South America.

Location: Bright to semi-shade; never sunny. In a location that's too dark the variegated leaves turn green. Keep warm all year around; in winter, never under 46° F (8° C). Avoid drafts and fluctuations of temperature.

Watering, Feeding: Keep damp throughout the year with soft, room-temperature water. In winter water more sparingly. In summer fertilize weekly with a low dosage.

Further Culture: Provide for indirect humidity (see page 43) or mist often. Repot every 2 years in spring, using all-purpose potting soil mixed with Styrofoam flakes. Cut back older plants that have completely lost their leaves. They will put out new growth.

Propagation: By tip cuttings or pieces of stem, in heated propagation flats or at a soil temperature of 77° F (25° C). Place pieces of stem horizontally on the surface of the potting medium with the eyes facing upward.

Pests, Diseases: Spider mites, thrips, and aphids from dry centrally heated air. Root rot from wet soil and fungus diseases from poor location and conditions.

Warning: All parts of the plant are poisonous. Its juice is irritating to skin and mucous membranes.

Dizygotheca
False Aralia

Dainty and elegant—*Dizygotheca elegantissima.*

The false aralia is a child of the exotic South Sea islands and there develops into evergreen bushes or trees. *Dizygotheca elegantissima* is, as its botanical name indicates, a very elegant sight with its fili-greelike foliage. As a rule, it grows from a central stem and even in the house it can reach a height of almost 7 ft (2 m). The seven to eleven narrow, long simple leaves are arranged like the fingers of a hand on a thin stem. In the juvenile stage they are reddish and delicate, later, dark olive green and somewhat broader. Only recently available commercially is *Dizygotheca veitchii* 'Castor'.

Family: Araliaceae (aralia family).

Origin: South Seas.

Location: Bright, but not sunny. All year requires soil and air temperatures that are uniformly warm-over 68° F (20° C). Ideal is a warm, humid flower window. Avoid drafts, or leaves will drop!

Watering, Feeding: Keep uniformly damp with soft, room-temperature water. No sogginess or dryness; both are lethal to the plants. In winter water less. From March to August feed every 14 days.

Further Culture: Mist often. Repot young plants every 2 years in all-purpose potting soil, older plants only as necessary. Can be cut back if growth is too leggy. This does, however, interfere with the plant's naturally characteristic growth.

Propagation: From seed, which must be fresh; or from tip cuttings. Difficult.

Pests, Diseases: Spider mites and scale in a winter location with dry air and too little light. Leaf drop in too wet or cool a location and dried leaf tips from low humidity or dried root ball.

Dizygotheca veitchii 'Castor'.

Bushy-growing—*Dracaena surculosa* 'Florida Beauty'.

The fragrant *Dracaena fragrans* 'Massangeana'.

Although dracaenas in their native habitats and in maturity look very similar

Charming Diversity of Dracaenas

1 *Dracaena draco*
2 *Dracaena sanderiana*
3 *Dracaena surculosa* 'Florida Beauty'
4 *Dracaena fragrans* 'Massangeana'
5 *Dracaena deremensis* 'Warneckii'
6 *Dracaena marginata* 'Tricolor'
7 *Dracaena congesta*
8 *Dracaena marginata*
9 *Dracaena glauca*
10 *Dracaena sanderiana*
11 *Dracaena fragrans* 'Victoria'

to palms, they are no more related to that plant family than are the yuccas. Indeed, they are frequently confused with *Cordyline* (see page 154). The best distinguishing feature is the roots. Dracaenas have orange-yellow, smooth roots, whereas those of the *Cordyline* species are white and thickened like clubs. Dracaenas are among the most popular and frequently propagated foliage plants. Therefore there are numerous species and varieties on the market.

• *Dracaena marginata* may be the best known. It forms heads of very narrow, arching, pendulous leaves, which can be green or, as in the variety 'Tricolor', striped with pink, cream, and green.

• *Dracaena fragrans*, the fragrant dracaena, is also frequently cultivated. It has broad, greenish-yellow or green-and-white-striped leaves.

• *Dracaena deremensis* has blue-green leaves with decorative white edges.

• *Dracaena sanderiana* is striped with whitish-yellow or silver gray.

• *Dracaena reflexa* has olive-green, cream-color-edged foliage. Its most beautiful variety is 'Song of India'.

• *Dracaena surculosa* (syn. *Dracaena godsefiana*) is a tropical beauty, a priority for a flower window.

Family: Agavaceae (agave family).

Origin: Canary Islands, tropical and subtropical Africa, Madagascar, Asia, and southeast Asian islands.

Location: Bright to semi-shady but not full sun. Colored-leaved varieties basically as bright as possible so that the leaves won't turn green. Warm all year around, 64° to 77° F (18°–25° C).

Watering, Feeding: Keep slightly damp at all times. No sogginess or ball dryness, otherwise, leaves may drop. Feed every 2 weeks from March to August.

Further Culture: Mist often. Repot every 2 years in all-purpose potting soil. Cutting back is possible at any time.

Propagation: The colored varieties can only be propagated vegetatively, that is, from pieces of stem, tip, or stem cuttings. Use a heatable propagation flat at a ground temperature of 77° F (25° C). Other species (for example *Dracaena surculosa* and *Dracaena draco,* the dragon tree) are propagated from seed.

Pests, Diseases: Browned leaf edges, scale, and spider mites from dry centrally heated air. Dried up leaf tips from incorrect watering. Root rot from cold, damp feet.

My Tip: Dracaenas will not tolerate any sprays for glossy leaves.

Pothos

Epipremnum pinnatum

Pothos is decorative and undemanding.

Pothos develops long shoots up to 33 ft (10 m) long and is suitable for hanging plants and for lush covering of room dividers or conservatory walls. Almost exclusively the variety available in the market is 'Aureum'. The juvenile form develops heart-shaped, green-and-gold-patterned leaves, which with age can be considerably larger and lobed. The plant is sometimes sold under its old name of *Scindapsus*.

Family: Araceae (arum family).

Origin: Solomon Islands in the Pacific.

Location: Light, semi-shady to shady. But: In too dark a location very long intervals develop between leaves, the leaves get green and remain small. Room temperature or warmer all year around; in winter, not under 61° F (16° C).

Watering, Feeding: Keep uniformly damp. From March to August feed weekly.

Further Culture: Repot every 2 years in all-purpose potting soil. Cutting back is possible at any time.

Propagation: From tip or stem cuttings, which also root in water. Put several young plants in one pot.

Pests, Diseases: Root rot and leaf drop in too damp or too dark a location.

My Tip: If you want to grow pothos on a trellis or wall, you may manage better with hydroculture, since that way you avoid the need for repotting.

Warning: Contains irritants to skin and mucous membranes.

Spindle Tree, Japanese Spindle Tree

Euonymus japonica

Euonymous japonica and variety 'Aureovariegata' (left).

The European spindle tree (*Euonymus europea*), the winter-hardy species of the genus *Euonymus,* is a well-known garden plant. For house culture and for the cool conservatory, only the Japanese species, *Euonymus japonica,* is suitable. It can attain a height of 39 in. (1 m) in pot or tub, sometimes even more. The leaves are oval, slightly toothed, and glossily leathery. Popular are colored-leaved varieties like 'Aureomarginata', 'Macrophylla', 'Pyramidata', as well as the small-leaved variety 'Microphylla'. They all are available as houseplants, but they only retain their beauty if they are treated like tub plants, that is, summered over out of doors after the middle of May and kept quite cool over the winter.

Family: Celastraceae (staff-tree family).

Origin: Japan, Korea, Ryukyu Islands.

Location: Bright to semi-shade, even sunny in winter so that it doesn't lose the leaf coloring. From March to August at around 64° F (18° C); from October to February no warmer than 50° F (10° C). Provide more warmth for higher humidity. Summer outdoors.

Watering, Feeding: From March to September water freely and feed every 14 days. Afterward, water less and do not fertilize anymore.

Further Culture: In spring repot as necessary, in all-purpose potting soil. Cutting back or trimming for shape can be done at the same time.

Propagation: By tip cuttings, from August to September. Use a heatable propagation flat at ground temperatures between 68° and 77°F (20°–25°C).

Pests, Diseases: Scale, leaf drop, and mildew in too warm a winter location.

Euphorbia
Spurge

Cactuslike *Euphorbia pseudocactus.*

The spurge family, the fourth largest plant family, also includes cactuslike leafless succulents. They are bizarre, undemanding plants, not a few of which look enough like cacti to be confusing. Those most commonly seen on the market are: *Euphorbia pseudocactus, Euphorbia tirucalli, Euphorbia erythraeae, Euphorbia balsamifera,* and *Euphorbia grandicornis.*
Family: Euphorbiaceae (spurge family).
Origin: Africa.
Location: Bright to full sun. Warm in summer; in winter 59° to 64° F (15°–18° C). Can be placed outdoors for summer in a rain-protected spot.
Watering, Feeding: In spring and summer water only a little, in fall and winter, much less indeed. Best to water from the bottom. Feed from April to September with cactus fertilizer in weak concentration.

Further Culture: As necessary, repot in spring in cactus soil with ¼ all-purpose potting soil.
Propagation: Depending on species, from seed, cut-off parts, or cuttings. Hold cut surfaces under lukewarm water (stops flow of milky juice and keeps it from gumming up the cut surfaces). Allow cut areas to dry before planting.
Pests, Diseases: Rare.
Warning: Euphorbias are poisonous to humans and animals. The milky juice contains irritants to skin and mucous membranes. Do not allow juice to get into eyes and be careful about open cuts or scratches! With some species you can receive injury from the thorns.

Euphorbia tirucalli thrives in hydroculture.

Fatshedera lizei
Aralia Ivy, Tree Ivy

Fatshedera does well in the shade.

The botanical name of the tree ivy results from the fact that it is not an established genus but a cross of the *Fatsia japonica* and English ivy (*Hedera helix*). The aralia ivy grows about 5 ft (1.5 m) tall and forms upright stems with dark-green, glossy leaves, which have mostly three and up to five lobes. The variety 'Variegata' has beautiful white leaves and is a little less vigorous in its upward growth.
Family: Araliaceae (aralia family).
Origin: None, since it's an entirely hybrid form.
Location: Bright to semishady, the variety 'Variegata' always bright, or the colored leaves will turn green. Room temperature all year around, well-grown specimens even somewhat cooler. Keep the plants cooler in winter (they will tolerate cold as low as 50° F [10°C]), in warmer winter quarters provide for humidity.
Watering, Feeding: From spring to fall keep uniformly damp; in winter water little in a cool spot, in a heated area give more water and mist often. From March to August feed every 14 days.
Further Culture: Repot young plants every spring, older ones only when completely pot-bound, in all-purpose potting soil. Cut back stems by ¼ so that the plant will bush out.
Propagation: In August, from mature tip or stem cuttings, which root in water or potting medium; or by air layering.
Pests, Diseases: Spider mites and scale in winter location with too much warmth and dry air.
Note: The much larger Japanese fatsia, *Fatsia japonica,* has similar requirements, but it needs somewhat more water.

White and green variegated climbing fig.

Ficus pumila clings fast with clinging roots.

Currently, the leading *Ficus* is the weeping fig (*Ficus benjamina*). Like the old familiar rubber plant (*Ficus elastica*) it grows to ceiling height and is obtainable in many green- and colored-leaved varieties.

The Rubber Tree and Its Relatives

1 *Ficus deltoidea*
2 *Ficus elastica* 'Doescheri'
3 *Ficus benghalensis*
4 *Ficus pumila*
5 *Ficus pumila* 'Sonny'
6 *Ficus benjamina* 'Exotica'
7 *Ficus sagittata*
8 *Ficus benjamina*
9 *Ficus lyrata*

•*Ficus lyrata*, the fiddle-leaf fig, with its wavy, lyre-shaped leaves, which occasionally are violin shaped, is in the long run only suitable for high, large spaces or entryways.
•*Ficus retusa* has leaves similar to the weeping fig and is preferred for bonsai training.
•*Ficus deltoidea* grows slowly and remains small. It is also a favorite bonsai plant.
•*Ficus pumila*, the creeping fig, and the white *Ficus sagittata* 'Variegata' on the other hand are gorgeous hanging plants.
•*Ficus buxifolia*, the box-leaf rubber plant, is a fast-growing shrub with almost triangular leaves and copper-colored stems.
•The warmth-loving *Ficus aspera* 'Parcelli', a small shrub from Polynesia, has projecting branches with short-stemmed, large, white-and-green-marbled leaves that feel rough.
•*Ficus benghalensis*, the Indian banyan tree, becomes huge and has beautifully shaped leathery leaves.
•*Ficus rubiginosa*, the rusty fig, likes it rather cooler. In its Australian habitat it grows as a branching shrub 13 ft (4 m) tall. There, its branches bow to the ground, take root, grow up, and soon cover a large area. Best known is the variety 'Variegata'. *Ficus rubiginosa* grows slowly and likes a cool, bright location in winter.

Family: Moraceae (mulberry family).
Origin: Tropics and subtropics.
Location: Very bright, but not sunny. Room temperature all year around, but green-leaved plants can be cooler too. Important: Warm soil and humidity.

Watering, Feeding: Water moderately in spring and summer, still more sparingly in fall and winter. Avoid sogginess or leaves will drop. Feed every 14 days in summer.
Further Culture: Mist often. Repot, as necessary, in spring; use all-purpose potting soil. With most species, cutting back and trimming will lead to branching.
Propagation: By cuttings, in a heatable propagation flat at 77° to 86° F (25°– 30°C). Or by air layering.
Pests, Diseases: Scale, spider mites, or thrips in dry centrally heated air. Leaf drop in winter as a result of too cool and damp a winter location.

Fittonia verschaffeltii
Mosaic Plant

Grevillea robusta
Silky Oak

Silver-veined *Fittonia* variety 'Argyroneura'.

Grevillea robusta is a marvelous tree for the house.

This charming small foliage plant is named for the Englishwomen Elizabeth and Mary Fitton. There are several varieties in culture, such as the silver-veined 'Argyroneura' or the red-veined 'Pearcei'. Both have leaves about 3 in. (7 cm) large and are proven ground covers for warm, humid flower windows, vitrines, greenhouses, or warm beds in a conservatory. The particularly small-leaved, silver-green variety 'Minima' was developed for bottle gardens and mini-greenhouses. Mosaic plants, whose ancestors came from the rain forests of South America, need humidifiers.

Family: Acanthaceae (acanthus family).

Origin: Colombia to Bolivia.

Location: Bright to shady, but no sun. Room temperature or warmer all year around. Even in winter never keep the mosaic plant below 64° F (18°C). No drafts, otherwise leaves will drop.

Watering, Feeding: Keep uniformly damp with soft, room-temperature water. Fertilize with a weak concentration every 14 days from April to October.

Further Culture: Provide high humidity. Mist often in houseplant culture. Repot only as necessary in shallow containers, in spring; use all-purpose potting soil mixed with Styrofoam flakes.

Propagation: In spring, from tip cuttings, use heatable propagation flats. Frequent pinching back makes the plants bushier.

Pests, Diseases: Wood lice and snails, which are especially likely to appear in greenhouses and conservatories.

This easy-care plant with its silvery-green pinnate leaflets is more reminiscent of a fern than an oak. In any event, it does have size in common with the oak. *Grevillea robusta*, which—as the species name says—is strong and solid, actually in its natural habitat in Australia it grows as a tree 164 ft (50 m) tall and is used for lining avenues. We know that this tropical shrub gets more than 6 ft (2 m) tall in 2 to 3 years, and thus is best placed in a roomy conservatory. Unfortunately, the splendid flowers never appear in pot culture.

Family: Proteaceae (protea family).

Origin: Australia.

Location: Very bright; in winter even sunny. Good air circulation all year around and fresh to cool rather than warm. The plants can be placed in a shady spot in summer. In winter, if possible, keep no warmer than 59° F (15°C) or ugly lanky growth will result.

Watering, Feeding: Water copiously in summer, in winter, more sparingly. From March to October feed weekly.

Further Culture: Repot as necessary in spring, in all-purpose potting soil. Plants that have grown too tall may be cut back severely in spring, but they then lose their treelike growth and become bushy instead.

Propagation: From seed, which must be fresh. The *Grevillea* is considered a poor sprouter. Professional gardeners usually sow them in heated sawdust. In August, a semimature stem cutting may be taken, but it often needs months to root.

Pests, Diseases: Blanching leaves indicate an unbalanced supply of nutrients. Aphids and whitefly.

Guzmania
Guzmania

Velvet Plant
Gynura

One of the numerous *Guzmania* hybrids.

The purple-red of *Gynura* is unique.

The name of this genus, of which some 100 species are identified, comes from the name of Spanish apothecary Guzman. Some of these species have been modified horticulturally and today great numbers of them are in cultivation. The beauty of guzmanias is in their strikingly colored bracts. Of the hybrids that are available, *Guzmania lingulata* is the best known. It attracts interest with green leaf rosettes some 20 in. (50 cm) in diameter, from whose center appear brilliant red young leaves that shine like satin. The flower itself is not as spectacular as in other *Guzmania* varieties. Guzmanias can be bound to ephiphyte supports or cultivated in pots.
Family: Bromeliaceae (bromeliad family).
Origin: Central and South America.

Location: Bright to semishady. Warm all year long, more than 68° F (20°C), and humid. Best if kept in a flower window or greenhouse.
Watering, Feeding: Water with soft, room-temperature water in the leaf cup and on the soil. In summer, keep cup filled; in winter, water less. From March to August, every 14 days, use a weak solution of fertilizer when watering or misting.
Further Culture: Provide indirect humidity (see page 43). Repotting not necessary since mother plant dies after blooming.
Propagation: From offsets, which must be half as large as the mother plant before they are separated. Pot in orchid potting medium. Seeds may be sown also.
Pests, Diseases: Scale and spider mites from dry air. Root lice.

The purple, furry leaves of the velvet plant, *Gynura aurantiaca*, are the charm of this tropical half-shrub. It is native to the mountain forests of Java, grows upright at first, later climbing, and there grows to a height of 20 to 39 in. (50–100 cm). *Gynura aurantiaca* was introduced to Belgium in 1880. Newer in the trade is *Gynura scandens* from tropical East Africa. Its leaves are also purple-haired, but, in contrast to the Java gynura, are coarsely toothed. Both are somewhat rare, but extraordinarily attractive hanging plants. The small orange flowers, which appear in summer, smell unpleasant and are unattractive, so it is better they be pinched off.
Family: Compositae (composite family).
Origin: Java, East Africa.
Location: Very bright and in winter sunny also, but avoid midday sun. In too dark a spot the leaves lose their coloration and long spaces develop between the leaf pairs. Room temperature all year around, between 64° and 68° F (18°–20° C), also warmer in summer.
Watering, Feeding: Water somewhat more in spring and summer; in fall and winter water sparingly. In summer feed weekly with low dosage.
Further Culture: Provide indirect humidity (see page 43), but do not spray directly on the plants. In spring, repot in all-purpose potting soil. After 2 years replace the plants with self-raised young plants, since they usually grow unsightly. Keep trimming back so that they will keep branching.
Propagation: In spring or fall, from cuttings, which root without any problems.
Pests, Diseases: Frequently aphids.

Young plants of the gynura are easier to winter over than older ones. Anyone who doesn't have the optimal winter location is better off taking cuttings in the fall.

167

Haworthia
Wart Plant, Star Cactus, Cushion Aloe

Haworthias are gems for the succulent collector.

These small, succulent leaf plants are coming into fashion again. They originate in South Africa, where as a rule they hide in bushes or under boulders. *Haworthia truncata* even creeps into the ground up to the tips of its leaves. Under culture are chiefly *Haworthia fasciata*, with horizontally striped rosette leaves, as well as *Haworthia glabrata*, whose leaves are densely set with tiny pearllike white tubercles. The flowers appear on long stems and are rather dull. Other unusual species such as *Haworthia attenuata, Haworthia limifolia,* or *Haworthia reinwardtii* can be found in a well-stocked cactus nursery.

Family: Liliaceae (lily family).

Origin: South Africa.

Location: Bright, but not full sun. The cushion aloe loves the fresh air of summer in a place protected from rain. Keep warm in summer; in winter, preferably around 50° to 59° F (10°–15° C). But it will also tolerate room temperature— around 64° F (18° C).

Watering, Feeding: In spring and summer water little, in fall and winter, only sporadically. <u>Avoid sogginess without fail.</u> From March to August feed with cactus fertilizer every 4 weeks.

Further Culture: Repot every 2 years in spring or summer, in all-purpose soil, but mix it with 1/3 sand from time to time.

Propagation: From seed and from side shoots, which arise from the axils of the lower leaves. Take off side shoots and allow to dry before planting.

Pests, Diseases: Rare.

Note: The similar-looking gasteria is cultivated exactly the same except that it will tolerate more sun.

Hedera helix
English Ivy

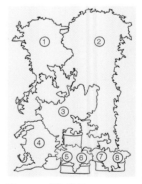

The varieties of ivy that have been developed can scarcely be counted. The large-leaved white variety 'Gloire de Marengo' has become famous. Two others, the hybrid forms of *Hedera helix ssp canariensis* and *Hedera colchica,* are important in houseplant culture. All have the typical ivy leaf with three to five lobes, but still show differences in color for each variety: Sometimes leaves have white, sometimes cream, sometimes yellow markings, or are plainly and simply green. Ivy is self-climbing and holds fast to anything offered it. All varieties are excellent hanging plants.

Family: Araliacaeae (aralia family).

Origin: Europe, Asia, North Africa. Only hybrid forms are in commerce.

Location: Bright to semishady. Room temperature all year long; in winter cooler also, but colored-leaved varieties not below 59° F (15° C). Rule of thumb: The greener the leaves, the greater the plant's tolerance for a shadier and cooler location; the more color in the leaves, the more sun and warmth the plant needs.

Watering, Feeding: Use room-temperature water. In spring, summer, and fall keep slightly damp all the time. In winter water somewhat less. From March to August feed weekly with low concentration.

Further Culture: Provide indirect humidity (see page 43) in heated rooms and mist often. Repot yearly in all-purpose potting soil.

Propagation: From end cuttings, which root easily in water or soil. Or by layering (see drawing, page 60). Always put several young plants in one pot. This way the plant will grow bushier.

Pests, Diseases: Scale from heated air. Spider mites from wintering too warm.

My Tip: When winter location is too warm and there is too little light at the same time, ivy develops weak stems, which it is better to cut back in the spring.

Warning: The berries are very poisonous. Of course they only form on older plants that are planted outdoors or in a conservatory.

Beautiful Ivy Varieties

1 'Ingrid'
2 'Eva'
3 'Gold Child'
4 'Gertrud Stauss'
5 New Danish hybrid, bred from 'Gold Child'
6 Typ Schäfer III
7 'Konigers Auslese'
8 'Calico'

Hypoestes phyllostacya
Polka-dot Plant

Polka-dot plants are wonderful ground covers.

In its Madagascar habitat the *Hypoestes* grows as a decorative shrub 20 in. (50 cm) tall. The leaves are covered with red or pink dots or spots of variable size, or they are variegated white and green. In our climate it stays rather herbaceous and as a rule is only cultivated as an annual, since the foliage pales with time and the plant becomes leggy when subjected to insufficient light.

Family: Acanthaceae (acanthus family).
Origin: Madagascar.
Location: Very bright, but no sun. Warm and humid all year around; in summer, around 68° to 73° F (20°–23° C); in winter, not under 64° F (18° C). Best is an enclosed flower window.
Watering, Feeding: Keep root ball only moderately damp all year around. From March to August feed every 14 days with a weak solution.

Further Culture: Provide high humidity and ground warmth. Repot in spring, in all-purpose potting soil mixed with Styrofoam flakes. Cutting back promotes new growth and bushy development.
Propagation: From tip cuttings, at a ground warmth of 77° to 86° F (25°–30° C). Keep trimming back young plants so that they'll branch. Seeding is possible too.
Pests, Diseases: Seldom.
Note: The reddish *Pseuderanthemum* and the silver-gray *Chamaeranthemum* are both close relatives of the *Hypoestes* and are cultivated exactly the same way.

Iresine
Bloodleaf

In time it becomes bushy—*Iresine herbstii.*

Would you like a bright spot of red on your windowsill? Then the bloodleaf is exactly the right thing. Its leaves look as if they were each dipped a couple of times into the paintpot labeled wine red. Two of the entire 70 species are popular annuals, either as houseplants or for outdoors: *Iresine herbstii*, with roundish leaves, and *Iresine lindenii*, with pointed oval leaves. In the variety 'Aureoreticulata' only the stems and principal veins are dark red, whereas the leaf surfaces are variegated with green and gold. All of them grow no taller than 12 in. (30 cm) in a pot and in a few months develop into a dense bush.

Family: Amaranthaceae (amaranth family).
Origin: South America.
Location: In the house, as bright as possible all year around; outside, sunny as well. In a dark location the iresinas turn very dark red. Keep warm and airy, in winter not under 59° F (15° C).
Watering, Feeding: Water well in summer, in all other seasons, only moderately. Dry heated air is poorly tolerated. Feed weekly from March to August.
Further Culture: Repotting not necessary. It's better to start new plants every year.
Propagation: From terminal cuttings, which root easily in water or soil. Trim young plants a number of times so they will branch nicely.
Pests, Diseases: Rare, occasionally aphids.
My Tip: The bloodleaf looks especially interesting in a red or a black cachepot. In a location with cross light, its color glows like burgundy.

Leea guineensis
Leea

Especially different—the red-leaved variety 'Burgundy'.

Maranta
Maranta, Prayer Plant

Maranta leuconeura 'Kerchoviana'.

The Scottish gardener James Lee is the godfather of this beautiful foliage plant, which was brought to England in 1880, slipped into oblivion for a long time, and today is again being sold. It is the only genus in the family. Of the 70 species, which grow as small shrubs in the tropical forests of southern Asia, it is primarily *Leea guineensis* and its red-leaved variety 'Burgundy' that are seen. The leeas sometimes develop umbrellalike cymes that are a little bit reminiscent of grape flowers. In fact, the grape family is very close.
Family: Leeaceae (leea family).
Origin: Southern Asia.
Location: Bright but no sun. More than 68° F (20° C) all year around; in winters, never below 61° F (16° C). The plant loves high humidity so it thrives best kept in an enclosed flower window.

Watering, Feeding: Keep moderately damp, but <u>avoid dry root ball and sogginess</u> to prevent sudden leaf drop. From March to August fertilize with weak dosage every 14 days.
Further Culture: Mist often. In spring, repot in all-purpose potting soil. Mix in Styrofoam flakes or sand so that the earth is more permeable.
Propagation: From seed, tip, or stem cuttings. Use a heated propagation bed. Difficult.
Pests, Diseases: Aphids and spider mites from dry, heated air.
My Tip: The secretion of sugar droplets is not disease but characteristic of the species and therefore a sign that the plant is feeling well.

The maranta family is at home in the tropical rain forests. The genus *Maranta* numbers 23 species with tuberous roots and terminal inflorescences. Here, *Maranta leuconeura* (the prayer plant) is the best known. There are numerous varieties of it, for instance 'Kerchoviana' with dark spots on emerald-green leaves. Other foliage beauties are 'Massangeana' with small leaves with red under-sides and 'Erythroneura', also with emerald-green leaves, light scallops along the middle vein, and red lateral veins. All are wonderful ground covers for tropical windows.
Family: Marantaceae (maranta family).
Origin: Rain forests of South America.
Location: Bright but no sun, very warm all year around, never under 64° F (18° C).

Watering, Feeding: In summer water freely, in winter, more sparingly. Feed every 14 days with weak dosage from April to August.
Further Culture: On the windowsill, mist daily with soft water or provide indirect humidity (see page 43). Repot as necessary in spring, in all-purpose potting soil. Add Styrofoam flakes.
Propagation: By division, at time of repotting in spring or by tip cuttings.
Pests, Diseases: Leaf margin necrosis from too cool a location. Spider mites when air is too dry. Bleached-out leaves from too much light.
My Tip: Curled leaves in the daylight are a sign that culture is too dry. At night it is "behavior" typical of the species; that is, at night marantas do roll up their leaves hornlike in a "sleep" position.

Maranta cuttings root relatively quickly in the greenhouse climate provided by a transparent plastic bag.

Monstera deliciosa
Swiss-cheese plant, Monstera

Monstera deliciosa develops strong aerial roots.

Beautifully perforated leaves and imposing stature have made the Swiss-cheese plant one of our most popular foliage plants. With good care this twining plant will develop stems up to 16 ft (5 m) long and numerous aerial roots. Therefore, it needs a trellis or an epiphyte trunk to fasten itself to. The heart-shaped juvenile leaves, and later the perforated mature leaves are dark green and glossily leathery. Older specimens bloom every year with a spadix surrounded by a white spathe, from which develops a violet-colored fruit that smells like pineapple. In addition to the green-leaved kinds there are also the smaller-growing variety 'Borsigiana' and the white form 'Variegata' available.
Family: Araceae (arum family).
Origin: Mexico.

Location: Bright but not sunny (thrives also in shade). All year around between 64° and 72° F (18°–22° C). The Swiss-cheese plant loves high humidity and warm soil.
Watering, Feeding: Keep only moderately damp all year long. From March to August fertilize with low dosage every 14 days.
Further Culture: Wash off leaves every so often so that the plant can "breathe." Mist often. As necessary, carefully repot in all-purpose potting soil. Do not injure aerial roots or cut them off.
Propagation: From tip cuttings, in heated propagation bed; or by air layering.
Pests, Diseases: Scale or spider mites from dry air.
Warning: Contains irritants to skin and mucous membranes. Therefore do not eat the fruit either.

Myrtus communis
Myrtle

Myrtle loves a sunny place out of doors.

The evergreen myrtle from the Mediterranean regions grows scarcely more than 39 in. (1 m) tall in pot or tub. It was once sacred to the Greek goddess Aphrodite and held as a symbol of youth and beauty. Three hundred years ago the Greek and Roman custom of crowning a virgin bride with a wreath of myrtle became ours too. Since that time myrtle has been under cultivation. It exists as shrubs or as elegant tree standards. The plant blooms in high summer with numerous small white blossoms and with good culture can live for many, many years. The small leaves smell spicy when bruised.
Family: Myrtaceae (myrtle family).
Origin: Mediterranean regions.
Location: Bright to full sun and good air circulation. Myrtle loves to be outside in summer.

Keep warm in summer; in winter, if possible, not more than 50° F (10° C).
Watering, Feeding: Use only soft water. In summer keep uniformly damp. Water freely out of doors. In winter keep barely damp. Avoid sogginess and dried-out root ball. Feed weekly from March to August.
Further Culture: Mist often indoors. Repot young myrtle yearly; older ones, as necessary in spring. Use all-purpose potting soil. Trim plants regularly. But if you cut back too severely there will be no flowers.
Propagation: From not-yet-woody end cuttings, in spring or summer. Trim young plants a number of times so they will branch.
Pests, Diseases: Whitefly or scale in poor locations.

Neoregelia carolinae with red inner leaves.

The pitcher plant is an ingenious insect trap.

In the rain forests of eastern Brazil, neoregelias grow as epiphytes. The rosette leaves form a large cup, in which the short-stemmed flowers "nest," as with the *Nidularium* (see page 174). The most striking thing is the color of the inner leaves, which often retain their brilliant coloration for months at a time. Best known are *Neoregelia carolinae* with red inner leaves and, in the variety 'Tricolor', creamy-white-striped outer leaves. *Neoregelia concentrica* has purple inner leaves. All are occupants for a warm, humid flower window.

Family: Bromeliaceae (bromeliad family).

Origin: Brazil.

Location: Very bright and in winter also sunny. Warm all year around, in winter, never below 64° F (18° C).

Watering, Feeding: Use only soft water and always pour it into the cup. Keep the cup full in summer, but in winter, barely full. During the growing season, every 14 days add a weak dosage of fertilizer to the irrigation water. Also every 14 days empty the water from the cup and replace it with fresh.

Further Culture: Mist often. Even better, provide indirect humidity (see page 43).

Propagation: From seed or from offsets, which should be half as large as the mother plant before they are separated. Plant in a mixture of peat and Styrofoam flakes.

Pests, Diseases: Dried-out leaf tips when air is too dry.

My Tip: The insignificant flowers that nestle among the strongly colored inner leaves do not last long. The inner leaves remain attractive for months. When they die down, the mother plant dies.

Of the few meat-eating plants that exist in the world the pitcher plant is the most striking. The pitchers are not flowers at all but metamorphosed leaf surfaces and the most refined insect traps that one could imagine. In their tropical habitat they are always $1/3$ full of water. A "cover" prevents rain from getting in. It has scent glands that attract insects, which slide across a smooth slippery area into the water containing concentrated poisonous secretions and are digested. The pure botanical species are available from specialty nurseries and the hybrids, from garden centers. They are sold in hanging pots so that the dangling pitchers can display freely.

Family: Nepenthaceae (nepenthes family).

Origin: Malay Archipelago, Sumatra, Borneo, Philippines, Australia, Madagascar.

Location: Very bright but not sunny. Over 68° F (20° C) all year around. The plants need high humidity. Ideal: a bay window greenhouse, vitrine, or a warm, humid greenhouse.

Watering, Feeding: Use only softened, room-temperature water. Keep potting medium uniformly slightly damp. In the growing season fertilize with a low concentration every 3 to 4 weeks.

Further Culture: Provide high humidity, mist the plants all over frequently. As necessary, repot in spring in orchid substrate. Use pots with good drainage or baskets. Take care that the roots are not injured when repotting.

Propagation: From cuttings, but very difficult for the layperson.

Pests, Diseases: The plant does not last long in a room with dry air.

Nidularium
Nidularium

Outside green, inside explosive red—*Nidularium*.

Of the some 25 *Nidularium* species, which are epiphytic inhabitants of Brazil, only a few are seen in trade. *Nidularium fulgens* is one that is very well known. As with the *Neoregelia*, the flowers of this cup bromeliad also nestle in the middle of the rosette; hence the name, from Latin *nidus* = nest. The *Neoregelia* is particularly like *Nidularium innocentii*. *Nidularium billbergioides*, on the other hand, displays yellow inner leaves and inflorescence, which peeks up out of the nest to as much as 8 in. (20 cm). The leaves are green, glossy, and may also be striped or spotted.
Family: Bromeliaceae (bromeliad family).
Origin: Brazil.
Location: Bright all year round but not sunny; if kept at room temperature, it should never sink below 64° F (18° C). The plant loves high humidity.
Watering, Feeding: Use only softened, room-temperature water. Keep the cup filled all year around and never let the substrate dry out entirely. Water copiously in a warm environment. In summer feed weekly with low concentration. Spray leaves with the fertilizer solution.
Further Culture: Provide high humidity (see page 43). Every 2 years repot in weakly fertilized potting soil mixed with Styrofoam flakes.
Propagation: From seed or by offsets, which are separated at repotting time when they are sufficiently large. It usually blooms after 2 to 3 years.
Pests, Diseases: Dried-out leaf tips from dry air. Rot from cold, wet feet.
My Tip: In too dark a location the cream-white striped leaves of some species turn green.

Pachira macrocarpa
Guiana Chestnut, Water Chestnut

The wild chestnut is very unusual and of easy culture.

In its native habitat the Guiana chestnut grows to become a small tree with a broad crown. The carmine-red flowers, up to 14 in. (35 cm) in size, rise like a plume of egret's feathers over the leathery, hand-shaped compound leaves. Unfortunately, the plant doesn't bloom indoors, but it is still a decorative little tree, with a reputation for being undemanding and satisfactory. What many do not know: The water chestnut is a close relative of the baobab tree (*Adansonia digitata*) and of the Madagascan baobab (*Adansonia madagascariensis*) and like them has a trunk that stores water. Thus the old term *Pachira aquatica* for the species that is today sold as *Pachira macrocarpa*.
Family: Bombacaceae (bombax family).
Origin: Mexico to Costa Rica.
Location: Sunny to semishady. Room temperature all year around, in winter also somewhat cooler, but not under 54° F (12° C). The plant loves high humidity.
Watering, Feeding: Keep only moderately damp all year around. Fertilize with low concentration every week from March to August.
Further Culture: Provide indirect humidity (see page 43), especially in winter. Repot as necessary in spring, in all-purpose soil. Cut back plants that grow too large.
Propagation: From seed or by tip cuttings, in a heated propagating bed at ground temperatures over 77° F (25° C).
Pests, Diseases: Sudden leaf drop from dry, warm heating-system air.

Pachypodium
Madagascar Palm

The flower is always a surprise.

The Madagascar palm tolerates heated air and does not need cool wintering over. In trade are *Pachypodium geayi*, with narrow, silvery-gray leaves, and *Pachypodium lamerei*, with broad, bright-green leaves. Both grow in their native habitat to trees of some 20 to 33 ft (6–10 m) in height. Indoors, after about 10 years they may attain 39 in. (1 m), and according to my experience, you may count on a very beautiful white star of a blossom when it reaches 47 in. (120 cm.)

Family: Apocynaceae (dogbane family).
Origin: Madagascar.
Location: Bright to full sun and warm all year around. In winter, not below 64° F (18° C). Tolerates warm, dry air, can thus be placed over a radiator without fear of harm.
Watering, Feeding: In summer, always keep slightly damp; in winter keep almost dry. Never soggy. From May to August feed every 4 weeks with cactus fertilizer.

Further Culture: Repot every 1 to 2 years in ¹/₂ cactus soil and ¹/₂ all-purpose soil.

Pests, Diseases: Root rot and blackened leaves from cold, wet feet in winter. Total leaf drop from too much water or dryness. Dropping of lower leaves is normal for the species. Plants enjoy 2 to 3 months of dry dormancy. As soon as the first new leaflets appear, start watering again.

Warning: Trunk and leaves of the Madagascar palm contain a highly poisonous milky juice. You can also receive injury from the thorns. Anyone who has children or pets had better avoid this plant.

Pandanus
Screw Pine

The screw pine needs lots of room around it.

Newly bought screw pines, usually juvenile plants of *Pandanus veitschii* or of *Pandanus sanderi*, look almost like dracaenas (see page 160), with their straplike, cream- or white-striped leaves. With increasing age, however, they develop the typical spiral arrangement of the leaves; the bizarre prop roots emerge from the stem, become woody, and anchor themselves in the ground. The screw pine develops to an impressive breadth and height. Therefore, you eventually need a great deal of room and free air space for this exotic, whose spiny leaf margins can easily tear stockings.

Family: Pandanaceae (screw-pine family).
Origin: Polynesia.
Location: Very bright, also sunny. Shade from summer midday heat. Keep warm all year long, even in winter—above 64° F (18° C).

Watering, Feeding: During the summer growing season always keep well dampened; in fall and winter water sparingly. From March to August fertilize weekly.

Further Culture: Repot young plants yearly, older ones as necessary in all-purpose potting soil mixed with a little sand.
Propagation: From offsets of about 8 in. (20 cm) in length with rootlets.
Pests, Diseases: Rare.
My Tip: Uneven whitening of the leaf surfaces is normal. You can receive injury from the spiny leaf margins. When repotting, tie up the tuft of leaves.

The screw pine grows at high speed and in a few years reaches the diameter of an automobile tire.

Pelargonium
Fragrant Geranium, Leaf Geranium

These leaf geraniums give off scent when their leaves are bruised.

Do you already know these sisters of the balcony geranium? Their flowers are small, but they have an exciting array of leaf patterns or leaves that smell of roses, oranges, apples, lemons, almonds, pine, mint, nutmeg, or camphor. The leaf geraniums include botanical wild species and hybrids of the bedding geraniums (*Pelargonium*

Zonale hybrids). The latter have more or less toothed leaves with white-red, white-green-red, very dark green, or greenish-yellow markings. The simple, dainty flowers are white, yellow, red, white-red, white-pink, or pink and appear in summer.

Scented geraniums:
• *Pelargonium blandfordianum* (almond, sage scent)
• *Pelargonium x citrosum* (citrus scent)
• *Pelargonium crispum*
• *Pelargonium* 'Els' (strong flower scent)
• *Pelargonium x fragrans* (citrus-pine scent)
• *Pelargonium gibbosum* (musky scent)
• *Pelargonium graveolens* (citrus scent)

• *Pelargonium odoratissimum* (lemon scent)
• *Pelargonium quercifolium* (camphor scent)
• *Pelargonium* 'Prince of Orange' (orange scent)
• *Pelargonium radens* (rose scent)
• *Pelargonium* 'Scarlet Pet' (orange scent)
• *Pelargonium tomentosum* (mint scent)

Leaf geraniums:
'Masterpiece', 'Dolly Vardon', 'Madame Salleron', 'Bird Dancer', and 'Freak of Nature'.

Family: Geraniaceae (geranium family).

Origin: South Africa.
Location: Full sun to bright, and airy. In summer also outdoors in a place protected from wind. Winter over in bright, cool spot at 50° to 54° F (10°–12° C).
Watering, Feeding: Water copiously in summer, in winter keep relatively dry. Fertilize weekly from March to August.
Further Culture: Tolerates dry air well. In spring or fall cut back severely and repot in all-purpose potting soil.
Propagation: Tip cuttings, in spring or fall.
Pests, Diseases: Aphids, whitefly, fungus and bacterial diseases.
Warning: Anyone who gets headaches from perfume or other odors should not keep too many scented geraniums in a closed room.

Pelargonium gibbosum, gouty pelargonium.

Pelargonium hybrid 'Prince of Orange'.

Pelargonium Stellar hybrid 'Els'.

Pelargonium hybrid 'Scarlet Pet'.

Peperomia, Radiator Plant

Peperomias invite collection and grouping.

The small, herbaceous peperomias are favorite plants of collectors. No wonder, with the multiplicity of pretty leaf structures and colors that they provide. More than 1,000 species are said to exist. Characteristic are the thick stems and their upper leaf sides formed like water cushions. If you cut through a leaf of one of the thick-leaved species you can see this very clearly. Peperomias grow upright, hang, or creep. Many are epiphytes. The flower spikes that appear with some species are white. Here are the well-known species and varieties:

• *Peperomia argyreia*, with green-silvery-striped foliage on red stems, is propagated from leaves like the African violet.

•*Peperomia arifolia* has oval, strongly pointed leaves, whose upper sides are glossy dark green.

•*Peperomia caperata* (see photograph, top row left and bottom row, second and fourth from left) has puckered leaves; the variety 'Tricolor' has white bordered foliage.

• *Peperomia clusiifolia* only shows its beauty when fully mature, when its fleshy leaves take on a strong red color.

• *Peperomia fraseri* has fragrant leaves.

• *Peperomia griseo-argentea* has silver-green leaves on red stems (see photograph, top row right).

• *Peperomia incana* can be easily recognized by the gray tomentum that overlies the fleshy leaves and is retained only in a bright location.

• *Peperomia maculosa* has unusual lanceolate leaves over 8 in. (20 cm) long, which display an ivory-colored central vein. Sprigs and leaf stems are dotted with brownish red.

• *Peperomia obtusifolia* (see photograph, bottom row, first from left) is a very common species that can be found with green-and-white- or yellow-marbled leaves. Best-known varieties: 'Jeli', 'Green-gold' (see photograph, bottom row, third from left), 'Albo-marginata', and 'Minima' (dwarf form). They must be trimmed from the time they are small so that they will grow nicely bushy. Very pretty hanging plants:

• *Peperomia rotundifolia* has small round leaves, which develop from disks the size of the head of a knitting needle and sit on threadlike stems.

• *Peperomia serpens* and its colored-leaved form 'Variegata' is also known under other names.

• *Peperomia scandens*. It bears heart-shaped leaves on long, creeping shoots.

Family: Piperaceae (pepper family).

Origin: Tropical America.

Location: Green-leaved species and varieties, bright; in summer, also semishady. Colored-leaved plants, very bright but not sunny; warm all year around. Species with fleshy leaves tolerate dried heating air, those with smooth leaves need higher humidity.

Watering, Feeding: Keep only slightly damp. Avoid cold feet in winter. Danger of rot. Feed every 3 weeks from April to September.

Further Culture: Provide high humidity, especially for the smooth-leaved species, from April to September. Mist often. In spring or summer repot in all-purpose potting soil. Carefully cut back plants that look bare in the spring.

Propagation: From tip and leaf cuttings.

Pests, Diseases: Leaf drop, leaf and stem rot from poor culture. Leaf eelworms.

177

Around 1850 the two most important species—*Philodendron erubescens*, the red-leaf philodendron, and *Philodendron scandens*, the climbing heart-leaf philodendron, were introduced and cultivated. Here are the best-known for house-plant culture of the approximately 275 species:

- *Philodendron bipennifolium* with heart-shaped to spear-shaped, compound leaves
- *Philodendron bipinnatifidum* with broadly oval, large leaves
- *Philodendron melanochrysum* with black-green foliage
- *Philodendron pedatum*, the tough species
- *Philodendron selloum*, trunk-forming philoden-dron, and the nonclimbing species *Philodendron martianum* and *Philodendron wendlandii*. Best known varieties are 'Red Emerald', 'Green Emerald', and 'Burgundy'. All climbing species need a support.
- *Philodendron 'Lynette'*, with leaves utterly atypical for philoden-drons, is new in the trade.

Rich Green from the Rain Forest
On the wicker table a magnificent specimen of *Philodendron selloum*, next to it *Philodendron erubescens* 'Red Emerald'.

An indefatigable climber—*Philodendron scandens*.

The best-known variety—*Pilea cadierei* 'Minima'.

Family: Araceae (arum family).
Origin: South America.
Location: Bright to semishady. Warm all year round, never under 64° F (18° C). Important: The soil temperature should never be below the air temperature.
Watering, Feeding: Always keep slightly damp. Feed every 14 days from March to August.
Further Culture: Mist often, especially when new growth begins. Important: <u>Do not use leaf polishes</u>. Repot young plants yearly, older ones as necessary, in all-purpose potting soil. It's all right to cut back the tips of shoots as soon as the plant gets too tall.
Propagation: From tip or stem cuttings, by air layering, or from seed.
Pests, Diseases: Scale, thrips from indoor air that is too dry. Root rot from wet, cold soil.
My Tip: Look at the old specimens of philodendron in a botanical garden. In many species the young forms look very different from the old ones.
Warning: Contains irritants to skin and mucous membranes.

New, with gorgeous leaves— *Philodendron* 'Lynette'.

Some species of pilea are called artillery plant. There's a reason for the military-sounding name. Touching the mature flower buds causes the filaments of the stamens to snap back elastically and propel the pollen away in a little puff. The artillery plants, which are very closely related to our stinging nettles, are herbs scarcely more than 8 in. (20 cm) in height with attractive pointed or round-oval leaves. They are especially good as ground covers for flower windows and for dish gardens. The important species and varieties are *Pilea cadierei* with silver-green, slightly bumpy leaf structure; *Pilea crassifolia* 'Moon Valley', with black-veined, crinkled leaves; and *Pilea spruceana*, with silver stripes on gray-green or bronze-green leaves. A pretty small-leaved hanging plant is *Pilea nummulariifolia*.
Family: Urticaceae (nettle family).
Origin: Tropics.
Location: Bright to semishady. Warm all year around. High humidity is desirable.
Watering, Feeding: In spring and summer water somewhat more, from fall and in winter more restrainedly. <u>Do not allow water to get on the leaves</u>. From March to August feed weekly.
Further Culture: Provide indirect humidity (see page 43). Repot in spring and cut back. These procedures seldom pay, however, since without artificial light in winter the plants soon lose their lower leaves and become unsightly.
Propagation: Possible from tip cuttings all year long. Pinch back young plants and keep bright and warm over winter.
Pests, Diseases: Spider mites from dry heated air.

179

Pisonia umbellifera
Bird-Catcher Tree, Para-Para

Variegated—*Pisonia umbellifera* 'Variegata'.

The bird-catcher tree looks something like a color-leaved rubber plant, but it is related to the *Bougainvillea* and to the four-o'clock (*Mirabilis jalapa*). Of the 50 species, only *Pisonia umbellifera*, the "umbel-bearing" pisonia, is cultivated as a houseplant. In its home-land it grows as a 20 ft (6 m) high tree or shrub with thin-skinned opposite leaves arranged almost in a whorl, up to 16 in. (40 cm) long. The variety available here, 'Variegata', has green, white, and silver marbled foliage. In the house it grows to be about 47 in. (1.2 m) high, provided you make sure that this South Seas beauty never has to complain about cold feet.
Family: Nyctaginaceae (four-o'clock family).
Origin: Australia, New Zealand, South Seas.
Location: Very bright so that it doesn't lose its variegation, but no sun. Warm air and soil all year round, temperature never under 64° F (18° C). The plant loves floor heat or a heating mat as an under-lay. The roots rot when cold!
Watering, Feeding: Always keep root ball uniformly damp. From March to August feed every 14 days.
Further Culture: Mist leaves often and wash off so that they can "breathe." As needed, repot in spring; use all-purpose potting soil. Cut back branches that are too long to old wood.
Propagation: From tip or stem cuttings, in heatable propagation flat with ground temperatures between 68° and 77° F (20°–25° C).
Pests, Diseases: Scale and aphids from dry, heated air. Dry or soggy root ball can lead to brown leaf edges, yellowed leaves, and leaf drop.

Plectranthus
Swedish Begonia, Swedish Ivy

A hanging plant—*Plectranthus coleoides* 'Marginatus'.

Over the decades since its introduction in 1817, *Plectranthus fruticosus* has been by far the most prominent representative of the genus. Our forebears successfully used the violet-flowered plant with its penetrating camphor odor to combat clothes moths. These are scarcely important as pot plants anymore today. Instead they have been replaced by two other species: on the one hand, by *Plectranthus oertendahlii*, with small, round, bright-green, white-veined and red-margined leaves; on the other, by *Plectranthus coleoides* and its variety 'Marginatus', with white-bordered leaves. Both develop slightly trailing shoots and are lovely hanging plants or ground covers.
Family: Labiatae, also Lamiaceae (mint family).
Origin: South Africa.
Location: Bright to sunny and in a room with good air circulation. Can summer outside well. In winter keep no cooler than 59° F (15° C), *Plectranthus fruticosus* even to 50° F (10° C).
Watering, Feeding: Keep uniformly damp. Water freely on hot summer days, in winter, quite sparingly. From March to August feed every 14 days.
Further Culture: Repotting is not rewarding, since older plants are often not particularly attractive.
Propagation: In early spring or summer, from tip cuttings, which root easily. Pinch back often so that nice bushy plants will develop.
Pests, Diseases: Rare.

Pogonatherum paniceum
House Bamboo

Polyscias
Aralia

The house bamboo should never dry out.

Polyscias balfouriana has non-pinnate foliage.

The house bamboo has the graceful elegance of evergreen culms in common with the bamboos and the subfamily of the sweet grasses. The fact that this plant, introduced around 1980, belongs to a different grass clan can be seen by its yearly flower, for as is well known, the bamboos bloom very seldom. In fact its old name *Saccharum paniceum* points to close relationship with the sugar cane. The house bamboo has a bushy habit and forms thin, woody stalks, 6 to 23 in. (15–60 cm) in length, with narrow leaves 3 in. (7 cm) long. The culms last quite a while when cut and are good for use as plant stakes.
Family: Gramineae, also Poaceae (grass family).
Origin: Southeast Asia.
Location: Bright to full sun. Warm all year around, even in winter- never under 59° F (15° C). Loves high humidity, but also tolerates dry air. May spend the summer outdoors in a semishady spot.
Watering, Feeding: Water copiously. Never let the root ball dry out. Dryness can be lethal. In summer even footbaths are permitted. From March to August feed every 2 to 3 weeks.
Further Culture: Repot yearly in spring. Use all-purpose potting soil.
Propagation: By division or from root runners when repotting in spring.
Pests, Diseases: Rare.

The aralia's name indicates that it is a shade plant (Greek: *poly* = much, *scias* = shade). This preference is also indicated by the fernlike character of the leaves of many species. *Polyscias filicifolia, Polyscias guilfoylei*, and *Polyscias paniculata* have pinnate or deeply incised foliage. To keep them successfully for any length of time, you need a warm, humid greenhouse window. *Polyscias balfouriana* is more robust and therefore more widely distributed. It has round to kidney-shaped leaves with white margins, spots, or veins.
Family: Araliaceae (aralia family).
Origin: Tropical Asia, Polynesia.
Location: Bright to semishady. Never sunny. All year round at 68° F (20° C) and warmer, never under 64° F (18° C). The plant loves high humidity.

Watering, Feeding: Keep only slightly but uniformly damp with soft, room-temperature water. Avoid sogginess absolutely. From March to August fertilize every 2 weeks.
Further Culture: Provide indirect humidity (see page 43) and mist often. Repot every 2 years in a not-too-large pot with all-purpose soil.
Propagation: From cuttings, in heated propagation bed. Difficult.
Pests, Diseases: Aphids and scale, as well as spider mites from dry heated air.

The odd-looking aralia, especially the species *Polyscias fruticosa*, is wonderfully suited for shaping into an attractive indoor bonsai.

Radermachera sinica
Radermachera

The *radermachera* doesn't like cigarette smoke.

The radermachera is one of the new houseplants that has won many admirers; this exotic with its doubly pinnate, glossy green leaves looks really very decorative. In its homeland it grows as a small evergreen tree and blooms with large sulphur-yellow flower bells. We know that in a roomy pot it will easily reach a height of 5 ft (1.5 m). It will probably never set flowers under houseplant culture, but it's easy to care for as a foliage plant. There's only one thing it doesn't like— cigarette smoke. It reacts to it with dropping leaves. If you cannot find the plant under this name, look for it under its former name, *Stereospermum sinicum*. Because of its graceful leaves that closely resemble the ash; it is popularly called house ash.

Family: Bignoniaceae (bignonia family).
Origin: Southwestern China, Taiwan.
Location: Bright and airy all year around. Keep warm in summer, in winter at 59° F (15° C).
Watering, Feeding: Keep only moderately damp. In winter only water enough so that the leaves do not fall. From March to August feed every 3 weeks.
Further Culture: Mist often. Repot young plants every year, older ones as necessary, in all-purpose potting soil. There is still very little experience available as to whether it is suitable for water culture.
Propagation: From seed or from cuttings.
Pests, Diseases: Aphids and scale, as well as spider mites and thrips after wintering over too warm.
My Tip: Put the radermachera outside from June to September in a sunny, wind-protected spot; it clearly does it good.

Rhoeo spathacea
Moses in the Bulrushes, Boat Lily

Rhoeo spathacea develops "little flower boats".

Without flowers the *Rhoeo* might appear at first glance to be a dracaena or a bromeliad. But when the small flowers appear in June/July, it immediately becomes clear that it is a strange, unique genus we are dealing with. For the inflorescences with the delicate white "tongue flowers" are situated in pocket- or boat-shaped bracts deep down in the leaf axils, directly on the stem. *Rhoeo spathacea* is the only species of the genus. The most widely distributed is the variety 'Vittata', whose sword-shaped leaves, about 12 in. (30 cm) long, have a green-and-white-striped upper side and glowing purplish-red undersides.
Family: Commelinaceae (spiderwort family).
Origin: Central America.
Location: Bright but not sunny. Room temperature all year long never below 64° F (18° C). The plant loves high humidity, especially during its growing season in summer.
Watering, Feeding: Only use soft, room-temperature water for watering. Always keep slightly damp in summer, keep drier in winter. Feed weekly from March to August.
Further Culture: Provide indirect humidity (see page 43). Repot as necessary in spring, in all purpose potting soil.
Propagation: From side shoots, tip cuttings, and seeds.
Pests, Diseases: Curling of leaves and brown leaf tips in air that is too dry. Crown rot from too much water, especially in winter.
My Tip: *Rhoeo* looks especially attractive when it has only one stem. Remove the side shoots. If you want branching, you need to pinch the plant back often.

Rhoicissus capensis
Cape Grape, Evergreen Grape

The Cape grape is a very vigorous vine.

The Cape grape is a vigorous climber, for which you need a sturdy trellis. It develops up to 7 in. (18 cm) wide, heart-shaped, single, glossy green leaves, whose undersides are reddish and hairy. The soft, woody stems are hairy too. In Mediterranean regions you frequently see it as a lush vine drapery on balconies and pergolas. It tolerates cool temperatures, as low as 41° F (5° C), and can be used for greenery in cool, frost-free conservatories.
Family: Vitaceae (grape family).
Origin: Cape Colony, South Africa.
Location: Bright to semishady, and airy. No sun. In summer not too warm; in winter best between 43° and 50° F (6°–10° C). But room temperatures are certainly tolerated. The plant loves shady summer quarters.
Watering, Feeding: Keep moderately damp, in winter water less. The Cape grape has round tubers, storage organs, with which it can survive the dry spells of its homeland. Avoid sogginess, for wet feet will kill it. Feed every 14 days from May to August.
Further Culture: Remove dust from leaves often with careful washing. In spring, repot in larger containers. Use all-purpose potting soil. Cutting shoots back is possible if overgrown.
Propagation: From stem or tip cuttings.
Pests, Diseases: Mildew and other fungus diseases from too much water. Spider mites.

Sansevieria trifasciata
Snake Plant, Mother-in-Law's Tongue

Sansevierias are almost indestructible.

The snake plant was already in cultivation in 1770, in Austria. Today it still enjoys great popularity, which certainly is because of its proverbial tenacity. Bowstring hemp is the name given to the genus on account of its hemplike fibers, from which the West Africans made bowstrings. Of the 70 recognized species, *Sansevieria trifasciata* is the one primarily cultivated by gardeners. There are tall varieties with stiffly upright leaves close to 39 in. (1 m) long, like the yellow-margined 'Laurentii', and lower-growing rosettelike ones such as the golden-yellow-stripped "Golden Hahnii' and the white-variegated 'Silver Hahnii'. All sansevierias have rhizomes, which become so tightly entwined with each other that they burst the pots.
Family: Agavaceae (agave family).
Origin: Tropical West Africa.
Location: Sunny to semishady. Room temperature all year round, which can go as low as 59° F (15° C).
Watering, Feeding: Water only a little. Always let the soil dry out. Tolerates hard water. Feed from March to August every 2 weeks with flower or cactus fertilizer
Further Culture: Repot yearly in shallow containers (because of the rhizomes) with all-purpose potting soil.
Propagation: By division and side shoots or by leaf cuttings (but colored-leaf varieties propagated this way produce only green offspring).
Pests, Diseases: Rare. Only too much water can kill the sansevieria.
My Tip: Old specimens can surprise you with wonderful-smelling flowers.

183

Saxifraga stolonifera
Strawberry Begonia, Strawberry Geranium

colored green-white-pink leaves. The stems grow from a rosette. The threadlike runners, which can be up to 20 in. (50 cm) long, have young plantlets (offsets) at the end. In summer, panicles of tiny white star-shaped flowers appear.

Family: Saxifragaceae (saxifrage family).

Origin: China, Japan.

Location: Bright to semi-shady, airy, and cool; in winter frost-free. In mild regions with appropriate protection is even winter-hardy. The colored variety 'Tricolor' is suited for indoor cultivation all year around and must be kept brighter and warmer (even in winter, at least 59° F [15° C]).

Watering, Feeding: Keep only moderately damp; in winter, in a cool situation water less. From March to August fertilize weekly.

Further Culture: Repot as necessary in summer in all-purpose potting soil.

Propagation: By offsets, which are often already rooted. Plant several of these young plants to a pot to produce lusher clumps.

Pests, Diseases: Aphids in too warm a location. Root rot from too much water.

My Tip: The runners of the strawberry begonia can dangle free (as with hanging plants) or lie on the ground (for example as a ground cover in a conservatory).

The strawberry begonia is one of our prettiest hanging plants.

Saxifraga stolonifera means something like "runner-growing stonebreaker." In fact, the first characteristic property has made the little plant into a popular hanging plant. Aside from the pure species with roundish- to kidney-shaped hairy leaves (which are dark-green on the upper sides with gray-white veins and purplish on the undersides), also seen in trade is 'Tricolor', a variety with three-

Schefflera
Umbrella Tree, Rubber Tree, Starleaf

Schefflera arboricola grows well on a moss stake.

The Schefflera grows as a shrub or tree in its habitat. Here one mainly encounters two species: *Schefflera arboricola* and *Schefflera actinophylla*, which is now classified under the botanical name of *Brassaia actinophylla*. The first's growth habit is daintier, its leaves are narrower, and recently it has also become available in a variegated form. The *Brassaia's* long-stemmed leaves, which look as though they were lacquered, can grow up to 12 in. (30 cm) long. The handlike arrangement of the leaflets is characteristic of both.

Family: Araliaceae (aralia family).

Origin: Taiwan, north-eastern Australia, New Guinea.

Location: Bright to semishady. In summer, airy; temperatures of 50° to 64°F (10°–18°C), in a place protected from sun and wind, are good. Also possible to keep out of doors. In winter, keep green species cool—54° to 61° F (12–16° C), variegated ones not under 64°F (18°C).

Watering, Feeding: Keep slightly damp at all times. In a cool winter location water sparingly. From March to August feed every 14 days.

Further Culture: Mist often in a warm location. Repot young plants yearly in all-purpose potting soil; older ones, only as necessary. If you don't want the plants to become too large, cut them back or pinch out.

Propagation: From seed (August and September or from December to February), air layering, or tip cuttings in a heatable propagation flat. Difficult.

Pests, Diseases: Scale in too warm and dry a winter location. Leaf drop at temperatures under 54° F (12° C).

Warning: Contains irritants to skin and mucous membranes.

Scirpus cernuus
Bulrush, Sedge

Sedum
Stonecrop

Instead of leaves, grasslike culms.

Sedum morganianum with succulent leaves.

Like the umbrella sedge, the bulrush belongs to the sedges and was recently sold in a brown plastic or cardboard tube as "grass tree." This is not the natural growth habit. In its native situation, the rushlike culms, at 8 in. (20 cm) long, are in full light and therefore grow smartly upright. Only in shade do they grow longer and droop gently. This trailing growth makes the rush suited for use as a hanging plant, but it unfortunately also makes it subject to the above-mentioned frivolity, which does not exactly prolong the life of the plant. All year long tiny little flower spikes form at the tips of the thin culms.

Family: Cyperaceae (sedge family).

Origin: Mediterranean area, subtropics and tropics.

Location: Bright to semishady, no sun. Room temperature all year long.

Watering, Feeding: Water copiously. <u>Never allow it to dry out.</u> Like the umbrella sedge, the plants love footbaths. From March to August feed with weak concentration every 2 weeks.

Further Culture: In a heated living room provide indirect humidity (see page 43). Repot every spring in all-purpose potting soil with ¼ part sand.

Propagation: From seed or by division (at time of repotting in spring).

Pests, Diseases: Dry tips from too little humidity and soil moisture. Aphids. Caution: The bulrush finds many insecticides intolerable.

My Tip: *Scirpus cernuus* is wonderfully suited for planting of swampy areas in a terrarium or indoor water garden. But it should not have its entire root ball in water.

Of the some 600 succulent species, the ones from Mexico have acquired the most importance. *Sedum morganianum* (burro's tail) is an attractive hanging plant, whose stems trailing 20 in. (50 cm) or longer are densely packed with gray-frosted, cylindrical leaves. Unfortunately, the little leaves drop easily at the slightest touch, as they do in the other species. One of the most exciting growth habits belongs to *Sedum rubrotinctum*, whose leaves turn red in the sunlight. Very well known too is the winter-hardy *Sedum sieboldii*, which comes from Japan and whose rounded blue-green leaves with a reddish border are not so dense as those of the first-named species. With the proper cool culture these plants go dormant in fall and sprout anew again in spring.

Family: Crassulaceae (orpine family).

Origin: Mexico, *Sedum sieboldii* from Japan.

Location: Bright to full sun. Warm in summer, also in a protected spot outdoors. In winter keep cool—41° to 50° F (5°–10° C). Warm room temperatures will also be tolerated if need be in an extremely bright location, but it is not good for it in the long run. *Sedum sieboldii* should be cultivated as cold as possible.

Watering, Feeding: Water sparingly in summer, in winter only dampen the plants a little now and then. In summer, give cactus fertilizer every 4 weeks. Too much fertilizer changes the plant shape and the color of the leaves.

Further Culture: Repot in cactus soil as necessary.

Propagation: From stem cuttings or single leaves. Allow cut surfaces to dry for a few days before planting.

Pests, Diseases: Rot from too damp a location.

185

FOLIAGE PLANTS

Soleirolia soleirolii
Baby's Tears, Irish Moss, Corsican Curse

Baby's tears wants constant moisture.

From Corsica to Sardinia this small-leaved carpeting plant is found in cracks of walls, between stepping stones, and on rocks. Anyone who has a greenhouse knows how fast it can spread on the benches there. But the baby's tears (formerly *Helxine soleirolii*) is a decorative plant for growing in pots and hanging baskets.
Family: Urticaceae (nettle family).
Origin: Mediterranean region.
Location: Bright to semishady. Will accept room temperature in winter as well as cooler temperatures. The plants even tolerate cold, down to the limits of frost.
Watering, Feeding: Water moderately but uniformly. In cool winter locations keep only slightly damp. <u>Do not allow plants to dry out</u>; they react to irregular watering with leaf spots and loss of leaves. Feed from March to August every 4 weeks.
Further Culture: Mist often. Not necessary to repot, since by division you can easily get new plants, which quickly thicken up nicely.
Propagation: By division. Plant pieces in pots with all-purpose potting soil. Or from cuttings, which root very easily. Always plant several in one pot.
Pests, Diseases: Rare.

Sparmannia africana
African Hemp, Indoor Linden

With the increase in installation of conservatories, there is again a place for decorative trees like the indoor linden—a decidedly solitary plant. With increasing age they need much space to unfold to their full beauty. Moreover, they like a generous supply of light. The large velvety leaves of the treelike shrub are linden-green, hairy on both sides, and hang on long stems. In larger plants, white umbels of flowers with yellow and red stamens develop from winter to spring. However, the flowering is very variable—some plants don't bloom at all.
Family: Tiliaceae (linden family).
Origin: South Africa
Location: Very bright, but not full sun. In a place that does not have optimal light, the plant develops unsightly long leaf stems. Keep moderately warm all year long, but preferably briskly cool; in winter maintain it at between 50° and 59° F (10°–15° C).
Watering, Feeding: The large leaves indicate that the plant evaporates much moisture. Therefore, keep the potting medium damp at all times, but <u>avoid any sogginess at all</u>. In summer water more, in winter less, depending on temperature. From March to August fertilize weekly, in winter in a bright spot, every 2 months.
Further Culture: Repot young plants yearly, older ones as necessary in all-purpose potting soil. Cutting back is possible for older plants with bare stems.
Propagation: In spring, from soft cuttings in a heatable propagation flat. From shoots with flowers you can expect compact, flowering plants; cuttings from shoots with leaves only will produce vigorously growing plants that only flower as older specimens.
Pests, Diseases: Lack of leaves and leaf drop from deficiencies of light and nutrients and too warm a location. Spider mites and thrips from poor air circulation. Whitefly.
My Tip: The indoor linden roots thickly and tips easily when it is in too small a pot. It's best to set the potted plant in a much larger outer pot and fill the space between them with a great quantity of water-permeable clay gravel (see drawing, page 40). This will give the indoor linden more support and in warmer areas will also provide increased humidity at the same time.

Small and delicate—the flowers of the indoor linden.

The Gentle Green Tree
The indoor linden grows fast; its large, furry leaves evaporate much water.

Syngonium
Syngonium

Exotic climber—the *Syngonium*.

Green-white or green-silver variegated leaves are the identification mark of the syngonium, which can easily be confused with the *Philodendron* (see page 178). At an advanced age, when this plant produces its green arum flower with the glowing-red spathe, the leaves take on a purplish tinge. And this is not the only unusual thing. While juvenile plants generally have arrowhead-shaped, simple leaves, older specimens sometimes have compound or lobed leaves. But in any case the syngonium is an attractive, exotic climber, which thrives best in a hanging pot, on a trellis, or on an epiphyte board. The commonest species by the way is *Syngonium podophyllum,* of which colored-leaved varieties are also available.

Family: Araceae (arum family).

Origin: Central America.

Location: Colored-leaved varieties bright, green-leaved species and varieties bright to semishady, no sun. Warm all year around, even in winter not below 64° F (18° C). The plants need high humidity and warm soil.

Watering, Feeding: Keep slightly damp all year around with soft, room-temperature water. From March to August feed every 14 days.

Further Culture: Mist often and now and then wipe dust off leaves with a damp cloth. As necessary, repot in all-purpose potting soil mixed with Styrofoam flakes.

Propagation: From tip or stem cuttings, in heatable propagating flat at soil temperature around 77° F (25° C).

Pests, Diseases: Scale from dry, heated air.

Warning: Contains irritants to skin and mucous membranes.

Tetrastigma voinierianum
Chestnut Vine, Lizard Plant

The chestnut vine grows tumultuously.

The chestnut vine is a twining plant that grows in rampant spurts and can easily develop 16 to 20 ft (5–6 m) in a year; therefore it needs a sturdy trellis for climbing. Because of its growth pattern the chestnut vine is mounted among the evergreen lianas and forms spirally twining tendrils. It has three to five leaflets per serrated leaf, whose upper sides are dark-green and undersides have a brown tomentum; leaves are carried on sturdy stems. In pot culture it seldom comes into bloom.

Family: Vitaceae (grape family).

Origin: Vietnam

Location: Bright to shady. Room temperatures all year around are endured, also cooler in winter, but never below 50° F (10° C). Tolerates dry indoor air.

Watering, Feeding: Water freely in summer (especially during a growth spurt), in winter more sparingly, depending on temperature. Fertilize weekly during growth period.

Further Culture: Repot every spring in all-purpose potting soil; can be cut back as necessary at the same time.

Propagation: In spring from cuttings with at least one eye and one leaf in a heatable bed at a ground temperature of 77° F (25° C).

Pests, Diseases: Rare.

My Tip: The young shoots are quite brittle. Best if you keep tying to a trellis. Take care when drawing over a hoop not to break the young shoots. If you tie them firmly but carefully, they will quickly harden.

Tolmiea menziesii
Piggyback Plant

Tolmeia likes it airy and cool.

The piggyback plant is a botanical curiosity: Brood buds develop at the base of the heart-shaped, hairy leaf and grow to be small plants and form roots as soon as the old leaf touches the earth. It has been given other similarly cheerful popular names such as "thousand mothers" or "youth-on-age plant." The large winter-hardy plant grows 10 to 12 in. (25–30 cm) high and is a splendid hanging plant, but it only blooms in its native habitat. There, the racemes of greenish brown and orange flowers appear from May to June.

Family: Saxifragaceae (saxifrage family).
Origin: Northern Pacific coast.
Location: Bright to semishady and airy. In winter, cool, at 40° to 50° F (5°–10° C); in summer, outdoors in a shady spot.

Watering, Feeding: In summer water freely, in winter keep barely damp. From March to August feed every 14 days.
Further Culture: Repotting not necessary. Best to put new plantlets in all-purpose potting soil every year in the spring.
Propagation: From plantlets (see photograph, below) which can be set in the soil with or without the mother leaf. Runners also develop.
Pests, Diseases: Brown leaf margins from too warm a winter location.

A leaf with offsets "piggybacked."

Tradescantia
Spiderwort

Green-leaved *Tradescantia fluminensis.*

Tradescantia is a green plant that can be recommended to anyone. It grows quickly, requires scarcely any care, and is a lovely hanging plant besides. Of the up to 60 species, the following have shown themselves to be best for houseplant culture:
• *Tradescantia albiflora* with tiny, pointed oval leaves, and its hybrid forms 'Rochford's Silver' and 'Alba-vittata' with silver-striped leaves, 'Tricolor' with three-colored leaves, and 'Aureo-vittata' with yellowish leaves.
• *Tradescantia blossfeldiana,* whose fleshy leaves have red undersides, and its variety 'Variegata', whose cream-green leaves are tinged with pink.
• *Tradescantia fluminensis* 'Variegata' looks very much like *Tradescantia albiflora.*
Family: Commelinaceae (spiderwort family).

Origin: South America.
Location: Colored-leaved species and varieties only bright, but not sunny; green ones bright but also semishady if necessary. Room temperatures all year around, also cooler in winter, may go as low as 50° F (10° C) in a location that's not too damp.
Watering, Feeding: Always keep slightly damp. In a cool location in winter water less. From March to August feed every 14 days.
Further Culture: Mist often at room temperature. No need to repot. Better to raise new plants each year. It is very easy to do.
Propagation: All year around from cuttings, which root easily in water or in soil. Pinch back young plants and always put several in one pot.
Pests, Diseases: Aphids rarely.

Yucca

Age-old favorites as house- and tub plants are *Yucca aloifoilia*, with a dense head of gray-green, hard, sharp leaves, and *Yucca elephantipes*, with a tuberously thickened stem at ground level and a rather loose head of dark-green, sword-shaped leaves, 20 to 39 in. (50–100 cm) long.

Family: Agavaceae (agave family).

Origin: Mexico, Central and North America.

Location: Very bright and sunny. In summer warm, preferably outdoors on a sunny terrace, in winter cool—40° to 50° F (5°–10° C)—but room temperatures are tolerated.

Watering, Feeding: In summer out of doors, water copiously, indoors moderately. In winter water less, depending on temperature. Feed every 3 weeks from March to August.

Further Culture: Repot as necessary in all-purpose potting soil.

Propagation: From stem pieces or side shoots.

Pests, Diseases: Only in too warm or dark a location in winter. Leaf drop at lower levels is normal trunk development.

My Tip: In spring you can shorten yuccas that have grown too tall to the desired height. Powder the cut surface with charcoal or sulfur.

Warning: You can receive injury from the leaf tips, particular of *Yucca aloifolia*.

Sun Child
Yucca aloifolia with a particularly luxuriant leaf crown.

Xanthosoma lindenii
Indian Kale, Spoon Flower

Zebrina
Zebrina, Wandering Jew

Xanthosoma—an unusual foliage beauty.

Zebrina is also nice in a hanging basket.

Like its relative the Alocasia (see page 143), the Indian kale is one of the most gorgeous foliage plants we have. The tropical plant has wonderful, white-veined, arrowhead-shaped leaves (especially the variety 'Magnificum') and a tuberlike rhizome. Older plants develop the inflorescence common to the arum family with a white spathe. This foliage beauty thrives best in an enclosed plant window or warm, humid greenhouse.

Family: Araceae (arum family).

Origin: Colombia.

Location: Semishady to shady all year around, humid, and warm, over 68° F (20° C), in winter not below 64° F (18° C).

Watering, Feeding: Always keep slightly damp from March to September and feed every 14 days. In winter water sparingly (dormancy). Avoid sogginess.

Further Culture: Provide high humidity (70%). Repot every 1 to 2 years at beginning of new growth in all-purpose potting soil. Mix Styrofoam flakes or sand with the soil.

Propagation: By division of the rhizome at repotting. Succeeds only at high soil temperatures.

Pests, Diseases: Spider mites when air is too dry. Absolutely avoid cold, wet feet. The rhizomes are very susceptible to rot and can be attacked by bacteria and by fungus.

Warning: *Xanthosoma lindenii* contains substances that can irritate skin and mucous membranes. This seldom happens with cultivated plants, though.

The close relationship with tradescantia (see page 189) cannot be denied. All three recognized species also good for pot culture: (1) *Zebrina pendula* is, as the botanical name already says, an ideal hanging plant. But it is also very happy as a ground cover in a roomy flower window or in a soil bed in a warm conservatory. The four-colored-striped 'Quadricolor' is the variety chiefly seen in trade. (2) *Zebrina purpusii* is more vigorous in habit, overall, and has no stripes. (3) *Zebrina flocculosa*, a fluffy, white, and hairy species is harder to find.

Family: Commelinaceae (spiderwort family).

Origin: Central America.

Location: Bright, not sunny. In dark locations the beautiful colors pale. Room temperatures all year around, in winter, not under 54° F (12° C). Tolerates dry air.

Watering, Feeding: Water moderately. From March to August feed every 14 days. Too much water and fertilizer have a bad effect on the leaf colors.

Further Culture: Repot in spring in all-purpose potting soil, although it is better to bring on new young plants every year.

Propagation: From cuttings, which also root easily in water.

Pests, Diseases: Rare.

Green plants that not everyone has: Bizarre shapes with remarkable leaves, new arrivals from the Far East, old friends rediscovered.

Bambus vulgaris 'Striata'
Common Bamboo

Thick, yellow, green-striped culms, sawed-off and rooted, with lateral shoot or shoots bearing abundant foliage. The plant grows about 39 in. (1 m) tall. Diameter of the culm is 2 to 3 in. (6–8 cm). Family: Gramineae (grasses). Origin: Tropics. Location: In summer, very bright and warm; from June on place outdoors. Cooler in winter, but not below 40° F (5° C). Watering, Feeding: Water copiously in warm temperatures and less at cool ones. Avoid sogginess! Feed every 3 weeks in summer. Further Culture: Repot every spring in all-purpose potting soil. In too warm and dry a winter location, susceptible to spider mites. Propagation: Difficult. Note: Also thrives in hydroculture.

Bambusa vulgaris 'Striata'; the variety name 'Striata' comes from the green-striped culm, which can produce growth of varying lushness.

Dionaea muscipula
Venus's Fly Trap

Small, rosette-forming, meat-eating plants with trapping leaves that snap closed when touched by an insect or an object. The Venus's fly trap is an interesting plant, but in the house it will only last in a cool, damp spot and even in winter it must have brightness.

Family: Droseraceae (sundew family). Origin: South and North Carolina. Location: Bright, cool, and airy. In summer out of doors; in winter, at 40° to 50° F (5°–10° C). Watering, Feeding: Keep slightly damp with soft water at all times (plant is a swamp dweller). Fertilize weakly only every now and again during the summer. Further Culture: Repot every spring in a shallow dish of peat. Propagation: From leaf cuttings or division.

Dioscorea
Yam

Semi-shrubby climbing plant with hard, woody tubers that lie on the ground, with upper surfaces that can be bumpy *Dioscorea elephantipes* or smooth

Dioscorea sylvatica. Leaves kidney- to heart-shaped and a fresh green on shoots 39 in. (1 m) long. Family: Dioscoreaceae (yam family). Origin: South Africa. Location: Bright to full sun, all year long not below 64° F (18° C). Watering, Feeding: In summer the plant needs a resting period, during which keep it almost dry. In fall/winter, water moderately and feed with weak concentration every 4 weeks. Further Culture: Repot before new growth in August in cactus soil with pumice or perlite. Propagation: From seed or cuttings, but is difficult.

Senecio rowleyanus
String-of-Beads

Creeping plant with thin, long stems on which pealike leaves line up like beads. Blooms in spring with small cinnamon-scented flowers. Family: Compositae (composite family). Origin: South-western Africa. Location: Full sun and warm, in winter 50° to 54° F (10°–12° C). Watering, Feeding: Very little, in

winter keep almost dry, in summer feed once monthly. Further Culture: As necessary, repot in spring in a shallow pot in cactus soil. Propagation: Let broken-off stems dry for 2 days and root in sandy soil. Note: Similar in growth and appearance are *Senecio citriformis*, *Senecio herreanus*, and *Senecio radicans*—all unusual hanging plants.

Buddleia indica
Indoor Oak

Undemanding evergreen plant with oval, dark-green leaves with indented margins and insignificant yellowish-green flowers, which seldom appear in

houseplant culture. Family: Buddleiaceae (butterfly bush family). Origin: Madagascar. Location: Bright or semishady. The plant tolerates temperatures between 41° and 72° F (5°–22° C). Watering, Feeding: Water copiously; in winter and in a cooler location somewhat less. From March to October fertilize weekly. Further Culture: Shorten stems that are too long. Every spring repot in all-purpose soil. Cut back somewhat first and decrease the root ball. Propagation: From semi-woody cuttings.

Ophiopogon jaburan
Snakebeard

Evergreen, grasslike plant with green or golden-yellow-striped leaves ('Varie-gatus') and white to violet flowers. Very robust. Family: Liliaceae (lily family). Origin: Japan. Location: Bright and room temperatures all year round. Even cooler in winter. Watering, Feeding: Keep uniformly damp all year around, water less in winter in a cool

location, mist in dry, heated air. From March to August feed every 14 days. Further Culture: Repot, as necessary, in spring. Propagation: By division in spring.

Perilepta dyeriana
Perilepta

Herbaceous shrub with elliptical-lanceolate leaves, which are dark green and on the upper sides shimmer almost to the edge with a metallic blue-silver-violet; leaves are red on the undersides. Family: Acanthaceae (acanthus family). Origin: Burma. Location: Bright to semishady all year around; keep humid and warm, in winter not below 61° F (16° C). The plants tolerate neither sunlight nor heating system air. Watering, Feeding: Keep moderately damp with soft water. In summer feed

with a low dosage every 14 days. Further Culture/Propagation: Since the perilepta quickly becomes twiggy and only the juvenile plants are beautifully colored, take cuttings in spring; these root quickly in a heated propagating flat. Trim the young plants two or three times so they will become bushy.

Whether delicately feathery or stoutly leathery, a fern's beauty lies in its fronds and its gracefully arching, erect growth. Most ferns are typical forest plants, which love humid air, light shade, and ground that is always slightly damp.

FERNS

At once a dense parasol and a green tent roof, ferns spread their mighty fan of fronds and show the traveler who takes a midday rest beneath them the eternal blue of heaven through the most beautiful lace curtain that ever Nature wove or knitted. Thus wrote a botanist about the ferns in the rain forest over 100 years ago. These words bespeak the enchantment the exotic ferns offered to those of the previous century. They were far and away the first choice for green ornaments for salons and hotel lobbies. The English of the Victorian era loved them so much that they artfully worked cast iron and glass to create the so-called ferneries, in which humidity and soil dampness remained almost constant. Ferns are still today, despite their limited lifespan, among the most popular green plants. They have been separated from the other green plants in this book and are treated in their own chapter for two reasons:

1. They do not, like the other houseplants, belong to the highly developed flowering plants.
2. They possess a decorative magic of a sort that demands a special presentation. The houseplant ferns introduced on the following pages all belong to the class of Filicopsida. Not included are the Japanese fern (*Cycas*), also called the Sago palm, which belongs in another botanical category and is therefore found with the foliage plants.

What You Should Know About Ferns

Did you know that the ferns on your windowsill belonged to the plant kingdom at the time of the dinosaurs? They are 250 to 400 million years old and have scarcely changed at all since then.

Today the botanists number some 200 genera and 9,000 species in the division of fern plants (Pteridophyta), cosmopolitans that are distributed all over the world. Ferns live on the ground in light or deep shade of domestic or tropical forests, inhabit the branch forks of high primeval giants, settle on sunny cliffs, or water surfaces. The

floating fern (*Salvinia*) coats waters in southern Africa so densely that a person can walk on this blanket. Yes, shrubs are even supposed to grow on it.

Ferns do not flower. Mother Nature only invented flowers very much later. Unlike the highly developed flowering plants, ferns reproduce "primitively" like fungi, through spores. These are situated on the undersides of mature leaves and, depending on the species, are arranged like tiny dots, loose little heaps, or precise lines. The mature spore dust is powder-fine and can be carried on the wind. On a warm, damp surface (earth, for example) it develops a *prothallium*. This is furnished with male and female reproductive organs from whose fusion the young fern plants arise. Dominant characteristics of most species are the more or less finely pinnate fronds. They can be light

This bird's-nest fern has settled in the crook of a limb of a tropical tree.

or dark green, striped with silver-gray or tinged with red, leathery and robust or extremely delicate. Characteristic are the pretty curled "fiddleheads" or "croziers" from which the new fronds uncoil. By rolling up, the fern protects its leaf tip—the most susceptible part— from being eaten by animals.

Appropriate Culture

Most of our house ferns are forest dwellers from warmer regions. This means that they do best in a humusy, loose, nutrient-rich, moisture-retaining potting medium. They do not tolerate blazing sunlight and cold, especially cold feet. Through their numerous fronds, ferns develop a lush mass of green which evaporates much water. The soil should therefore be slightly damp at all times, the watering water soft and at room temperature. Almost all species, but especially the tender-leaved ones, are from habitats where high humidity prevails—the main reason why they often fail in rooms with heated, dry air. Unfortunately, many ferns do not like to be misted, so you must provide indirect humidity (see page 43). Hard-leaved species like the holly fern tolerate dry air, the staghorn fern protects its leaves from too much evaporation by a waxy coating, the cliff brake, as a xerophyte (plant that thrives in very dry locations) is used to dryness.

Ideal locations for all ferns are the bathroom, a damp, humid flower window, climate-controlled vitrine, or greenhouse. Also suitable are planted terrariums, paludariums, and of course mini-greenhouses.

Ferns that are epiphytic in their habitat can be bound to a fibrous piece of bark. There they feel at home, as can be seen.

Adiantum
Maidenhair Fern

Arachniodes
Arachniodes

Fragrant and delicate—the maidenhair fern

Arachniodes aristata tolerates heated air.

Most of the some 200 *Adiantum* species tolerate neither dry house air nor drafts. There are only a few species in trade. The best known are *Adiantum raddianum*, with its varieties 'Decorum', 'Fragrantissum', or 'Fritz Luth', and *Adiantum tenerum*, of which the variety 'Scuteum Roseum' has red-tinged leaves. Maidenhair ferns have the thin, almost wiry, dark-brown to black stems.

Family: Adiantaceae (maidenhair ferns).

Origin: Tropical and temperate regions of the earth, especially the Americas.

Location: Semishady. No sun. Temperature of air and soil never under 68° F (20° C) all year long. The plant needs high humidity and, therefore, lives longer in a vitrine, fernery, or in an enclosed flower window.

Watering, Feeding: Keep root ball damp all year round with soft, room-temperature water. The ball must never dry out—otherwise withered leaves and branches will result. From March to August feed every 2 weeks with low dosage. Use water-soluble fertilizer.

Further Culture: Provide for indirect humidity (see page 43). Mist often, especially in heated dry air. Repot larger plants in spring in American violet potting mix or add ¹/₂ peat to the standard all-purpose mix.

Propagation: By spores at ground temperatures between 75° and 79° F (24°–26° C). Place a flat with damp peat under the fronds. Also by division.

Pests, Disease: Faltering growth from too much dampness. Growth disturbances from cold feet and alkaline water. Watch for fungus gnat larvae.

This bushy fern has leatherlike leaves, which have two to three leaflets. The fronds can get to be as long as 27 in. (70 cm). The fern grows epiphytically in its habitat. The root stock is thick, creeping, and densely covered with long, red-brown scales. *Arachniodes adiantiformis* and *Arachniodes aristata*, along with its variety 'Variegatum', are the best-known species of the genus. They manage very well with central heating.

Family: Aspidiaceae

Origin: South Africa, Central and South America, Australia, Polynesia, New Zealand.

Location: Bright to semishady, no sun. The plant loves high humidity. Room temperatures all year around are tolerated, also somewhat cooler in winter, almost no growth below 54° F (12° C), however. Can take fresh air outdoors in summer.

Watering, Feeding: Keep uniformly damp with soft, room-temperature water. In winter in a cool location reduce water, but water somewhat more in a warm location. From March to August feed weekly with a low dosage.

Further Culture: Mist often in warm winter quarters. Repot as necessary in African violet potting mix or all-purpose mix with ¹/₂ peat added.

Propagation: By division and by sowing of spores in a heated propagating bed at 72° to 75° F (22°–24° C). Also by runners and rhizome division.

Pests, Diseases: Soft stems from light deficiency. Spider mites and scale from too warm and a dry winter location with poor air circulation, followed by sooty mildew infection.

Note: Sensitive to many insecticides.

Asplenium nidus
Bird's-Nest Fern, Nest Fern

Blechnum
Blechnum

The bird's-nest fern forms a rosette cup.

Blechnum gibbum is an unusual eye-catcher.

This tropical-forest fern, which in its natural setting develops leaves almost 39 in. (1 m) long, does best in a warm, humid environment, but it also manages astonishingly well in dry, heating-system air, especially the variety *Asplenium nidus* 'Fimbriatur'. The bird's nest fern grows and lives on trees like a bromeliad and collects nutrients and rainwater in its leaf-rosette nest. Especially attractive are the dark middle veins of the leaves. What many do not know: The bird's nest fern is closely related to wall rue (*Asplenium ruta-muraria*), a delicate fern that crowds out of the cracks of old walls.
Family: Aspleniaceae (spleenwort family).
Origin: Tropical rain forests of Asia, Africa, and Australia.
Location: Semishady. All year around room temperatures of 68° F (20° C) and more, never below 61° F (16° C). A warm, humid flower window is ideal. Important: Warm feet. Place a heating mat underneath on cold windowsills.
Watering, Feeding: Water regularly with soft water. In spring and summer feed once weekly with a weak dosage.
Further Culture: In heated areas mist often with soft water or provide indirect humidity (see page 43). Repot in summer every 2 years in all-purpose potting soil.
Propagation: By spores in a warm propagating flat.
Pests, Diseases: Brown leaf margins from too dry air or too low temperatures. Failure to grow because of cold feet. Susceptible to nematodes. Bacterial leaf disease.
My Tip: Don't use leaf polish sprays on the nest fern. It doesn't tolerate it.

These ferns from tropical and subtropical regions are very decorative with their sturdy rhizomes and feathery, dark-green fronds, sometimes even with split leaflets. The best-known species, *Blechnum gibbum*, thrives satisfactorily either in the house or in a conservatory. With increasing age, this fern grows over 3 ft. (1 m) and frequently develops a slant and thus looks very strange. *Blechnum brasiliense*, whose young fronds are brownish red, and *Blechnum moorei* need more warmth and humid air.
Family: Blechnaceae.
Origin: South America, New Caledonia.
Location: Bright to semishady. In summer, warm. In winter, never a temperature below 64° F (18° C). Tolerates neither cold feet nor drafts.
Watering, Feeding: Use softened, room-temperature water. In summer keep uniformly damp; in winter water somewhat less. Never allow root ball to dry out. From April to August feed every 2 weeks with low dosage.
Further Culture: Do not mist, rather provide indirect humidity (see page 43). Repot as necessary in spring in a mixture permitting air circulation composed of $1/2$ peat moss and $1/2$ all-purpose potting soil mixed with Styrofoam flakes.
Propagation: From spores, in a heatable propagation flat at ground temperatures between 68° and 77° F (20°– 25° C) or by division.
Pests, Diseases: Scale from poor air circulation, spider mites from dry air.
My Tip: An enchanting tub plant for shady terraces or balconies is *Blechnum spicant*, but it must be wintered over in the house at about 55° F (13° C).

The potting medium for Blechnum should have the character of the forest floor and be warm, airy, and water permeable, but at the same time also be water retentive.

Cyrtomium falcatum
Holly Fern

Davallia
Davallia

The leaves of the holly fern shine on their own.

Davallia mariesii with hairy rhizomes.

The holly fern is a sturdy, undemanding fern for cool areas and conservatories that also thrives in quite shady locations. In protected situations it even will go dormant under a cover of leaves to survive unharmed after a not very severe winter. Its finely serrated, leathery, hard leaves shine as if polished. They are therefore used like ilex branches for staking flowers. The most frequently cultivated variety is 'Rochfordianum', which has deeply incised finely serrated leaflets.

Family: Aspidiaceae.
Origin: East Asia, India, South Africa.
Location: Bright to shady, cool and airy. In winter, if possible, no warmer than 50° to 57° F (10°–14° C). Can summer over out of doors in a shady, airy place from middle of May on.
Watering, Feeding: Use soft, room-temperature water. From April to August, depending on temperature, water moderately to freely (baths now and then) and feed every 4 weeks. In winter, at lower temperatures, keep only slightly damp.

Further Culture: Mist often and repot as necessary in spring, in African violet soil mix or a blend of ½ peat and ½ all-purpose potting soil.
Propagation: By division or from spores. Place a flat with damp peat under the frond. Ripe spores will fall out and sprout.
Pests, Diseases: Rare. In a location that is too warm and has dry air, scale can appear.
My Tip: Rare, but especially unusual is *Cyrtomium caryotideum*, whose fronds look very much like those of the fishtail palm (*Caryota mitis*) (see page 207).

Of the some 40 *Davallia* species most often seen are *Davallia bullata* and *Davallia mariesii*. Both have bright green, finely pinnate fronds reminiscent of chervil and do not become very large. This epiphytic fern thrives best when it is bound to a trunk or a piece of bark and can enjoy the high humidity of a vitrine or an enclosed flower window. But there is a trick to cultivating it properly in the house as well. Bind its brown- or silver-haired rhizomes around a clay pot whose draining hole has been stopped up. The clay pot is filled with soft, lukewarm water, which continually evaporates a slight dampness into the air as well as to the outer wall of the pot, and this supplies the fern roots.

Family: Davalliaceae.
Origin: Canary Islands, tropical Asia.
Location: Bright, no sun. Warm all year, <u>never under 64° F (18° C).</u> The plant needs high humidity.
Watering, Feeding: Keep uniformly damp with soft, room-temperature water. The rhizomes should not dry out. In summer feed with a weak concentrate of fertilizer in water every 2 weeks.
Further Culture: Mist often. For culture in a shallow pot use coarse epiphyte mixture (materials available from nursery supply stores).
Propagation: By sowing spores or from rhizome pieces which grow on a damp sand-and-peat mixture (see page 43) with bottom warmth.
Pests, Diseases: Scale in dry, heated air.

Didymochlaena trunculata
Didymochlaena

Didymochlaena is easy to cultivate.

Didymochlaena trunculata, which freely translated means something like "shortened cloak," is found in all the tropical regions of the world and has every possible name in the different countries. In England, for example, it is called "cloak fern." In its habitat it develops a stem 20 in. (50 cm) high with a cluster of fronds a good 39 in. (1 m) long. The leathery, oval, doubly pinnate leaves are situated on brownish red stems. This ground-dwelling fern is of easy culture. In botanical gardens it is kept in the so-called warmhouse. The conditions there match those of a not-too-strongly heated conservatory. Only one handicap: Like all ferns, it does not tolerate dry, heated air.
Family: Aspidiaceae.
Origin: Tropical regions worldwide.

Location: Bright to semishady all year around. Keep warm from the beginning of new growth and over the summer; in winter keep cool–61° to 64° F (16°–18° C). A north window is ideal.
Watering, Feeding: Use only softened, room-temperature water for watering and mixing. Keep slightly damp the whole year over. From March to August feed with weak dosage every 14 days.
Further Culture: Mist often. Repot every spring in African violet soil mix or a half-and-half mix of peat and all-purpose potting soil.
Propagation: From spores or by division.
Pests, Diseases: With dryness of root ball and air, the fronds wither and the leaflets fall off. Scale from too warm a location with dry air.

Microlepia speluncae
Microlepia

In time, *Microlepia* develops very long fronds.

Of the 45 known species that occur in tropical and subtropical regions, *Microlepia speluncae* has become best known as a houseplant. It has soft, light green, sparsely hairy fronds and like *Davallia* (see page 198) has creeping, hairy rhizomes. The fronds develop very lushly and thus, of course, evaporate much water. This fern, which was described 100 years ago by the English botanist Thomas Moore, needs much free space to uncoil its fronds that grow up to 39 in. (1 m) long.
Family: Dennstaedtiaceae.
Origin: Tropical regions worldwide.
Location: Very bright all year around, but <u>never sunny</u>. In spring and summer around 68° F (20° C), in fall and winter not under 61° F (16° C). The plant loves high humidity.
Watering, Feeding: Use only soft, room-temperature water. Keep root ball quite damp, otherwise the fronds wilt. In winter, with cooler temperatures water less. From May to August feed every 4 weeks with a low dosage.
Further Culture: Provide indirect humidity (see page 43) and mist often. Divide each spring when growth is vigorous and repot in African violet soil mix or all-purpose potting soil.
Propagation: By sowing of spores at soil temperatures of 68° F (20° C). Or by division when repotting. Each portion of rhizome must show an actively growing point from which the new fronds can develop.
Pests, Diseases: Growth disturbances from too dry air.

Nephrolepsis exaltata
Sword Fern

Pellaea
Cliff Brake Fern

With its pale green, the sword fern is an all-around ornament.

The best known of the 30 species in this genus is *Nephrolopsis exaltata*. Countless large and dwarf cultivars with curly, wavy, or multiple pinnate fronds are in trade. Some form long runners that can be used for propagating.

Family: Nephrolepidaceae.

Origin: Distributed in tropical regions all over the world.

Location: Bright to semishady, warm and damp all year, in winter not under 64° F (18° C). In higher humidity even tolerates some sun.

Watering, Feeding: During the main growing season from March to August provide with plenty of room-temperature water and feed weekly with weak dosage. From June to September place out of doors. From October water somewhat more sparingly but <u>avoid drying out of root ball</u>.

Further Culture: Mist daily in winter. Every year in the spring or summer repot in all-purpose potting soil or African violet mix.

Propagation: Mainly by runners (cut off in summer and plant), more rarely by spores. Important: Soil temperature over 68° F (20° C).

Pests, Diseases: Rarely aphids, spider mites, scale.

Note: The plant is sensitive to many insecticides.

The cliff brake is ornamental and charming in hanging basket or pot.

One of the cliff brakes (*Pellaea rotundifolia*) is "button fern" because of its round, leathery leaves. The appearance of this species is utterly atypical of ferns. It also lives differently from its forest relatives. In contrast to most ferns, it grows in relatively dry locations. There it forms trailing stems up to 8 in. (20 cm) long, which look wonderful in a hanging basket. But there are also other species on the market that do not belie their fern origins: *Pellaea viridis* from South Africa and Madagascar with long green fronds, *Pellaea falcata* from southern Asia and Australia, and *Pellaea atropurpurea* from North America, an almost winter-hardy rock fern with long red-brown fronds.

Family: Sinopteridaceae.

Origin: New Zealand, Australia, Norfolk Island, North America, Asia, Africa, Madagascar.

Location: Bright but not full sun. Room temperature all year around. *Pellaea rotundifolia* and *Pellaea atropurpurea* in winter around 59° F (15° C).

Watering, Feeding: Water only moderately all year around. <u>Avoid sogginess at all costs</u>, for it quickly leads to death of the plant. From March to August feed every 2 weeks.

Further Culture: <u>Don't mist</u>. Repot newly acquired or young plants every spring in shallow containers in a blend of all-purpose soil and peat moss. Provide for good drainage.

Propagation. By division and from spores, which only appear on the undersides of leaves of older plants, however.

Pests, Diseases: Rarely, scale.

Phlebodium aureum
Rabbit's-Foot Fern, Golden Polypodium

Phlebodium scolopendrium 'Crispum'.

This tropical fern has heavily haired rhizomatous parts (that look like rabbit's feet), and bluish-green leaves with golden-yellow spore heaps on the undersides. The rabbit's-foot fern, which can grow to be quite large, comes from the warm, humid regions and with its tough leaves, which evaporate little water, can handle dry air astonishingly well. On the market are 'Areolatum' with broad wavy leaves, the most vigorously growing variety 'Mandaianum' with typical fern fronds, and the somewhat less vigorous 'Glaucum'.

Family: Polypodiaceae (polypody family).

Origin: South America.

Location: For an intense blue color, bright; semishade is also tolerated, but no blazing sun. Warm all year around, in winter cooler also but not under 54 to 61° F (12°–16° C). Thrives best in warm,

humid flower window, but manages well too in north, east, or west window.

Watering, Feeding: Keep root ball slightly damp at all times and feed every 14 days during the growing season with weak concentration.

Further Culture: Mist often in heated room or provide indirect humidity (see page 43). Repot every spring in African violet mix or ¹/₂ all-purpose potting soil with ¹/₂ peat added.

Propagation: By spores or division of rhizomes.

My Tip: Be careful in repotting to leave the rhizomes sticking out of the soil. If the fern becomes unbalanced for this reason, the rhizomes can be fastened with florists' wire (place around the rhizome and draw through the drainage hole of the pot) until the plant is firmly rooted.

Phyllitis scolopendrium
Hart's-Tongue

In a bright location the fronds turn blue.

This winter-hardy fern, which is native to Europe, used to be a popular houseplant, and there were countless variations of it, especially in England. Today, when more and more people are installing unheated conservatories, the hart's-tongue fern is coming into fashion again as an attractive green plant for cool, shady locations. It also thrives everywhere, with the exception of tropical heat and blazing sunshine. On the market are varieties, like 'Cristata' or 'Crispa', with attractively long, wavy leaves or some like 'Ramosa Marginata' or 'Ramosa Cristata', with almost parselylike leaves.

Family: Aspleniaceae (spleenwort family).

Origin: Europe, Asia Minor, North Africa, USA, Japan.

Location: Semishady to shady all year around; a north window is ideal. In summer 59° to 64° F

(15°–18° C), in winter around 50° F (10° C). The plant loves an outdoor stay from the middle of May to October.

Watering, Feeding: Keep uniformly damp but not wet. During the growing season from May to September feed with weak dosage every 14 days.

Further Culture: Needs high humidity. Mist all over often. Repot in spring as necessary in African violet mix or ¹/₂ all-purpose soil with ¹/₂ peat.

Propagation: The species by spores, the varieties by division or by rooting of stems with a little piece of rhizome.

Pests, Diseases: Scale and thrips in too warm a location with dry air.

Platycerium
Staghorn Fern

The staghorn fern is an extraordinary hanging plant.

The staghorn fern is a remarkable looking fellow that is clearly different from other ferns. Characteristic are the antlerlike branching leaves, often a yard (meter), long which develop brown-black, flat spore deposits (sporangia) on the undersides of the leaves at particular spots, according to the species. This epiphytic fern is also furnished with other, sterile leaves that serve to anchor it and for food storage. They stick up a little and form a kind of trough or niche for rain-water, but also for falling leaves and rotting plant parts, from which the fern gains its nutrients. An ideal place for the staghorn fern is an enclosed flower window, where it is bound to a sturdy epiphyte support. Just as satisfactory, however, is a sturdy lattice-work basket or a hanging pot. The genus *Platycerium* consists of some 17 species. In addition to *Platycerium bifurcatum*, the best-known species and the one easiest to culture, which was introduced to England in 1808, one encounters *Platycerium grande*, which is larger all over and comes from the Philippine island of Luzon. Its sterile leaves are lighter green, slightly wavy, and incised at the end. The fertile leaves grow to more than 39 in. (1 m) long and when juvenile are tomentosely fuzzy. Rarely seen in the market is the African species *Platycerium angolense* with simple fertile leaves.

Family: Polypodiaceae (polypody family).

Origin: Australia, Peru, Madagascar, New Guinea.

Location: Bright to semishady, not sunny. Room temperatures all year, in winter even cooler (but never below 61° F [16 °C]).

Watering, Feeding: Water into the trough using soft, room-temperature water or soak the fern once a week for 30 minutes. From April to August add fertilizer to the water or place a crumb of peat soaked in food solution behind the sterile leaves. One quarter of the prescribed amount of fertilizer per quart (liter) of water is enough.

Further Culture: Provide for high humidity. Do not use water to wipe off leaves or you will remove the pretty hairy covering. Repotting is not necessary for specimens on epiphyte supports. Potted plants should be planted in coarsely crumbled peat mixed with African violet potting soil and Styrofoam flakes.

Propagation: From spores (difficult for the layperson) or by side shoots that sometimes develop.

Pests, Diseases: Scale on the undersides of fronds from dry heating-system air. Scratch off carefully or dot with spirits-soap solution (see box, page 52) and then wash off with lukewarm water.

Note: *Platycerium* is sensitive to many insecticides.

A rarity—*Platycerium angolense*.

Brake, Dish Fern, Table Fern

Pteris ensiformis 'Evergemensis' (left) and *Pteris cretica* 'Albo Lineata' (right).

The genus *Pteris,* represented by about 280 species in the tropics and subtropics, offers a rich choice of colored-leaved, green, small but also vigorously growing species and varieties. Its name comes from the Greek word **pteron** = wing. Characteristic for the brakes are the bushlike fronds, which arise from short, underground rhizomes. They grow upright at first and then bend with their tips pointing downward. Some species have two kinds of fronds: short sterile ones and longer fertile ones on which the sporangia are situated along the edge of the underside of the leaf. Others have only fertile or only sterile fronds. Best way to tell: fertile fronds curl the edges of their leaflets under to protect the sporangia, so that they appear to be smooth-margined. If you see the leaf serrations clearly, the frond is a sterile one. The best-known dish fern is the robust *Pteris cretica* and its green and variegated cultivars like 'Albo Lineata', the parsleylike 'Rowen', or 'Wimsettii'. *Pteris cretica* has either fertile or sterile fronds on black stems 6 in. (15 cm) long. Needing more warmth is *Pteris ensiformis*, a charming small fern for the bottle garden, mini-greenhouse, and fernery. This species has fertile and sterile fronds. In trade are exclusively varieties like the white-bordered "Evergemensis", which was developed in Belgium in 1956, or 'Victoriae', which has been around since 1890. Anyone with a climate-controlled flower window can also grow the especially beautiful *Pteris quadriaurita* as well as its cultivar 'Argyraea'. In roomy conservatories the brilliant green *Pteris tremula* from New Zealand and Australia makes a very good show. It can get to be at least 39 in. (1 m) tall. All are terrestrial ferns and must be kept in pots and not bound to boards.

Family: Acrostichaceae.

Origin: Tropical and subtropical regions worldwide, Mediterranean region.

Location: Semishady to shady. Delicate species like *Pteris quadriaurita* and *Pteris ensiformis*, all year round at 68° F (20° C); *Pteris cretica* in winter cooler also—variegated cultivars at 61° to 64° F (16°–18° C), green-leaved at 54° F (12° C). High humidity is important.

Watering, Feeding: Water only with soft, room-temperature water. In summer keep moderately but uniformly damp; in winter at lower temperatures water somewhat less. From April to August feed with weak concentration every 14 days.

Further Culture: Mist now and then. In spring repot in a mixture with equal parts of peat moss and all-purpose potting soil.

Propagation: By division, in spring, when repotting or by spores, which form so abundantly that young plants often settle on the surfaces of pots of neighboring plants. Transplant out the young plants into very small pots.

Pests, Diseases: Scale and aphids in too dry a location.

My Tip: Cut away the unsightly older fronds. The plant regenerates itself through the development of young fronds.

PALMS

Palms bring the bright atmosphere of southern vacation lands into the house and become as precious artworks. Some, reaching to the ceiling, over the years grow to be an integral part of our homes.

Palms are favorites of the interior decorators and are often used to soften the icy glitter of modern lobbies of glass and steel. With the exception of *Washingtonia*, the lady palm, and palmetto, all the palms considered here are species of indoor palms that should be kept warm all year round and not be placed outdoors in summer.

What You Should Know About Palms

More than 3,000 species and over 200 genera belong to the palm family. Palms grow in shady tropical rain forests, but also in the intense light on mountain massifs 10,000 ft (3,000 m) high. They are to be found on savannahs, steppes, deserts, and along seashores, and almost all are sensitive to frost. They are among the younger plants in the history of evolution of the botanical system. This is indicated by their being monocotyledonous as well as by their long, parallel leaf veins.

Their exceedingly decorative leaves are the palm's hallmarks. They are divided into feather-leaved (plumose) and fan-leaved (palmate) palms according to the way they look.

• Feather-leaved palms like the parlor palm develop what are ordinarily described as palm fronds.

• Fan-leaved palms like the *Washingtonia* have almost circular leaves.

In almost all palms, fronds or fans are borne at the end of an

The coconut, a giant seed, can float for thousands of miles and sprout on a new shore.

Only in a natural setting out of doors do palms develop their spadixlike inflorescences, often with vibrantly colored fruits, which contain the seeds.

unbranching trunk. With the exception of the parlor palm, palms do not bloom in the house, for in the confined space of their pot they never leave the juvenile stage.

The Right Culture

The best location for a palm is a very bright one, but never a sunny one. Species with hard, tough foliage tolerate dry air better than those with soft, filigree-fine leaflets. Fan palms offer larger surfaces for evaporation and must be provided with water more often. Moreover, dry heating-system air and dry root ball are the chief causes of brown tips, a frequent occurrence on palms.

When watering, the "heart" of the palm must be avoided. This bulblike, thickened stem contains the vegetative cone from which the new leaves develop. When it rots, the palm is done for. Standing water or cold in the root region can be just as lethal.

In their homelands palms grow in inorganic soil, on sand, limestone, serpentine rock rich in magnesium and silicic acid, as well as in the type of tropical red soil that is enriched with clay and iron. Inorganic fertilizers or horse-tail broth rich in silicic acid (see box, page 52) does them good, in my experience. As a potting medium, you can use all-purpose potting soil, which can be made more permeable with added sand, perlite, or Styrofoam flakes.

PALMS

Archontophoenix cunninghamiana
Piccabeen Palm

Archontophoenix is an Australian house palm.

○ 🪣 🧴

This palm species, in which the fronds broaden with increasing age, is frequently sold under its old botanical name *Seaforthia* or *Ptychosperma*. Moreover, its name is easy to confuse with *Acanthophoenix*, a less well known species that is native to Mauritius. *Archontophoenix cunninghamiana* is native to Australia and there its trunk attains a height of 59 to 72 ft (18–22 m). If you are lucky, you may see the grown plant in a botanical garden blooming with lavender-blue flowers, from which later red berries develop.

Family: Arecaceae (palm family).

Origin: Eastern Australia.

Location: Bright but not sunny. Room temperatures all year around, but in winter rather cooler—not below 50° F (10° C). Tolerates dry heating-system air poorly, therefore better to place in a bright stairwell or in the conservatory beginning in fall.

Watering, Feeding: Keep uniformly damp but avoid sogginess. From April to August feed with weak solution.

Further Culture: Mist often, especially after heat is turned on. Repot as necessary in all-purpose potting soil.

Propagation: By seed, in a heated propagating bed.

Pests, Diseases: Spider mites and scale in a warm, dry location.

My Tip: In the juvenile stages you can easily confuse *Archontophoenix* with the Assai palm (*Euterpe*), the sentry palm (*Howea*, see page 209), or the yellow palm (*Chrysalidocarpus*, see page 208). Best key to recognition: The tips of the fronds of *Archontophoenix* look like a cut-out *V* on top.

Areca catechu
Betel Palm

The betel palm looks very different when it is mature.

○ 🪣 🧴

In its habitat the betel palm grows to a height of 98 ft (30 m). Here you frequently acquire it as a relatively small seedling that has two to four leaves. Only with greater age does it develop the twiggy pinnate leaves. Unfortunately the life expectancy of this slender-stemmed palm, also sold here as a "mini-coconut palm," is limited if you can't offer it a warm, humid flower window or a roomy vitrine. The betel palm—famous because of the betelnut cud chewed as a stimulating drug by 300 million people between the tropics of Cancer and Capricorn in the old world—grows very slowly.

Family: Arecaceae (palm family).

Origin: Philippines, Southeast Asia.

Location: Bright but not sunny all year around and warm (over 68° F [20° C]). The plant needs high humidity and ground warmth.

Watering, Feeding: Keep uniformly damp. In a window give it an undersaucer constantly filled with water. From April to August feed with weak dosage every 14 days.

Further Culture: Provide indirect humidity (see page 43) and mist often. Repot seldom.

Propagation: From seed, which sprouts after 2 to 3 months at ground temperature of 77° F (25° C).

Pests, Diseases: Growth disturbances in too cool a location with dry air.

My Tip: With a warming pad underneath, this plant will survive for a long time even on the windowsill.

Caryota mitis
Burmese Fishtail Palm

Chamaedorea elegans
Parlor Palm

Leaves like nibbled fish tails—*Caryota*.

The parlor palm blooms even when it is a young plant.

Of the 27 species that belong to this genus, to date only *Caryota mitis* has become known as a houseplant. It has long been a prized houseguest in the United States and since 1850 in Europe. Its doubly pinnate leaves looking like gnawed fishtails make it unmistakable. It grows busy, relatively slowly, and develops numerous runners, which can be removed and used for propagating. In an optimally warm, humid situation it can grow to a height of 58 in. (1.5 m) and almost as wide. Its striking deep-green fruit clusters, which look like bunches of nut necklaces, do not develop in pot culture. But often you can admire them in botanical gardens.

Family: Arecaceae (palm family).

Origin: Burma, Java, Philippines.

Location: Bright and warm all year around. No sun and never under 64° F (18° C). The plant needs high humidity. A climate-controlled flower window or greenhouse is ideal.

Watering, Feeding: Keep root ball slightly damp at all times. Avoid sogginess and dry root ball. From spring to fall fertilize weakly every week.

Further Culture: Provide for high humidity. Best to mist daily. Only repot when completely potbound. Use all-purpose potting soil. First place a drainage layer of pebbles, Styrofoam flakes, or sand in the new pot.

Propagation: From seed or by layering.

Pests, Diseases: Spider mites when air too dry. Brown tips after dried root ball or sogginess.

The delicate parlor palm, *Chamaedorea elegans*, has a stiff, closely ringed little trunk, which reaches 79 in. (2 m) at the most, and fresh-green, gracefully weeping feathery leaves. It is at home in the thick, impenetrable mountain forests of Mexico and Guatemala and adept at surviving in shade. Moreover, it is one of the few palms that bloom in their juvenile years. The female flowers of the dioecious plant give off a lovely scent; the male ones are odorless. In good culture the pale-yellow flowers keep on appearing regardless of the time of year. Newly offered: *Chamaedorea cataractum* from Mexico and Hawaii, with darker fronds.

Family: Arecaceae (palm family).

Origin: Mexico, Guatemala.

Location: Bright to semishady. A north window is ideal. Keep at 68° F (20° C) in summer, cooler in winter. May be placed outdoors in a shady place from June on.

Watering, Feeding: Keep root ball uniformly damp. From March to September feed with a weak fertilizer every 3 weeks.

Further Culture: Mist often. Only repot as necessary in all-purpose potting soil.

Propagation: From seed.

Pests, Diseases: Attacks of spider mites in dry heating-system air. Possible root rot with too much dampness in too dark a location.

My Tip: If the parlor palm blooms too often and you don't want the plant to be unnecessarily weakened, it's better to cut the flowers off before they unfold.

Remove flowers. The parlor palm invests all its strength in the subsequent development of seeds because maintaining the species is its most important goal.

207

PALMS

Chrysalidocarpus lutescens
Areca Palm, Yellow Palm

The Areca palm has supplanted the sentry palm.

Under its old name of Areca palm, at one time this was one of the most frequently propagated palm species. In fact, the elegance of the Areca palm is quite the equal of that of the sentry palm (*Howea*, see page 209). It differs from the *Howea* in its lighter, green-yellow foliage and in the "freckled" leaf shafts. In its Madagascan habitat it can reach heights of 33 ft (10 m). In the house, with good culture, it will easily grow 8 in. (20 cm) per year. The fronds are 39 in. (1 m) long, comblike pinnated, and very decorative. The plant is sold in all sizes and usually as a clump. It blooms and fruits after several years, even in houseplant culture.

Family: Arecaceae (palm family).

Origin: Madagascar.

Location: Bright but not sunny; all year round very warm, never under 61° F (16° C).

Watering, Feeding: Always keep slightly damp. At high soil temperatures will even tolerate foot baths. From March to beginning of August feed weekly with a low concentration solution.

Further Culture: Avoid dry air, provide humidity at all costs. In winter mist daily. Every 2 to 3 years repot in all-purpose potting soil.

Propagation: From seed or by division. The Areca palm develops runners.

Pests, Diseases: When air is too dry, leaf drop, yellowed leaves, or brown spots may occur.

My Tip: Do you live in an area that is hot and humid in summer? If so, put the Areca palm in a shady place out of doors at the beginning of June. It loves thunderstorms.

Cocos nucifera
Coconut Palm

Coconuts need much light, humidity, and warmth.

The coconut palm is the embodiment of the exotic palm. What we buy are forced plants, tiny in comparison to the mother. Most are still tied to the nut that gives them nourishment. The threadlike so-called floating body that is located under the smooth outer skin of the nut and helps the nut to travel thousands of kilometers in the seas, does not rot so quickly with us as it does in the warm, humid native habitat. It becomes dry and hard and can hinder the growth of the young plant. This and because the coconut palm lacks the high light intensity and the damp warmth of its home at the Equator are the reasons that most specimens never get very old here.

Family: Arecaceae (palm family).

Origin: Tropics worldwide. Origin unknown.

Location: As bright, warm, and humid as possible. The plant tolerates full sun. In summer, shade at midday. In winter do not keep below 64° F (18° C).

Watering, Feeding: Keep root ball slightly damp at all times. From April to September fertilize every week with a weak solution.

Further Culture: Provide humidity. Mist often. Repot as seldom as possible.

Propagation: From seed, or coconuts.

Pests, Diseases: Rare. Wilting of the lower leaves is normal, since this is the way the trunk develops. Brown tips indicate dry air.

My Tip: In winter I place my coconut palm under a plant light and mist it daily with soft, warm water. This way it lives longer.

Howea
Sentry Palm, Kentia Palm

Microcoelum weddelianum
Weddel Palm

The broadly overhanging *Howea forsteriana*.

The Weddel palm loves high humidity.

On the market are two species: *Howea forsteriana* and *Howea belmoreana*. As young plants both are scarcely distinguishable from each other. Only later can you tell by the growth: While *Howea forsteriana* grows faster and spreads wider, *Howea belmoreana* develops slowly and becomes stiffly upright. Both bear pinnate, dark-green fronds, have a single trunk, and are mostly offered in clumps of three.

Family: Arecaceae (palm family).

Origin: Lord Howe Island, Australia.

Location: Bright to semishady. The plant tolerates no sun, can get by with little light, but then grows very little. All year long room temperatures, in daytime up to 77° F (25° C), cooler at night. Older plants may be set outside at the end of May in a wind-protected, shady place.

Watering, Feeding: Water copiously but always allow soil to dry out between waterings. Absolutely avoid sogginess. From March to September feed weekly with a weak solution.

Further Culture: The Kentia palm tolerates dry heated air relatively well. Nevertheless, in winter mist often. Repot in all-purpose potting soil only when plant is completely potbound. Important: Make a drainage layer of pot shards or expanded clay pellets.

Propagation: From seed at ground temperatures between 77° and 86° F (25°– 30° C).

Pests, Diseases: Spider mite and scale infestations in air that is too dry. The heart rots with constant sogginess.

My Tip: At least twice a year wash off dusty fronds with lukewarm water so that it can "breathe" better. Advisable: A gentle May rain.

The Weddel palm is one of the best-selling palms for the house, frequently even being offered as a "beginner's palm." But rather, this filigreed plant from the tropical rain forest is something for the advanced gardeners who already have other exotics like orchids or bromeliads in warm, humid flower windows, vitrines, or conservatories. For these are the conditions under which the Weddel palm feels at home and where it can thrive for a long time, since even the oldest plants grow scarcely larger than 5 ft (1.5 m).

Family: Arecaceae (palm family).

Origin: Tropical Brazil.

Location: Bright and warm, never under 68° F (20° C). Protect from sun. The plants love warm feet.

Watering, Feeding: Keep constantly damp; in winter water somewhat less. In spring and summer feed once a month with weak dosage.

Further Culture: Must be sprayed often and regularly in winter. Repot as necessary in all-purpose soil mixed with Styrofoam flakes—as a rule every 2 to 3 years.

Propagation: From seed at ground temperature of 86° F (30° C).

Pests, Diseases: Spider mites when air too dry. Brown tips with dried out root ball and too little humidity, stunted growth with cold feet.

My Tip: Your Weddel palm has a chance at longer life if you surround it with constant humidity. To do so, encase the plant in a larger pot filled with expanded clay pellets or peat (see drawing, page 43).

PALMS

Phoenix
Date Palm

Phoenix roebelenii makes an elegant appearance.

Of the 13 recognized *Phoenix* species there are mainly 3 that are interesting to the houseplant fancier: the true date palm (*Phoenix dactylifera*, see photograph, page 64), the Canary Island date (*Phoenix canariensis*), and the miniature date palm (*Phoenix roebelenii*). The first two are only suitable for the house as young plants. They quickly become large and are then wonderful tub plants for the terrace or the cool conservatory. The miniature date palm, on the other hand, hardly grows taller than 59 to 79 in. (1.5 – 2 m), even in age, and needs a great deal of warmth. Humid vitrines or flower windows and warm conservatories are its favorite spots. It produces slender fronds, which droop elegantly. The young shoots look as though they were dusted with flour, the young fronds have white fibers. The plant develops a handsome trunk with a bushy crown of fronds.

Family: Arecaceae (palm family).

Origin: Laos.

Location: Very bright but not full sun. Warm all year around, in winter never below 59° F (15° C).

Watering, Feeding: Keep root ball slightly damp at all times but never wet. From April to August feed with low dosage.

Further Culture: Mist often, daily after heat is turned on. Repot as necessary in all-purpose soil with plenty of Styrofoam flakes.

Propagation: From seed, in a heated bed.

Pests, Diseases: Chlorosis when watered with hard water. Spider mites when air too dry. Growth disturbances and brown fronds in a location where feet get cold, too much dampness in winter, or hard water.

Rhapis
Lady Palm

The lady palm is the embodiment of Far Eastern flair.

The small *Rhapis humilis*, which only grows to 39 in. (1 m), is suitable for a room; for the conservatory or as a tub plant, there is *Rhapis excelsa*, which in a large container can reach 79 in. (2 m). Both have bamboolike, slender trunks with brown fibers and were very popular as long ago at the turn of the century. The fronds become 6 to 12 in. (15– 30 cm) across. The individual leaflets in *Rhapis humilis* are narrower and more delicate and numerous than in *Rhapis excelsa*. *Rhapis* is the only palm genus that has been used successfully for bonsai. In the United States it is so popular that some nurseries deal exclusively in the Lady Palm.

Family: Arecaceae (palm family).

Origin: China, Japan.

Location: Bright to semishady, no sun. In summer warm, in winter cool at 41° to 50° F (5°– 10° C). From middle of May can be set outside in a semishady spot for the summer. Thrives well in stairwell, provided there are no drafts.

Watering, Feeding: Water freely in spring and summer. In winter water more sparingly. From May to August use weak fertilizer.

Further Culture: Mist fronds occasionally. Repot in all-purpose soil with sand added when the root ball begins to squeeze itself out of the pot.

Propagation: From seed or by runners that are separated from the mother plant and planted.

Pests, Diseases: Dried and browned fronds from too warm a location with dry air. Yellow leaves from attack of spider mites.

Sabal
Palmetto

Washingtonia
Washington Palm

The palmetto loves a bright location.

The petticoat palm needs much space.

Palmettos are striking primarily because of their deeply incised fans. There are stemless, bushy species and ones with mighty trunks that have steeply tapered sides. In their habitat, the largest, with a trunk diameter of 39 in. (1 m), reach a height of 82 ft (25 m). There are some 25 known species, whose distribution area extends from Venezuela through Central America, Mexico and the southern United States. In Cuba these ornaments command the landscape, and even in Italy there were palmettos during the geological miocene epoch. On the market there is *Sabal minor*, which grows to a height of barely 79 in. (2 m), is rather bushy in habit, and forms runner-like rhizomes. Its deeply cut leaves are larger than 39 in. (1 m) and sometimes appear bluish-frosted. There is also *Sabal palmetto*, whose leaf-stalk scars make a beautiful trunk pattern.

Family: Arecaceae (palm family).

Origin: Subtropical America.

Location: Very bright all year round, especially in winter. Keep warm in summer, cooler (50°–59° F [10°–15° C]) in winter. May be set outside in a warm, sunny place from the middle of May.

Watering, Feeding: Water abundantly in summer, in winter only enough so that the root ball doesn't dry out. From May to August fertilize with a weak solution every week.

Further Culture: Repot as necessary in all-purpose potting soil with sand added.

Propagation: From seed, also may attempt with runners of *Sabal minor*.

Pests, Diseases: In a bright location, rare.

The splendid Washington palm can only be kept as a houseplant for a limited time. Then it becomes too large and imposing and needs as least a conservatory. It grows very quickly and even in a tub can become over 79 in. (2 m) wide and 10 ft (3 m) tall. Available are the Mexican species *Washingtonia robusta* and the California *Washingtonia filifera*, also called "threadbearing palm." Both, because of the pattern made by the base of the leaf-stalk, have particularly picturesque trunks. The leaves of *Washingtonia robusta* are glossy green, those of *Washingtonia filifera* gray-green.

Family: Arecaceae (palm family).

Origin: Arizona, California, Mexico.

Location: Bright and airy. In summer warm, in winter cool, at 50° F (10° C). Will not tolerate any heating at all. Place outside from the middle of May.

Watering, Feeding: Water copiously in summer, more sparingly in winter. Feed with weak solution every 14 days from April to August.

Further Culture: Repot young plants yearly, older ones rarely. All-purpose potting soil with sand is suitable.

Propagation: From seed, in a heatable propagation bed.

Pests, Diseases: Aphids and brown leaf tips in dry, stagnant air.

Warning: Washington palms bear sharp thorns on the leaf stems that can cause injury. Place the plant in the conservatory or on the terrace so that a person doesn't brush the palm when passing by.

A petticoat of old leaves that haven't fallen wraps the trunk of the Washingtonia and has earned it the name of petticoat palm in the United States.

You don't absolutely have to have a greenhouse or a climate-controlled flower window to fulfill a dream of growing orchids. Many modern cultivars will grow and bloom even on a windowsill.

ORCHIDS

The blooming of the African violets or clivia is a joyous occasion. But let the *Coelogyne* rain down its cascades of white flowers punctually in March, let the light-craving cymbidiums be successfully brought into bloom or the bulk of lady's slipper orchids be increased with each year, and for the ambitious houseplant gardener this is truly a cause for celebration.

As a rule, the modern hybrids are the easiest to cultivate. Produced from various species and genera, these beauties are selectively bred to be better adapted to our climate and light conditions and usually bloom more profusely and more willingly than the wild forms. Anyone who buys them also is not supporting the destruction of the species and thus helps to practice conservation. The orchids introduced on the following pages are primarily hybrids that are easy to obtain and to grow. Anyone who is interested in more striking and demanding species will find them with appropriate tips on culture in the last section (see pages 220–221).

What You Should Know About Orchids

Not only are orchids the youngest flowering plants in terms of evolutionary history, they also represent the largest plant family, with some 750 genera and 10,000 to 30,000 species and more than 70,000 hybrids. With the exception of the ice-cold polar region and the hot, dry desert regions, they are represented all around the globe. They settle primarily in tropical rain or mountain forests, cool, moisture-saturated foggy forests, as well as in rocky or coastal wastelands near the seas. Most of them come from Asiatic regions, many from Central and South America. There, they mostly live in trees, some grow on the ground, a few also on rocks.

Growth forms: Orchids have two growth forms:
• Monopodial species like the *Phalaenopsis,* which forms one main stem that grows vertically from the root and develops flowers at the side of the main axis.

• Sympodial species like the *Cattleya,* which continue to grow on a horizontal axis, from which numerous sprouts arise. The new growth comes sideways from the base and at some point shoves itself over the edge of the pot. Sympodial orchids have pseudobulbs. These storage organs for water and nutrients are evidence that in their natural habitat the plants have to survive periods of dryness.

The leaves are supplied with veins that run parallel and are usually smoothly edged. Color and constitution give evidence as to the desired location. The intensity of color in the leaves indicates their light requirements; dark green, low light; bright green, normal; and gray-green, extremely high. Additionally, orchids that tolerate cold or sun have rather hard leaves, whereas shade- and warmth-loving ones have rather soft leaves.

Orchid blossoms are of perfect beauty and most are astonishingly long lasting.

Correct Culture

Always ask when you are buying an orchid whether you are dealing with a species or hybrid for cool, temperate regions or warm ones.

Orchids living on or in trees derive their nutrients from the humus of decaying plant parts.

Orchids from cool regions are the most difficult to keep, those from the warm areas, the easiest. The required humidity is achieved through electric humidifiers or other measures (see page 43). Of course all orchids thrive best of all in climate-controlled flower windows or greenhouses. The magic formula for successful blooming is: rest, cooler temperatures at night, much light in fall, and enough humidity at all times.

Rule of thumb: Orchids with tough leaves and thick bulbs need a dry resting period; those with soft, tender leaves must never get completely dry.

In late winter/spring the new growth begins. This means give more water now.

In early summer/summer the orchid grows and needs food (fertilizer), water, and warmth.

In late summer/fall the bulbs develop, the new growth matures, the development of the ability to flower takes place. Important: Nightly temperature drop of about 7° to 11° F (4°–6° C), full fall light, less water.

In fall/winter the rest period occurs. This corresponds to the tropical dry season. Give your orchids plenty of light now and little water.

Unlike most houseplants, orchids will not grow in potting soil. They need a special orchid potting medium (see page 40), which is loose, light, and air permeable on the one hand, but on the other can store nutrients and water.

Orchids probably have the most bizarre flowers of all. These of *Encyclia cochleata* resemble mysterious insects.

Cattleya
Cattleya

Cattleya bicolor comes from Brazil.

More *Laelia* than
Cattleya—*Laeliocattleya*
hybrid Creamton.

In their natural setting cattleyas usually grow epiphytically on branches or tree trunks. The flowers are large, magnificently colored, and have a conspicuous lip. The buds develop from a sheath. On the market are *Cattleya* species, *Cattleya* hybrids, and so-called multigeneric hybrids, for example, *Brassolaeliocattleya*, *Epicattleya*, *Potinara*, or *Sophrolaeliocattleya*. The

flowers appear in white, yellow (in many shades), pink, and various shades of red. Particularly good orchids for the house are crosses of *Cattleya* and *Laelia* (see page 216), so called *Laeliocattleya* hybrids, for example Alma Wichmann (spring bloomer), as well as Max, Moritz, and Winter's Tale

White *Laeliocattleya*
hybrid with yellow
column.

Particularly intensely
colored—*Laeliocattleya*
hybrid 'Culminari
Recital'.

The readily flowering *Cattleya bowringiana*.

(winter bloomers). They are cultivated like cattleyas.

Blooming Season:
Depending on species and variety, in spring, summer, fall, or winter.

Family: Orchidaceae (orchid family).

Origin: Central and South America.

Location: Very bright but not blazing sun. Ideal is an east or a west window. In summer and during growing season warm all day to 77° F (25° C) and airy. Important: The drop in temperature of some degrees during the night. In winter 64° F (18° C) in the daytime, and 57° F (14° C) at night are enough.

Watering, Feeding: In summer water as needed or soak the plants; in winter water only enough to keep the roots and pseudobulbs from drying out. In summer add an orchid fertilizer to every third watering.

Further Culture: Mist

leaves frequently from May to October. Every 2 to 3 years repot in orchid potting medium. Spring and summer bloomers after flowering, fall and winter bloomers in March, April.

Propagation: By division of the pseudobulb when repotting.

Pests, Diseases: Scale from dry house air. Watch out for ants, which are drawn by the sticky sweet excretion from the spathe and have aphids in train. The brown color of the flower sheath is typical of the species. So is the fibrous development around the bulb. It serves as a sunshade.

My Tip: To ensure that your *Cattleya* will bloom every year, you must put the plant in a cooler place as soon as the growth is mature and reduce the amount of water. In too warm a location the *Cattleya* will bolt and form only leaves.
Of all the orchids, the

Brown hybrids are especially sought after.

Color kaleidoscope of *Cymbidium* flowers.

cymbidiums provide the most cut flowers. From Thailand, mainly, come thousands of panicles to the flower markets of the whole world. This is no wonder. Cymbidium flowers last a particularly long time in a vase and offer a color spectrum without equal. Most cymbidiums are cultivated as terrestrials and have thick, fleshy roots and hard, long rein-like leaves, which usually grow out of oval pseudobulbs. The racemes of flowers appear at the bottom of the bulb and are very long lasting. The market offers the so-called standard type, *Cymbidium* hybrids that in a conservatory grow more than 39 in. (1 m) tall, and the miniature cymbidiums for the house, which grow to a height of 31 to 39 in. (80–100 cm). The latter have warmth-loving forebears, bloom from fall, and tolerate heated rooms far better. The palette of flower colors ranges from cream-white through yellow, orange, pink, red, violet, brown to green. Well-known miniature cymbidiums, which bloom in winter/spring, are: Agnes Norton, Show-off, Dag Oleste, Excalibur, March Pinchess 'Del Rey', Miniatures Delight (wonderful hanging plant!), Minneken, 'Pink Tower', 'Lemförde Surprise'.

Blooming Season: According to species and variety, in spring, summer, fall, or winter.

Family: Orchidaceae (orchid family).

Origin: Tropical Asia, Australia.

Location: All year around airy, very bright, and sunny. Put standard types and older mini-cymbidiums out of doors from June to end of September in a bright spot but not in full sun. Keep warm in summer but definitely cooler at night from August on.

Watering, Feeding: Water copiously from March to the end of September and provide the plant with orchid fertilizer every 4 weeks. In late fall and winter water less, do not feed.

Further Culture: Provide high humidity. Mist often. Every 2 years repot after blooming in orchid potting medium.

Propagation: Through division of the pseudobulb at the time of repotting.

Pests, Diseases: Spider mites in dry air. Yellow spotted leaves and lighter leaves indicate a virus disease. Isolate plant so that it can't infect any others, or destroy it. There are no remedies for virus disease.

My Tip: In cymbidiums the flowers that bloom from September to January are set in May/June, those blooming from February to May are set in September. During these periods the plants need much warmth in the daytime and plenty of fresh, cool air at night.

The *Cymbidium* Hybrids in the photographs:
The Cymbidium Hybrids in the Photographs:
Top left: Green hybrid with spotted lip.
Bottom left: Silvia Müller Citronella.
Top right: Cream-white hybrid with orange-red lip.
Bottom right: The well-known Starbright Capella.

Laelia
Laelia

Laelia purpurata—the national flower of Brazil.

In their habitat the some 50 species of *Laelia* mostly grow as epiphytes in tropical forests. But there are also some species that grow on rocks or on sandy ground, as for instance the stone laelias. Among them are the cinnabar-red *Laelia cinnabarina*. These are recommended for the beginner and, like the magnificent *Laelia purpurata,* bloom in spring. *Laelia crispa* blooms in summer. Included among the fall bloomers is the huge-flowered *Laelia pumila* (violet pink), and *Laelia harpophylla* (orange) flowers in winter. Laelias produce relatively few hybrids by crossing of the species, with the exception of the laeliocattleyas (see Cattleya, page 214).

Blooming Season: According to species and variety, in spring, summer, fall, or winter.

Family: Orchidaceae (orchid family).

Origin: Tropical America.

Location: Bright to semi-shady, airy (but no drafts). In fall full sun for *Laelia cinnabarina*. In spring and summer days 64° to 75° F (18°–24 C), nights and in fall/winter around 12° F (7° C) lower.

Watering, Feeding: In summer in very hot weather, water abundantly or soak. Only water again when the potting medium is well dried out. In winter give only enough water to keep the plants from wilting. At every third watering during the growing season add orchid fertilizer.

Further Culture: Provide for high humidity. Repot every 2 to 3 years in fresh orchid substrate. Epiphytic laelias can be bound to cork or tree-fern supports.

Propagation: Division of the pseudobulb at the time of repotting.

Pests, Diseases: Beware of stagnant, suffocating air; it is not well tolerated by laelias.

Miltonia, Miltoniopsis
Pansy Orchid

The pansy flowers of *Miltoniopsis.*

Characteristic of miltonias are the open, flat flowers with a short column, which at first glance look like pansies or violets. Today, miltonias are roughly divided into two groups: *Miltonia* species, which are good for house-plant culture, and *Miltonipsis* species, the so-called pansy miltonias, which come from the cool, damp cloud forests.

Both genera embrace 15 to 20 species. The epiphytic plants usually bear bright-green flattened pseudobulbs with one or two small leaves. The flowers always arise from the base of the youngest pseudobulb. The flowers are multicolored, often white with red or pink. Primarily found on the market are the summer- or fall-blooming *Miltonia clowesii, Miltonia flavescens,* and *Miltonia spectabilis,* as well as various hybrids.

Blooming Season: Summer/fall, some all year around.

Family: Orchidaceae (orchid family).

Origin: South America.

Location: Bright all year round but not sunny. Also tolerates semishade. In summer not over 77° F (25° C), in winter around 68° F (20° C), at night 59 to 64° F (15°–18° C).

Watering, Feeding: Always keep slightly damp. In winter water sparingly. In spring and summer feed every 3 weeks with a weak dosage.

Further Culture: Provide high, indirect humidity (see page 43), but <u>do not spray on the plants</u>. Repot rarely and when you do, use orchid potting medium for epiphytes in spring or fall.

Propagation: By division of pseudobulbs at repotting.

Pests, Diseases: Only with poor cultivation. At a slightly red tinge to the leaves, move to a brighter location.

Odontoglossum

The familiar *Vuylstekeara cambria* 'Plush'.

Yellow-spotted hybrid.

Most of the more than 100 species of *Odontoglossum* are cool mountain beauties. They grow at heights of 5,000 to 9,000 ft (1,500–3,000 m). Some of them can even stand freezing temperatures for a brief time. From the unusual flowers, which sometimes have a tooth-like process at the bottom, comes the botanical name (Greek/Latin: *odontos* = toothed, *glossa* = tongue). The pseudobulbs are smoothly oval, have one to three leaves at the tip, and at the base develop racemose inflorescences, which as a rule point upward. One of the least demanding species is *Odontoglossum grande* (tiger orchid), which today is classified in a special genus as *Rossioglossum.* The following hybrids and multiple-genera hybrids of *Odontoglossum* are of particular interest for houseplant fanciers:

• *Odontioda* (from *Odontoglossum x Cochlioda*)
• *Odontonia* (from *Odontoglossum x Miltonia*)
• *Ondontocidium* (from *Odontoglossum x Oncidium*)
• *Vuylstekeara* (from *Odontoglossum x Cochlioda x Miltoniopsis*)
• *Wilsonara* (from *Odontoglossum x Cochlioda x Oncidium*)

They are bred especially for windowsill requirements and outdo themselves with luxuriantly produced, frequently multicolored panicles of flowers, which come in yellow to brown (flecked or striped), white with pink, or red. Of the pure species, *Odontoglossum bictoniense, Odontoglossum pulchellum,* which has a lily-of-the-valley fragrance, and *Odontoglossum crispum* are good for culture as houseplants.

Blooming Season: Depending on species and variety, in spring, summer, fall, or winter.

Family: Orchidaceae (orchid family).

Origin: Central and South America.

Location: Bright to semi-shady. East, west, or north window; in winter, south window. In summer, 68° to 75° F (20°–24° C), cooler at night. In winter, 57° to 64° F (14°–18° C).

Watering, Feeding: During the growing season keep uniformly damp. In winter water only enough that the substrate and the pseudobulb never dry out. From June to August fertilize every 14 days through the leaves (protect potting medium and roots from salt damage).

Further Culture: Provide for high humidity with misting. Every 2 to 3 years repot in fresh orchid potting medium after blooming.

Propagation: By division of the pseudobulb at repotting.

Pests, Diseases: Leaves grow wavy when humidity is too low.

My Tip: If you have a garden, hang your *Odontoglossum* in a thinly foliaged tree, beginning in June. The orchid loves the summer fresh air, but particularly the summer warmth after a cool night. Important: Don't forget to water in dry spells. On the other hand, it's best to bring the plant indoors again during protracted rainy spells to keep the potting medium from becoming moldy.

Give the plant full sun from September on. This promotes the development of flowers and the maturation of the pseudobulbs. Let it fill up on sunlight into the middle of October, but be careful of night frosts! Then bring it into the house and place it in a bright, cool spot. There won't be a long wait for the beginning of new flower buds.

The odontoglossum is an important forebear of many a house orchid that is known under a different name, such as the Vuylstekeara.

Oncidium
Dancing-Lady Orchid

Oncidiums—there are about 100 species—are at home in various temperature zones and are correspondingly various in form. The inflorescences bear delicate single flowers that are often banded or spotted. There are both hybrids and pure species on the market. When buying always ask whether the oncidium you have chosen is at home in temperate or warm regions.

Blooming Season: Depending on species and variety, spring, summer, fall, or winter.

Family: Orchidaceae (orchid family).

Origin: Subtropical and tropical America, West Indies.

Location: In summer, bright to semishady. No direct sun. Days warm, nights cool. In winter keep temperate oncidiums at 59° F (15° C), warmth-needing ones at around 68° F (20° C) and full sun.

Watering, Feeding: Keep plant slightly damp constantly from March to October. From November to March only water enough to keep the pseudobulbs and the leaves from wilting. During the vegetative period give orchid fertilizer every 3 weeks.

Further Culture: Provide for high humidity but mist carefully in winter and spring, since new growth rots easily. When the pseudobulbs swell out of the pot, repot plant in orchid potting medium.

Best time: At the end of rest period (March) when the roots and the new shoots begin to grow.

Propagation: By division of pseudobulbs at repotting time.

My Tip: Do not cut off the flower stalks of *Oncidium kramerianum* and *Oncidium papilio* (*Psychopsis*) after they bloom. New buds develop on the same stem the next year.

Oncidium hybrid with mottled flowers.

Paphiopedilum
Cypripedium, Lady-slipper

Paphiopedilum hybrids are of easy culture.

There are about 60 species of *Paphiopedilum*. Erroneously, some call them lady-slippers, which is the name of our native *Cypripedium* orchids. Far larger, however, is the number of hybrids, to which plant fanciers should turn for reasons of conservation. These cultivars are much tougher than the botanical species and even thrive in heated areas. *Paphiopedilum* has a special program of growth: Each leaf rosette produces only one flower shoot. Then new rosettes develop in the leaf axils, which bloom the following year. The flowers are white, yellow, green, brown, or purple, and often striped, spotted, or speckled.

Blooming Season: Depending on species and variety, spring, summer, fall, or winter.

Family: Orchidaceae (orchid family).

Origin: Tropical Asia.

Location: In summer semishady, in winter bright but not sunny. Room temperatures all year round, cooler at night. Exception: In September, after growth stops, keep cool at night and sunny during the day for 2 to 3 weeks.

Watering, Feeding: Provide moderate dampness. Water only when the potting medium has dried out. In winter water more sparingly. From April to September feed every 3 weeks with a low dosage.

Further Culture: Provide for high humidity. Mist the leaves often. Repot the plant after blooming but only if the potting medium has clumped or smells musty.

Propagation: By division at repotting.

Pests, Diseases: Possible attacks by spider mites and scale. Bud, leaf, and root rot from continued dampness.

My Tip: *Paphiopedilums* thrive best when they can grow luxuriantly in a clump. Thus, it's better not to divide!

Phalaenopsis has broad leaves.

Phalaenopsis hybrids flower almost all year around.

Orchids that close at night, such as *Phalaenopsis,* do not develop pseudo bulbs but have roots that cling to whatever is offered them. The leaves are tonguelike and quite wide and the flowers have various forms, colors, and markings. They appear almost all year around in white, yellow, pink, red, violet, brown, and green. On the market are species hybrids (ideal for beginners), and multigeneric hybrids like *Asconopsis, Doritaenopsis,* or *Renanthopsis,* all of which require the same culture.

Blooming Season: Depending on species and variety, spring, summer, fall, or winter; hybrids bloom almost all year long.

Family: Orchidaceae (orchid family).

Origin: India, Southeast Asia, Indonesia, Philippines, and northern Australia.

Location: In summer semishade, in winter bright. Never sunny under any circumstances. Warm all year around. Days around 68° to 72° F (20°–22° C) (even warmer in summer), nights not below 64° F (22° C). Exception: In fall keep plants around 61° F (16° C) for about 4 to 6 weeks. This stimulates the formation of flowers.

Watering, Feeding: Keep moderately damp all year around. The potting medium should never dry out completely but should dry before it is watered again. Never water into the heart of the plant— danger of rot. Feed with weak dosage every 14 days in summer.

Further Culture: Mist the leaves often. Provide high humidity for *Phalaenopsis* species. The hybrids are better suited to dry house air. Repot the plants in May every 2 years in coarse, airy orchid potting medium. Do not injure roots.

Propagation: From offsets that occasionally develop on the flower stems.

Pests, Diseases: Fungus infections from overwatering; scale in too dry a location; bud drop in too dark a spot. Danger of snails in a greenhouse.

My Tip: *Phalaenopsis* can bloom two to three times on the same stalk if you cut off the flower stalk above the third or fourth stem node before it has entirely finished blooming.

Mambo is the name of this green-gold hybrid.

Spattered flowers— *Phalaenopsis* hybrid Hokuspokus.

The hybrid Cassandra with a purple-red lip.

From warm, humid tropical regions and damp, cool mountain forests, choice orchids with special requirements.

Coelogyne cristata
Coelogyne

For temperate areas, Coelogynes are epiphytic orchids with narrow, dark-green leaves 6 to 12 in. (15–30 cm) long, oval pseudobulbs, and trailing white flowers with golden-yellow crests that appear in clusters of several on stems up to 12 in. (30 cm) long.

Blooming Season: November to March. Family: Orchidaceae (orchid family). Origin: Himalayas, Nepal. Location: Bright and airy all year around. No midday sun. Outdoors in summer. In winter 57° F (14° C) during day, 46° F (8° C) at night. Watering, Feeding: Water moderately from May to September and feed with weak solution every 2 weeks. From October to April keep almost dry. Further Culture: Don't mist new growth, or it may rot! Repot plant, as necessary, after blooming in orchid potting medium. Propagation: By division. My Tip: The *Coelogyne* blooms better when it has been outside in the full fall sun.

Brassia verrucosa
Brassia

Brassia is a temperate area orchid species with flat pseudobulbs, oblong, leathery leaves and flowers that often have taillike long petals and are situated

on stems 20 in. (50 cm) long.
Blooming Season: Spring or summer, depending on species. Family: Orchid-

aceae (orchid family). Origin: Tropical America. Location: Very bright to semishady. In summer room temperature with drop to from 61° to 64° F (16°–18° C) at night. In winter not over 64°F (18°C) in the daytime, 57°F (14°C) at night. Watering, Feeding: Water copiously with soft water from April to September and feed with weak solution every 2 weeks during this period. From October to March water only enough to keep the bulbs from shriveling. Further Culture: Mist regularly. Scale attacks when air is too dry. Propagation: Through division of pseudobulbs.

Dendrobium densiflorum
Dendrobium

For temperate areas, *Dendrobium* is an epiphytic species with bamboolike

pseudobulbs and golden-yellow clusters of flowers.
Blooming Season: March to May. Family: Orchidaceae (orchid family). Origin: Himalayas, Burma, Indochina. Location: Very bright, but not sunny, all year around. In spring/summer warm, from October 12 to 59°F (15°C). Watering, Feeding: In spring/summer water copiously and feed with low dosage every 14 days. From October water less; in winter water only enough to keep the bulbs from shriveling. Further Culture: Mist often, especially in summer. Propagation: By division of pseudobulbs after blooming.

Zygopetalum

Zygopetalum Artur Elle

An orchid for temperate areas, *Zygopetalum* has thick roots, 2 or more narrow lanceolate leaves, oval pseudobulbs, and strikingly patterned and colored flowers. The remarkable name comes from the Greek and alludes to the thickened welt at the base of the lip, which holds the petals together like a horse yoke (Greek: *zygo* = yoke, *petalon* = petal). Both species and hybrids are available. <u>Blooming Season:</u> Winter. <u>Family:</u> Orchidaceae (orchid family). <u>Origin:</u> South America. <u>Location:</u> Bright to semishady and airy. Room temperature all year around. In winter, 59° to 64° F (15°–18° C). <u>Watering, Feeding</u>: Keep moderately damp continuously. From March to September feed with low dosage every 2 weeks. <u>Further Culture:</u> Provide indirect humidity (see page 43), but do not mist or you will have spotted leaves. Repot yearly after flowering. <u>Propagation:</u> Through division of pseudobulbs with leaves.

Masdevallia

Masdevallia militaris

Masdevallias prefer cool, damp areas. Only keep in a cool greenhouse! Orchids with fleshy root stock and unusual flowers in which the corolla is almost completely reduced and the calyx has developed to a three-pointed structure. <u>Blooming Season:</u> Spring or summer, depending on species. <u>Family:</u> Orchidaceae (orchid family). <u>Origin:</u> Central and South America. <u>Location:</u> Bright to semishady. Airy and damply cool all year around. <u>Watering, Feeding:</u> Always keep orchid slightly damp, no rest period. In summer feed with low dosage every 3 weeks. <u>Further Culture:</u> Repot in spring in orchid potting medium, as necessary. <u>Propagation:</u> By division of rhizomes; leave large clumps.

Bulbophyllus longiflorum is also called *Cirrhopetalum.*

Bulbophyllum

Bulbophyllum longiflorum

The bulbophyllum is for warm areas. These epiphytic orchids have elongated, creeping rhizomes and slanted pseudobulbs, on which a leathery leaf is situated (thus the name, from Greek: *bolbos* = tuber and *phyllon* = leaf). The bizarre flowers are always clusters of several in an umbel. <u>Blooming Season:</u> July. <u>Family:</u> Orchidaceae (orchid family). <u>Origin:</u> Evergreen rain and monsoon forests of the tropics. <u>Location:</u> Bright all year around, 68° F (20° C) in the daytime, never under 61° F (16° C) at night. <u>Watering, Feeding:</u> Keep uniformly damp, feed every 14 days with weak dosage during the growing season. <u>Further Culture:</u> Provide indirect humidity (see page 43). <u>Propagation:</u> By division of the pseudobulbs.

They require little space and care, turn into brilliant flowering beauties overnight, and excite a desire to collect them like no other plant group. Anyone who has ever fallen under the spell of the children of the light is captive forever.

CACTI

Anyone who has a bright, sunny windowsill and cool, bright winter quarters can collect cacti and experience these thorny fellows at close range. Even a tray offers a place for a small collection. Perhaps you are beginning with the easy-to-grow cacti—as are shown on the following pages. Or you may prefer the exclusive group of epiphytic leaf cacti. For the fancier with experience (and possibly also a greenhouse) we also include here a small selection of more demanding cacti. The intentional grouping of plants with nearly identical culture requirements should give you a chance to acquire more than a half dozen different species at once that take the same care. For cacti are not really charming individually but rather as a colorful group.

The magic of the cactus lies in its contrariness. Defiant, very nearly repelling, is the impression given by the flowerless "thorn balls." Yet when their flowers suddenly appear one after the other, shining like silk and joyously colored, they reveal an irresistible charm.

Around the year 1500 the first cactus specimens are believed to have been introduced to Europe with Christopher Columbus's *Santa Maria*. By about 1700, the melon, pillar, leaf, and fig cacti were already known, and the passion for these plants reached a peak in the first half of the nineteenth century. Today the Cactus and Succulent Society of America alone, founded in 1921, has over 7,000 devoted members.

What You Should Know About Cacti

Cacti are "Americans." Their distribution area ranges from Canada to Patagonia. Most of them inhabit prairies and blazing hot, desertlike, dry regions. Only relatively few penetrate the warm, humid tropical areas, creeping under bushes or growing in the forks of tropical forest trees. The cactus family, botanically named Cactaceae, embraces some 200 genera and several thousand species. They are flowering plants like African violets and azaleas— so why do they look so different? The characteristic cactus structure developed over millions of years through adaptation to a dry location. In order to keep the evaporation surface as small as possible and to protect themselves against sun and ultraviolet light, the cacti "invented" the spherical and pillar form, turned leaves into thorns, and developed a thick skin, which they additionally furnished with a waxlike coating, cork deposits, dense thorns, or a coating of silvery hairs. Some species form broadly extending, flat subsurface roots that can make the most of even the briefest downpour of rain, others grow thick beetlike roots for water storage. A true achievement is succulence (from Latin: *succus* = juice). This means that tissue, the cortex, and pith serve as water reservoirs. A common growth form of younger cacti is the round form. Besides this, there are species that form pillars or cushions. Mature specimens often take on a shrub, tree, or candelabra shape. Climbing cacti, like the queen-of-the-night, have long limbs and branchlike bushes. The few epiphytes in the family, like for example the Christmas and the Easter cactus, have leaflike stems. The flowers of the cacti develop—depending on the species—on 2- to 3-year-old specimens or only after they've reached a particular size. Blooming seasons for most species are spring and early summer. There is every possible color with the exception of black and blue.

The Right Culture

Cacti are robust, to be sure, but they can easily be cultivated to death with too much water. In summer the plants can comfortably be watered freely, but it's important that there be no residual dampness around the roots and that they are only watered again when the potting medium is completely dried out. In fall the amount of water is reduced, in winter a cactus should have nothing at all to drink in a cool location under 50° F (10° C), in a warmer spot only very, very little. Under no circumstances should growth be stimulated in the dark season. The potting medium should have the character of desert sand—that is, be very water permeable and aerated and be inorganic soil. Work fine and coarse sand into all-purpose potting soil, which is often too full of humus.

Be careful when repotting—danger of injury! Cacti are often furnished with extremely sharp thorns or spines and are best gripped with gloves, pieces of Styrofoam (see drawing, page 41), or canning or cooking tongs. Epiphytic cacti are cultivated entirely differently. They need a humus-rich, nourishing potting medium, more water, and high humidity. And in contrast to their desert brothers they say: Sun, no thank you!

Many cacti with a bushy growth habit only grow as pillars in a pot. Impressive candelabras like this are exclusive to the native location.

The giant barrel cactus (*Echinocactus ingens*) from Mexico can weigh as much as a ton in its native setting and earned a gloomy reputation among the Aztecs as a sacrificial altar.

Easy-Care Cacti

It isn't too hard to get these little fellows to bloom.

The cacti pictured here can be made to bloom over and over.

Family: Cactaceae (cactus family).

Origin: Southwestern United States, Central and South America.

Location: From spring to fall very bright to sunny and warm. From October bright and cool (41° to 54°F [5°–12° C]). From end of May outdoors in a sunny place. But: Protect from rain.

Watering, Feeding: From May to September water thoroughly, but always let potting medium dry first. From the end of October keep dry. Don't water if wintered over cool, under 50° F (10° C), if warmer, water very little. In spring carefully resume watering. As soon as new growth shows, give cactus fertilizer every 14 days. Shortly before the beginning of wintering, give a phosphorus-weighted fertilizer in the last watering, which will promote flowers.

Further Culture: Repot every 2 to 3 years in early summer. Add fine and coarse sand to cactus mix.

Propagation: By seed, in a heatable propagation flat at around 82° F (28° C); good seeding time around the end of February. When the seedlings become crowded, thin out or transplant.

Pests, Diseases: Only from overfeeding, wet culture, wrong wintering, pampering, or too little fresh air.

Gymnocalycium
Large-flowered, very profusely blooming flattened-spherical to spherical cactus. Sprouts from the base and grows about 6 to 8 in. (15–20 cm) tall and 6 in. (15 cm) thick. There are species with flat or projecting thorns. The flowers, up to 2 in. (6 cm) in size, often appear on 3-year-old plants.
<u>Recommended species:</u>
G. andreae (yellow),

G. Baldianum (red-violet),
G. bruchii (pink),
G. denuda-tum (cream-white), G. multiflorum (pink to pinky-orange),
G. quehlianum (white with red throat),
G. uruguayense (cream-white).
<u>Blooming Season:</u> Spring to summer.

Notocactus
Spherical to short pillar cactus genus about 6 to 8 in. (15–20 cm) in height and diameter. Usually sprouts only when it is older and is furnished with different-looking spines. The flowers appear near the crown and are about 3 in. (8 cm) across.
<u>Recommended species:</u>
N. apricus, N. concinnus, N. ottonis, N. submam-mulosus (all yellow), N. rutilans (carmine pink), N. uebelmannianus (yellow-red and wine-red to violet-red).
<u>Blooming Season:</u> Spring to summer.

Cacti in the photograph:
1 *Gymnocalycium uruguayense*
2 *Notocactus concinnus*
3 *Mammillaria zeilmanniana*
4 *Rebutia ritteri*
5 *Rebutia minusculua*
6 *Echinofossulocactus*
7 *Lobivia vatteri*

Mammillaria
The name in English, pin-cushion cactus, indicates that the mammillarias all have ribs studded with bumps that look like pin-heads. Depending on the species, they may be flattened spheres, spherical, thin or thick pillars and have various kinds of thorns. Almost all sprout vigorously and form cush-ions. There are species that are 20 in. (50 cm) tall.
<u>Recommended species:</u> All.
<u>Blooming Season:</u> Spring.

Admirers find the patterns of thorns just as attractive as the flowers.

Rebutia

At most 3 in. (8 cm) thick and under 3 in. (8 cm) tall, these cacti sprout very vigorously and soon develop small groups. Fine spines cover the entire body of the cactus. The cheerfully colored flowers, $^{3}/_{4}$ to 2 in. (2–5 cm) in size, are often so numerous that the entire cactus is covered with them.
Recommended species:
All, but especially *R. marsoneri* (yellow), *R. violaciflora* (violet), *R. senilis* and varieties (yellow, red).
Blooming Season: Spring.

Echinofossulocactus

Hallmarks of this spherical cactus genus are the deep, usually wavy ribs. Therefore, it is also called brain cactus. The marginal thorns are light and thin, the middle ones are sturdy and often curved like horns. The flowers are whitish to blue-violet with dark center stripes or yellow, whitish to cream-colored with dark back stripes.
Recommended species:
All. A particularly typical and attractive representative is *E. lamellosus*.
Blooming Season: Early spring.

Lobivia

Spherical to short-pillar and many-ribbed genus. At most 12 in. (30 cm) tall and rarely thicker than 4 in. (10 cm) in diameter. The pattern of thorns varies. The flowers, up to 4 in. (10 cm) across, appear at the side.
Recommended species:
L. backebergiana (orange), *L. rebutioides* and *L. famatimensis* (yellow), *L. jajoiana* (tomato red), *L. pentlandii* (white, yellow, pink to violet), *L. wrightiana* (pink).
Blooming Season: Spring to summer.

Cleistocactus

Pillar cactus with dense, mostly needle-fine thorns.

First blooms at from 12 to 31 in. (30–80 cm) in height. Exception: *Cleistocactus wendlandiorum* can bloom when it is only 6 in. (15 cm) tall. The tubular flowers, up to 3$^{1}/_{2}$ in. (9 cm) long, project perpendicular to, or pipe-like, from the cactus body and only open partway.
Recommended species:
C. laniceps (red), *C. strausii* (wine red), *C. wendlandiorum* (orange).
Blooming Season: Spring to early summer.

Echinocactus grusonii

The barrel or golden-ball cactus grows to a height of 5 ft (1.5 m) in its Mexican habitat. Its golden-yellow thorns are characteristic. The yellow flowers only appear in mature plants, at a diameter of about 23 in. (60 cm).
Blooming Season: Summer.

Parodia

Small-growing and relatively early-blooming

Cacti in the photograph:
1 *Cleistocactus straussii*
2 *Echinocereus pectinatus*
3 *Mammillaria bocasana*
4 *Echinocactus grusonii*
5 *Echinofossulocactus* spec
6 *Parodia mairanana*
7 *Mammillaria zeilmanniana*

cacti with flatly spherical, spherical to cylindrical bodies. Achieve maximum height of 8 in. (20 cm) and thickness of 3 in. (8 cm). Growth of parodias varies, depending on the species, but they sprout vigorously. The flowers appear on the usually woolly crown.
Recommended species:
P. chrysacanthion (yellow), *P. maassii* (red), *P. mutabilis* (yellow-orange), *P. sanguiniflora* (blood-red).
Blooming Season: Spring to summer.

Epiphyllum Hybrids
Orchid Cactus, Pond-Lily Cactus

Leaf cacti bloom luxuriantly when they are able to spend the summer outside.

The name *Ephiphyllum* means "on the leaf" and points to the fact that here, against all the botanical rules, the flower appears to arise from the leaf. In reality this leaf is a flattened stem, usually furnished with thorns, though insignificant ones. Epiphyllums live in their tropical habitats as trailing epiphytes. They can therefore be cultivated in hanging pots. Meanwhile there are, mainly in the Americas, more than 10,000 different hybrids. Depending on the species or variety, the flowers measure from 2 to 14 in. (5–35 cm) in diameter and are white, cream-colored, yellow, orange, pink, red, purple, or violet shades, and usually even bicolored. Small-growing varieties like 'Mimi' are especially in demand. Specialty nurseries have the largest choice.

Red *Epiphyllum* hybrid.

Yellow *Epiphyllum* hybrid.

Blooming Season: May to July.

Family: Cactaceae (cactus family).

Origin: Southern Mexico to tropical regions of South America. But only hybrid forms are marketed.

Location: Bright to semi-shady, depending on domestication also sunny. Should spend the summer out of doors. From spring to fall keep warm and humid; in winter, at around 50° to 59° F (10°–15° C).

Watering, Feeding: Keep moderately damp all year around with soft, room-temperature water. Fertilize from March to August.

Further Culture: Mist now and again. As necessary repot in bromeliad potting medium or soil with humus and peat. Cut out unsightly growth and thin spikes.

Propagation: From cuttings. Let cut surfaces dry.

Cacti in the photograph:
1 Red *Epiphyllum* hybrid
2 White *Epiphyllum* hybrid
3 'Empress-of-Germany' (*Nopalxochia phylanthoides*)

Pests, Diseases: Aphids (especially on buds), scale.

Note: The pink-flowering *Nopalxochia phylanthoides,* known as 'Empress-of-Germany', which has proved itself as a hanging plant, is cultivated exactly the same way.

My Tip: A dormant period from November to March in cooler temperatures is

Flower of *Marniera chrysocardium.*

Rhipsalidopsis Hybrids
Easter Cactus

Schlumbergera Hybrids
Christmas Cactus

Robust and eager to flower—the Easter cactus.

The Christmas cactus loves humidity.

the recipe for success for sure-fire development of flowers.
There are three "styles" of Easter cactus:
• *Rhipsalidopsis gaertneri,* with scarlet red flowers 1¹/₂ to 2 in. (4–5 cm) long.
• *Rhipsalidopsis rosea,* with five-sided, bristly hairy stems and somewhat smaller, pink flowers
• a cross of both of the above called *Rhipsalidopsis x graeseri* and obtainable with pink to violet flowers.
In spring all produce a profusion of brilliant flowers that sit at the end of the leaf member. The Easter cactus grows as an epiphyte in its habitat.

Blooming Season: March to May.
Family: Cactaceae (cactus family).
Origin: Brazil.
Location: Bright to semishady and warm all year around. Keep at 50° F (10° C) for 8 weeks from November to January.

This promotes flower development.

Watering, Feeding: During the growing season (February to October) keep uniformly damp with soft, room-temperature water; water only a little 4 weeks after blooming and during the rest period (November to January). In summer give cactus fertilizer now and then.
Further Culture: Mist often. Repot only as necessary in bromeliad potting medium, shredded peat, or all-purpose potting soil mixed with sand.
Propagation: From sprouting members, best in May (but possible all year round). Allow cut surfaces to dry, then cuttings root easily in damp potting medium.
Pests, Diseases: Root rot from too much water. Falling off of buds from too cool a location or too much warmth with a deficiency of light at the same time. Shrinking of

leaf members indicates culture too dry or root rot from too much water.
The Christmas cactus, as we buy it today, is the result of a cross of the true Christmas cactus (*Zygocactus truncatus*) and *Schlumbergera russeliana*. Both species grow as epiphytes on trees in the Orgel Mountains near Rio de Janeiro in Brazil at heights of 3,000 to 4,600 ft (900 to 1,400 m). There are enchanting hybrids on the market, with white, red, purple-red, and violet flowers. With some luck you might find one of the newly hybridized yellow varieties like 'Gold Charm'.

Blooming Season: December to January (occasionally to March).
Family: Cactaceae (cactus family).
Origin: Brazil.
Location: Bright to semishady, little sun. The plants love the fresh air outdoors in the summer

(to the end of September) in a semishady place.

Watering, Feeding: Keep moderately but uniformly damp in summer. Until the end of July feed every 14 days. From August on, water and feed less so that the leaves will mature.
Further Culture: Mist often. Bring the plants indoors again at the end of September and keep warm 64° to 72° F (18°–22° C). The shorter periods of daylight will stimulate the development of flowers.
Propagation: Accomplished easily by leaf cuttings, which should be dried before being planted in dampened potting medium.
Pests, Diseases: Bud drop from changing amount of light resulting from change of location.

Cacti for the Experienced

Melon Cactus

The genera pictured here represent a small cross-section of cacti for the experienced admirer and are somewhat the same in culture. A greenhouse is recommended to cultivate most of them successfully. This guarantees the greatest possible amount of light and a controlled climate, both requirements for sure-fire flowering. Some, like *Sulcorebutia* and *Mediolobivia* actually come from mountain regions and are accustomed to intense ultraviolet light.

Cacti in the photograph:
 1 *Astrophytum capricorne* var. *niveum*
 2 *Cephalocereus senilis*
 3 *Thelocactus bicolor*
 4 *Neoportaria villosa*
 5 *Mammillaria nepina*
 6 *Mammilaria laui*
 7 *Thelocactus bueckii*
 8 *Weingartia multispina*
 9 *Astrophytum myriostigma*
10 *Astrophytum asterias*
11 *Mammillaria yaquensis*
12 *Mediolobivia schmiedcheniana*
13 *Sulcorebutia steinbachii*

Blooming Season: Spring and summer in most of the genera. *Thelocactus* blooms from spring to late summer.
Family: Cactaceae (cactus family).
Origin: Southern United States to South America.
Location: From spring to fall very bright to sunny and warm. From October on, bright and cool—41° to 54° F (5°–12° C). From end of May, the cacti can also be cultivated in a sunny warm place outdoors. But protect from rain!
Watering, Feeding: As soon as they show new growth in spring, water regularly. But let potting medium dry out before each new watering.
Further Culture: Mist now and again in summer and fall. Repot every 2 to 3 years. Important: A good water-permeable, rather inorganic soil. Don't use any cactus soils with heavy humus content. Better: Compose a mixture of pumice granules, lava granules, perlite, and coarse sand with some all-purpose soil.
Propagation: From seed, at a ground temperature of about 82° F (28° C).
Pests, Diseases: Spider mites or mealybugs. Cactus rot from too much water, especially in winter.
My Tip: With the cacti shown here you can celebrate a festival of flowers even on a sunny windowsill.

The crown is the flowering area.

Tabernaemontanus described this curious creature as melon thistle as early as 1588. Melon cacti differ from many other genera in their development of an accumulation of bristles, hairs, and wool. This cephalium, which looks like a little crown, is the flowering area of the *Melocactus*. It develops after 7 years. The green cactus body winds up its growth with it and sets about blooming. Melocacti belong to the warmth-loving species and in winter prize a sunny place on the windowsill, which may even be above a heating unit.
Blooming Season: May to September.
Family: Cactaceae (cactus family).
Origin: Central and South America.
Location: All year around full sun, or at least very bright, and warm. In summer place outdoors in a warm, protected spot.

Watering, Feeding: Water regularly in summer; reduce amount of water from October to March, but keep potting medium slightly damp at all times. In summer feed cactus fertilizer every 4 weeks.
Further Culture: Mist frequently all year long. Repot every 2 to 3 years in shallow pot or generous dish with very sandy potting medium containing only a little humus. Do not injure the roots, especially of specimens that have a cephalium.
Propagation: From seed, in sandy soil at ground temperature of about 82° F (28° C).
Pests, Diseases: Cactus rot from too much water and temperatures that are too cool.
My Tip: The old-man cactus (*Cephalocereus senilis*) is cultivated exactly the same way; however, it may be kept cooler in winter, but not under 59° F (15° C).

229

INDEX

Numbers in **bold** indicate color photos and drawings.

INDEX

INDEX

Bibliography

African Violets

Coulson, Ruth, *Growing African Violets,* International Specialized Book Services, Portland, Oregon, 1987.

Powell, Charles, *African Violets and Flowering Houseplants,* Ortho Books, San Ramon, California, 1985.

Sunset Editors, *African Violets,* Sunset Books/Lane Publishing Company, Menlo Park, California, 1977.

Azaleas

Darden, Jim, *Great American Azaleas: A Guide to the Finest Azalea Varieties,* Greenhouse Press, Clinton, North Carolina, 1986.

Fairweather, Christopher, *Azaleas,* Globe Pequot Press, Chester, Connecticut, 1988.

Galle, Fred, *Azaleas,* Timber Press, Portland, Oregon, 1987.

Begonias

Catterall, E., *Growing Begonias,* Timber Press, Portland, Oregon, 1984.

Haegeman, J., *Tuberous Begonias: Origin and Development,* Lubrecht and Cramer Ltd., Forestburgh, New York, 1979.

Bonsai

Ainsworth, John, *The Art of Indoor Bonsai,* Trafalgar Square/David and Charles, Inc., North Pomfret, Vermont, 1989.

Anderson, Charles and Anderson, Ruth, *The Care and Feeding of Bonsai,* HarborCrest Publications, Bainbridge Island, Washington, 1988.

Daute, Horst, *The Macmillan Book of Bonsai,* Macmillan Publishing Co., Inc., New York, New York, 1986.

Bromeliads

Benzing, David H., *Biology of the Bromeliads,* Mad River Press, Eureka, California, 1980.

Padilla, Victoria, *Bromeliads,* Crown Publishers, Inc., New York, New York, 1986.

Cacti

Benson, Lyman, *The Cacti of the U.S. and Canada,* Stanford University Press, Stanford, California, 1982.

Cullman, Willy, *et al, Encyclopedia of Cacti,* Timber Press, Portland, Oregon, 1987.

Gibson, Arthur and Noble, Park S., *The Cactus Primer,* Harvard University Press, Cambridge, Massachusetts, 1986.

Haselton, Scott E., *Cactus and Succulents and How to Grow Them,* Desert Botanical Garden, Phoenix, Arizona, 1983.

Camellias

Noble, Mary and Graham, Blanche, *You Can Grow Camellias,* Peter Smith Publishing, Inc., Magnolia, Massachusetts, 1983.

Chrysanthemums

Brock, Wallace, *Growing and Showing Chrysanthemums,* David and Charles, Inc., North Pomfret, Vermont, 1984.

Randall, Harry and Wren, Alan, *Growing Chrysanthemums,* Timber Press, Portland, Oregon, 1983.

Skeen, Bruce, *Growing Chrysanthemums,* International Specialized Book Services, Portland, Oregon, 1985.

Ferns

Cobb, Boughton A., *Field Guide to Ferns and Their Related Families: Northeastern and Central North America,* Houghton Mifflin Company, Boston, Massachusetts, 1977.

Foster, F. Gordon, *Ferns to Know and Grow,* Timber Press, Portland, Oregon, 1984.

Brooklyn Botanic Garden, *Ferns,* Brooklyn, New York.

Geraniums

Shellard, Alan, *Geraniums for Home and Garden,* David and Charles, Inc., North Pomfret, Vermont, 1984.

_____ , *Growing and Showing Geraniums,* David and Charles, Inc., North Pomfret, Vermont, 1984.

Yeo, Peter F., *Hardy Geraniums,* Timber Press, Portland, Oregon, 1985.

Orchids

Hawkes, Alex D., *Encyclopedia of Cultivated Orchids,* Faber & Faber, Inc., Winchester, Massachusetts, 1987.

Hunt, P. Francis, *The Orchid,* Smith Publications, Inc., New York, New York, 1979.

Pinske, Jorn, *The Macmillan Book of Orchids,* Macmillan Publishing Co., Inc., New York, New York, 1986.

Palms

Blombery, Alec and Rodd, Tony, *Palms,* Salem House Publications, Harper & Row, Scranton, Pennsylvania, 1983.

McGeachy, Beth, *Handbook of Florida Palms,* Great Outdoors Publishing Co., Saint Petersburg, Florida.

Rhododendrons

Clarke, J. Harold, *Getting Started with Rhododendrons and Azaleas,* Timber Press, Portland, Oregon.

Cox, Kenneth and Cox, Peter, *Encylopedia of Rhododendron Hybrids,* Timber Press, Portland, Oregon.

Greer, Harold E., *Greer's Guidebook to Available Rhododendrons,* Offshoot Publications, Eugene, Oregon, 1987.

Addresses

Indoor Gardening Society of America
c/o Horticultural Society of New York
128 West 58th Street
New York, NY 10019

African Violet Society of America
P.O. Box 3609
Beaumont, TX 77704

Azalea Society of America
8610 Running Fox Court
Fairfax Station, VA 22039

American Begonia Society
P.O. Box 1129
Encinitas, CA 92024

American Bonsai Society
Box 358
Keene, NH 03431

Bonsai Clubs International
2636 West Mission Road, #277
Tallahassee, FL 32304

Bromeliad Society
2488 East 49th Street
Tulsa, OK 74105

California Cactus Growers Association
1701 South Palm Canyon Drive
Palm Springs, CA 92264

Cactus and Succulent Society of America
2631 Fairgreen Avenue
Arcadia, CA 91006

American Camellia Society
Box 1217
Fort Valley, GA 31030

International Camellia Society
P.O. Box 750
Brookhaven, MS 39601

National Chrysanthemum Society
10107 Homer Pond Drive
Fairfax Station, VA 22039

American Fern Society
Pringle Herbarium
Department of Botany
University of Vermont
Burlington, VT 95495

Gardenia Society of America
P.O. Box 879
Atwater, CA 95301

International Geranium Society
4610 Druid Street
Los Angeles, CA 90012

American Gloxinia and Gesneriad Society
9320 Labadie
St. Louis, MO 63120

American Orchid Society
6000 South Olive Avenue
West Palm Beach, FL 33405

International Palm Society
P.O. Box 368
Lawrence, KS 66044

American Poinsettia Society
Box 706
Mission, TX 78572

American Rhododendron Society
P.O. Box 1380
Gloucester, VA 23061

Important Note

This book deals with the care of plants in the house. Some of the plants described are more or less poisonous. In the introduction to the plant portraits (see page 87) the plant families that are particularly poisonous are named and the physical injuries and effects that can be caused by houseplants are listed. Furthermore, in the descriptions of the individual plants (see pages 84 to 229) under the heading "Warning" the specific health hazards are pointed out. Lethally toxic plants or less poisonous ones that can produce disturbances in the health of vulnerable adults or children are indicated with a skull-and-cross-bones danger symbol. Make absolutely sure that children and pets do not eat the plants that carry these Warnings. Some plants secrete skin-irritating substances, and these are also noted for the plants in question. Anyone who suffers from contact allergies should always wear gloves when handling these plants.